BRONSON 2
MORE PORRIDGE THAN GOLDILOCKS

Published by John Blake Publishing Ltd,
3 Bramber Court, 2 Bramber Road,
London W14 9PB, England

CHARLES BRONSON

D1472003

JOHN BLAKE

London W14 9PB, England

www.johnblakepublishing.co.uk

This edition published in paperback in 2009

Parts of this book have previously been published as Insanity My Mad Life.

ISBN: 978-1-84454-860-6

British Library Cataloguing-in-Publication Data:

A catalogue record for this book is available from the British Library.

Design by www.envydesign.co.uk

Printed in Great Britain by CPI Bookmarque, Croydon, CRO 4TD

1 3 5 7 9 10 8 6 4 2

© Text copyright Charles Bronson with Stephen Richards

Papers used by John Blake Publishing are natural, recyclable products made
from wood grown in sustainable forests. The manufacturing processes conform to
the environmental regulations of the country of origin.

Every attempt has been made to contact the relevant copyright-holders,
but some were unobtainable. We would be grateful if the appropriate people
could contact us.

BRONSON 2
MORE PORRIDGE THAN GOLDILOCKS

For John, my brother.
You fought hard against it,
you said you had no regrets
and that you'd been around the
world twice and seen it all.
We miss you and love you.

Charles Bronson

CONTENTS

INTRODUCTION
BY STEPHEN RICHARDS

Charles Bronson! Two words that conjure up conflicting thoughts: One – is he the great American *Death Wish* actor? Two – Oh, yeah, I know who he is, he's that madman in prison who keeps taking hostages ... I think. In this case, we're talking about Charles Bronson, the man dubbed the UK's hardest man, the man labelled the UK's maddest and baddest hostage-taker, self-confessed 'King of the Roofs' and one of the kindest men you could ever meet!

There are three sides to this man Bronson – good, mad and bloody bad, the good side very rarely being revealed to the person who has experienced the mad and the bloody bad sides. The mad and bad parts of Bronson's persona are usually held in reserve for those on the same side of the prison wall he's behind, particularly paedophiles and bully screws.

The able and willing part of Bronson's persona is generously bestowed upon those who have earned his kindness. As if some king giving his grateful subjects a royal wave, as if the Pope giving his papal blessing, as if a great wizard casting a lucky spell for his willing students, Bronson can equally give his heart and soul for those he believes in. But there is also a warning label attached to the Bronson kindness – 'Handle with care, treat with respect or you'll regret it!'

When you breed man-eating piranhas, they say you haven't been a successful breeder until you've been bitten by one of the killer fish. Piranhas don't actually bite as such – they scoop out the flesh of their victim, leaving a big messy hole! Once you've been blooded, then, and only then, have you received your rite of passage and you can declare yourself to be a successful breeder, displaying the healed wound as proudly as a newly promoted Hell's Angel shows off his newly won patches.

Very few people are able to say they have endured the wrath of Bronson after a close friendship and then, afterwards, were able to start all over again with the man. I, Steve Richards, have had that dubious honour.

Charlie Bronson and I have fallen in and out of friendship more times than I care to remember. I've been blooded and obtained my patches the hard way – Charlie respects me for my stance. Once, writing to the big man, I mentioned a particular subject that I was disgruntled about: 'I want you to bend over, 90 degrees, from the waist, take the document and ram it up your arse.'

Charlie sent the letter to one of his then close supporters and had written over the top of it, 'He's either mad or very brave!'

Our little fall-out lasted for quite a while. He'd write to me in a nasty and sarcastic, but funny, manner and I'd respond with an equally caustic reply – childish, really!

During the course of our love–hate relationship employing angry words, one thing became apparent – Charlie was able to express his anger by proxy. He wasn't able to pin me down and punch my lights out; he had to express his anger by letter. He dared, I thought to myself, to cross swords with the Golden Pen, a name given to me by some of the criminal fraternity. The man I was fighting was able to give as good as he got; as a consequence, both of us suffered the damage of our ever more daring penmanship and, I can tell you, he gave a good fight and became a great, great friend of mine, a friendship that I would not wish to lose.

I am the sole survivor of similar disagreements that he has had with those who have supposed him to be unable to comprehend what goes on in the outside world. I believe this special bond I have with Charlie gives me the authority to be able to speak so expertly about him.

Not once did I blame Charlie for his actions; always, instead, I blamed the penal system for what they had done to him. After reading this book, I'm sure you, too, will also blame the system for its mismanagement of one of its most misunderstood inmates.

During the course of being honoured in assisting Charlie with his work, I banished myself into solitary in order to experience what he must feel like and to get a better understanding of how it can make or break you as a person. Obviously, I couldn't endure the 24 years he's suffered in such solitary conditions, but what I was able to do was divest myself of all the worldly goods we, outside solitary, take for granted.

First, it was away with my mobile phone, my precious cigars ... oh, what the hell, they could go as well, as would my other daily luxuries. I even banished myself to a stark building with a steel door, locked from the outside, with no heating, no ventilation, no phones, no snacks, no newspapers ... nothing! With just my pen and a notepad, I was beginning to know what solitary felt like.

I did, however, grant myself two luxuries: One — soft toilet roll; Two — cans of Pepsi-Max. The Pepsi would help take away my craving for nicotine and now the fight was on. One hour into the venture I felt great — yeah, I can do this, no problem.

After a sleepless night on wooden pallets, stacked four high to represent Charlie's sleeping conditions, I was wondering if what I'd embarked on was, as Charlie would put it, a mission of madness. The following morning saw me standing by the steel door like an expectant dog waiting for its master to return home ... the door opened ... light, real light!

I decided to take an hour off, equivalent to the one-hour exercise Charlie is allowed. What would I do in this hour? Sneak off, look for a newsagent and buy a pack of cigars? After all, I still had money in my pocket. Yes, no, yes, no, yes ... so the inner battle went on. I walked up to the shop, went in and bought a tray of Mr Kipling's Apple Pies. Was I that mad after only one day! If I'd bought the cigars, I'd have let Charlie down. OK, he wouldn't have known, but in our new-found closeness it meant a lot to me not to lie to him, to keep the faith, bro'.

In the early stages of my captivity, I was like a giggling schoolboy on a mystery school outing ... this was going to be an adventure after all! Washed down with the Pepsi, the apple pies tasted good. I soon forgot about the cigars I had craved, and then I found myself looking at stark reality! The magical mystery tour had turned into a sudden realisation that this might be madness.

I was sitting looking at the bricked ceiling, the plain-bricked wall and a closed steel door. It dawned on me ... what if something happened, like if I developed appendicitis or I was to have a heart-attack or something equally life-threatening? At least if this happened to Charlie he could bring this to the attention of prison officers by pressing a call button in his cell. Hmmm, I thought.

The following day, I was supplied, at my request, with a new cheap throwaway mobile phone. New because it meant no one would be ringing me; it had £10 worth of credit on it. Charlie is allowed to make phone calls, which to date he refuses to do because of his fight to have open visits with his wife, Saira. The prison authorities will not allow Charlie any contact with visitors and all visits have been ordered to take place with Charlie behind a steel cell door, so, consequently, as a protest Charlie now refuses to make phone calls. I took up my entitlement to use £5 worth of calls in a seven-day period and that way, if need be, I could phone for help.

I felt a lot safer with the mobile phone, but what it did make me aware of was all of the times Charlie needed help and how he was refused access to a doctor, when he was left lying in a stinking cell trussed up in a restraining belt two sizes too small for him and with only a few cockroaches for friends. Nah, I wasn't prepared to go to those lengths to see what Charlie must have been feeling or thinking ... I'd use my imagination and, besides, the supplies of apple pies were running low!

Dinner had arrived ... mmmmmm, aaaaaaah ... the smell of fish and chips nearly brought me to my knees in appreciation. Hey, this wasn't too bad after all ... wasn't I doing well, my second day in solitary? No sweat.

I had to sort Charlie's handwritten notes into order so that would help while away the hours. Most people cannot read Charlie's scrawled handwriting ... me, I've got no problem. If I could read Reggie Kray's almost impossible, hieroglyphic-style handwriting, then Charlie's presented no problems. (After all, my scrawl is just as bad.) Time was flying! This made me aware that so long as Charlie was kept busy, then time would fly equally fast for him. I mean, after all, at least he had his art and his many hundreds of letters from fans to reply to. Yes, I had decided, that was the key to it all ... keep busy.

Charlie has had his art materials taken from him countless times by the prison authorities as a punishment for minor and major breaches of prison rules. Charlie even went on hunger strike at HMP Whitemoor for a 40-day period when the prison confiscated his art materials, but by doing this they were 'taking away his soul', his reason for living, and now, after only two days, I was beginning to understand what he meant!

Charlie once punished me by withdrawing all his art from me. He wrote, 'I'm not sending you any more art until January 2002 because you don't appreciate my art.' My misdemeanour was not to have sent him photographs showing his pictures hanging on my office walls! That's how much he values his art works. Charlie actually sent me more drawings before the period of withdrawal had expired ... he's such a softy!

Teatime had arrived! I stood by the door with baited breath ... what goodies could I expect? Nothing! What ... nothing? Yes, nothing. I was supposed to be brought a meal three times a day, but the person responsible for this had been called away on urgent family business and it was passed on to someone else. Now isn't that typical of what happens in Charlie's life? Others are delegated a job and that's when things go wrong – talking but not communicating.

So there I was, standing by the door arguing! The only thing I was handed was a list of urgent phone calls that had been left at the office for me! I blew my top. 'For fuck's sake, what am I supposed to live on until tomorrow morning?' I said with an aggression that surprised me.

'Hang on a minute ...' the person responded but, before they could say anything else, I apologised and said I didn't know what had come over me. I explained that I wouldn't be getting anything else until breakfast and needed my tea. Ten minutes later, I was brought a bag of crisps, a Mars bar and two cheese pasties ... oh well, better than nothing, I suppose.

Again, I was now made to think of the times Charlie had told me over the phone about his meals being messed up. He told me that if he was expecting a visit, when he was allowed open visits, he wouldn't have dinner because his visitor would be able to buy goodies from a vending machine in the visits room. But if the visitor didn't turn up, he would be starving by the time his last meal of the day was served. I was beginning to understand what this cock-up would mean to a solitary prisoner. I was beginning to understand why such a small thing as a missed meal could set him off.

The solitary conditions brought me even closer to Charlie and here I was reading his handwritten notes that were now very relevant to my own condition. I could also understand why actors have to become the person they are playing; they go and study the person in great depth.

I noted among the list of phone messages I'd been given some time earlier that one call in particular was from Charlie's wife, Saira. What was I to do? Break my code of silence and return her call? Would it matter if I did ... after all, it was Charlie's wife calling me?

No! I had to see it through; unless it was a life or death situation I would remain in solitary. Hey, hang on a minute, I thought to myself, Charlie has a radio in his cell ... I want one, too! I hadn't realised what interesting programmes there are on the radio; a great lifeline in such conditions, that radio became my friend.

Breaking point, I must admit, was near. Without a cigar, I was nearly climbing the walls, although at this stage I wasn't chewing my nails, but I noticed that I had developed the habit of playing about with my eyebrows. By doing so, I was making them look rather curly, and when the steel door opened I was greeted with laughter. Not knowing what it was about, I didn't find it funny, until it was pointed out what was making them laugh – my 'Dennis Healey' eyebrows; I, too, eventually saw the funny side.

This really was becoming insanity at its best! I imagined Charlie twiddling with his moustache, making the ends curly, as I had done with my eyebrows. A cigar, I'd love a cigar, I thought to myself. Charlie surely craved things as well; maybe it would be apple pies instead of cigars.

I had to make a brave decision. Nicorette patches were called for, one for each arm, I thought. No, maybe more to help me through, but the instructions said not to overdose by applying too many patches, so it was only the one patch to get me through the night.

That night, even though the chilly winter was biting into my toes, I was sweating. I tore off the patch and eventually by breakfast time I had found a friend in sleep.

I called for Nicorette gum and, some hours later, along with my dinner and more lists of urgent telephone messages that needed answering, I chewed on my first piece of Nicorette gum ... yuk! Fuck this for a lark! I thought in temper. Is this what Charlie really had to endure? Probably not half or even a quarter of it ... at least he didn't have to chew on Nicorette gum! No doubt about it – Charlie certainly didn't have it as bad as I had! I mean, he only had to endure beatings and the liquid cosh, while I had to endure cravings for nicotine! There I was, contemplating taking a hostage or two just so I could get my hands on a juicy Cuban cigar.

A change of clothing was to make me feel refreshed; I washed using a basin, no shower! Then again, Charlie gives himself a body wash up to three times a day; of course, he also does up to 6,000 press-ups, which generates a lot of sweat! I quickly dispensed with the idea of pumping out a quick 6,000 and found another method of keeping warm – running on the spot, lifting my legs high, and before long I was in a sweat.

I knew why I was doing this; I had an aim, I was not going to let it beat me. Everything was going great until I had a piece of sad news relayed by a note along with another list of 'urgent' telephone calls. Before long, I found it playing on my mind ... all day! The sad news was starting to consume me; my isolation had helped to magnify and enlarge this piece of news until it consumed my whole fucking mind!

Teatime arrived and, somehow, I had to break the solitary conditions I was enduring in order to attend to a very urgent matter.

Charlie, however, in such circumstances wouldn't be able to do this. He couldn't say, 'Hey, let me out for a few hours, I need to sort this problem out.' I had learned a valuable lesson from all of this and it brought it home to me how Charlie must have felt when he received a piece of bad news and was powerless to do anything about it. If only Jack Straw or David Blunkett could be put into isolation, then they'd understand how and why prisoners kick off.

I thought to myself that I had failed: failed myself and failed Charlie. The problem *was* of a delicate nature and involved another party; it wasn't my problem, but what if it was my problem, though? I could see how it would crack Charlie up if he wasn't able to help his friends and family.

Maybe in some way it had been a blessing in disguise. I was starting to experience all of the chains and shackles of solitary life. Solitary wasn't just about being locked in a room for 23 hours out of a 24-hour day. Solitary was about living with yourself, tolerating the things you couldn't change, being able to accept things going wrong, anticipating things going wrong, hoping they didn't go wrong!

That night, after being freed to solve the problem, I was back on the wooden shipping pallets, and for the first time in a week I was experiencing sound sleep. I made a point of stacking the pallets four high, leaving plenty of ground space to avoid the little creepy crawlies of the night! I'd read about an earwig lodging itself in Charlie's ear – fuck that!

What the hell was I doing here? How long would it last? What was the aim of being in solitary ... I really didn't know. What has come out of it, though, is a greater understanding of what has caused Charlie to display such a violent temperament and how it came about.

Some of the things I came across in Charlie's writing made for harrowing reading. How could I compete with what he was writing about? It became a challenge. I thought of the TV show *Survivor*, based on people being stranded on a desert island, the last one winning £1 million. Charlie would have won hands down. I mean, what torture the poor contestants must have suffered having to endure the agony of being stranded on a sun-kissed desert island and having to eat a fish's eyeball. I think Charlie deserves £1 million for each year of his life spent in solitary conditions. The pain of being branded a lunatic and enduring the ravages of Broadmoor, Ashworth and Rampton special secure hospitals couldn't be reinvented. I mean, what could I possibly do to get near to that? I just couldn't get to grips with what he'd gone through.

I was starting to feel angry at how he had been caged up like an animal; I was starting to blame everyone but Charlie. I began to have violent thoughts, such as, The system's a fucking joke, run by lunatics ... I caught myself mid-thought, realising that it would be easy to become extremely violent when put in isolation — but what about after 24 years of it?

I continued enduring the mock solitary conditions. How long before I would crack? Is this what happened to Charlie? I didn't have the disadvantage of people winding me up; I didn't have malicious prison officers tormenting me or the humiliation of losing my privacy; I didn't suffer the embarrassment of having to sit on my hands while someone shaved me; I was play-acting, trying to find the beast within me! I eventually started talking to myself, but didn't dare answer! They say when you answer yourself, it's the first sign of being mad. I wondered if Charlie talked to and then answered himself, but in another voice. I could see where he had got all of his ideas from and how they manifested themselves.

I would suggest to any writer that if you write about any subject then you would be advised to immerse yourself in your subject matter – fact or fiction. It doesn't bring a better understanding, it brings oneness, and until you achieve that oneness you cannot impart the subject matter to the reader with the artistic input and authority it deserves.

The first cigar, after it all ended ... brilliant, fan-fucking-tastic? No! The Havana Special tasted like an old sock! I endured the dried seaweed taste until, after a short while, the cool flavours the Cuban cigar imparted to me the thoughts of how the leaf had been gently rolled, traditionally, on the thigh of a virgin, which made me think about the 'S' word. I didn't get much sleep that night! Charlie Bronson deserves a medal as big as a house, and I hope that what I have been able to do to his handwritten manuscripts is enhanced by my own experiences of solitary.

Stephen Richards

FOREWORD

I think Charlie's had a rough deal and I think they're treating him all wrong. I know that if Charlie was free he could make a living; obviously he couldn't get a normal job, but he could make a living by being on the crime circuit like most of the other well-known characters from the underworld.

I go down to London every year, always ending up having a meal in the Blind Beggar pub. On one particular occasion, Frankie Fraser came in with a tour party, showing them the notorious haunts where shootings took place from the days of the Kray twins. I got talking to Frankie and said, 'I'm not on the tour, but I'm a big '60s crime fan,' and I introduced myself as Mick Peterson.

Frankie said, 'Oh, yeah, I know you.' We just left it at that because he was taking his tour around the sights.

A few years later, I went to a boxing tournament and caught Frankie's eye. I went over and said, 'All right, Frank, I'm Mick Peterson.'

Frankie said, 'I've never seen you for ages ... remember when we were in Dartmoor?'

'No, that wasn't me, you're thinking of Charlie Bronson,' I said.

Frankie was adamant it was me he'd met and said, 'No, no, no. You!'

Frankie was convinced I was his old prison pal, Charlie Bronson, and he was saying to this other guy, one of the organisers, 'Me and him ...' pointing at me, 'we were in Dartmoor together.'

The man pulled me to one side and said, 'Were you and Frankie really in jail together?'

'No, no, he's got the wrong bloke. I think he thinks I'm Charlie Bronson,' I replied.

Eventually, I read one of Frankie Fraser's books and he said he knew Mick Peterson, but not Charlie Bronson! So I don't know if there was another Mick Peterson besides the one who eventually changed his name to Charles Bronson.

I think if Charlie was free then he'd need someone to look after him and point him in the right direction. The last time he came out of prison he was left to his own means – no money and no prospects. Now, though, Charlie could earn a good living just from his books and going around giving talks and interviews. I don't think he would need to sign on at the dole office.

I'm a big Tottenham Hotspur fan, as is Charlie, although I've still got a soft spot for my local team, Hartlepool United. Charlie and I have a lot in common, in that we both like a drop of vodka and a pint or two of Guinness and, of course, our past links with the crime world. I was just as bad as Charlie when I was younger and my criminal record proves it. Charlie would bash people up and I would, too, but I paid the price and learned my lesson. Now that Charlie's remarried I think he'll realise what he's missing being behind bars, and that's what can drive the man on to win his freedom ... thinking of his family.

Good luck, Charlie.

Michael Peterson

1

INSANITY

This is a book about madness. Unbalanced minds. Disturbances of the brain. Unpredictable people. Uncontrollable, dangerous and fearless! Men I've lived with, eaten with, laughed with, cried with, fought with! Men of *insanity*. Lost souls inside the asylums of hell, criminal and lunatic asylums, such as Broadmoor, Rampton and Ashworth, all top-secure establishments in England. These three are the only ones in England that cater for the criminally insane. Scotland has only one — Carstairs. I've been an inmate in Broadmoor, Rampton and Ashworth. I was one of 'them'. I was once Britain's most unstable madman!

This book is a complete one-off! If you're a nervous type of reader, then don't read it. You've been warned! You are now entering the world of insanity; please keep hold of your sanity until the book comes to a stop!

Just imagine — you're on a stretcher in a hospital, being wheeled to the operating theatre; they inject you, put you to sleep ... anaesthetic. You drift into blackness, you're out and you're the closest yet to death.

Then a surgeon cuts into your body, rips you open, goes deep inside, looks within, pulls a bit out, puts bits in, sews you up.

Then, if you're lucky, you awake! Some don't wake, and this is my point ... will you wake? Why should you? How can you? That's the black hole of madness you're in, screaming to get out. 'Alive' or just 'sane'? You want out of it, you want to see the light!

Hope – without hope you never awake! This hope, I live in continuously, every day of my life I'm under such an anaesthetic! I'm drugged up with the system's madness, they pump more and more into my head; my brain is swimming with their shit! They're beyond explanation, beyond explaining and beyond approach! A law unto themselves. Evil bastards! That is insanity!

It is said that we all have a double or a soul partner or brother or sister, whatever; either you believe it or you don't. But when you read this, it's sure to blow your wig off!

Here I am, banged up in old HMP Durham, England, when many thousands of miles away, in Durham County, North Carolina, USA, my namesake, Michael Peterson, is banged up and awaiting trial for murder. Now you readers new to me will know me as Charles Bronson, but I used to be called Mick Peterson (yeah, we all know it's me) but is it?

At the exact same time I'm banged up here in Durham Prison, so is this other Michael Peterson geezer from America. Only he's banged up in Durham Prison, in Durham County, USA! Like me, he's a writer, only he's a novelist and former city council and mayoral candidate (I did try to run for the advertised job as London Mayor, but didn't Lord Archer beat me to it ... until he was rumbled). Michael Peterson is charged with first-degree murder of his wife. (Don't mix him up with the Michael Peterson who wrote the Foreword ... he's a third Michael Peterson.)

The American Peterson, a former *Sun-Herald* columnist, claims his wife died after a fall down a flight of stairs. Sounds like a nightclub doorman's worst nightmare. The copper asks, 'What happened, old son?'

'Well blow me, didn't he go and fall down the stairs, officer!'

The defence claim that police used false and misleading affidavits to get search warrants for the home and grounds of murder suspect Michael Peterson. Just like me, this man is being given a raw deal. Cor, doesn't it make you really angry? The defence said that such police tactics were 'unconstitutional' and that, as a result, any information obtained in the Peterson searches should be thrown out — too fucking right they should.

After the indictment, Peterson spent three weeks in jail and was released in mid-January 2002, when a judge set an $850,000 secured bond for him. Peterson put up his Cedar Street home, with a tax value of $1.2 million, to cover the bond. Good on you, mate; maybe they'll give me bail, too!

The discovery of a body — the wife (Kathleen Peterson) of an outspoken critic of the police — at the bottom of a staircase is obviously a very tragic story.

All right, it might look bad for Michael Peterson right now; there are still many more questions than answers in his case. That won't stop many law-abiding folk from jumping to conclusions, of course.

Michael Peterson, like me, has been a sharp critic of the Durham Police Department for years; only I was a critic of all the police departments throughout the world. Old ladies being mugged, mobile phones being taken in street robberies ... all for what, a few quid!

Peterson went after the Durham cops for, among other things, a 'cowardly' approach to the problem of the city's violent gangs and 'the lowest clearance rate in solving crimes of any police force in the State'. So, like me, he opposes bullying and what does he get for it? A raw deal. See, one minute you can be running for the job of mayor and the next minute you're in the slammer on a murder rap; that's what I call insanity. So all you good people out there, be careful when criticising me, 'cos by tomorrow you could well be in the cell next to me!

Now, you think that's mad, it gets madder! I know some of you will have read the Foreword and, if you have, you'll have some idea of what I'm going to say next when I mention the other Michael Peterson. You see, it could be that I'm innocent of all charges! Did I kill myself off years ago to free Michael Peterson? Maybe he doesn't exist and it's me going insane? Is he living my life out there? Fuck me, it's awesome! What a story, even as far back as 1974 he was in my life, and I never knew! He could be me and I'm him!

This guy is the hidden key to madness, we have to open it up, it's a gem! People say I'm mad; a few years ago, Michael Peterson met Screaming Lord Sutch! Anyone remember Lord David Sutch? He's the guy who was always running for MP and represented the Monster Raving Looney Party, my favourite political party.

Lord Sutch never won a seat, came close a few times, but that was it. Sadly, on 16 June 1999, the godfather of pop and British politics was found hanged at his home in South Harrow, London. Like all the loons, it had become too much for him and he took the way out that most of them do – he was only 58. David wanted to forget his past, but they wouldn't let him, they thought he was Lord Sutch 24/7. Now that can be too much for any man, even me! One day, I know

I'll have to hang my Charles Bronson handle up and head for the sunset ... but until then, let's have fun, yeeeehaaaaa!

In a set of amazing coincidences, it would seem I'm also leading another life. My name given to me at birth was Michael Gordon Peterson; the other Mick Peterson has the same initials as me, but his middle name is 'George'. I was born on 6 December 1952; the other Mick was born on 25 March 1954, 15 months after me. My favourite drink is vodka; Mick's favourite drink is ... you've guessed it right, vodka! We both love a Guinness, too.

I started offending in earnest in 1969, whereas Mick started offending in 1970. Yeah, we've both got criminal records that date back some time! We both have records for violence. Wait 'til you hear this one; in 1974 I was sent to prison for robbery ... nothing strange about that. Back then, Mick Peterson was my name; the other Mick Peterson was working around the country having lived in London for a time, not far from Charlie Richardson's yard in Camberwell. During the early '70s, Mick was working at Butlin's for a number of summer seasons and also on the fairgrounds, which meant working away from home.

Mick's dear mother, Barbara, only goes and reads in the newspaper that Mick Peterson (me) has been sent to prison for robbery in Luton. Mick's mother lived in Hartlepool, so, to her, Luton may as well have been in London. Anyway, her son, Mick, lands back home on his mother's doorstep and his mum has the shock of her life saying, 'You're supposed to be in prison, what are you doing here?'

Is that mad or what? So Mick knew of me way back then. I only got to know about him when he joined my fan club in March 2000. Can you believe Mick Peterson joined my fan club? I thought, someone's having a laugh here! So now we know what went wrong; they've sent the wrong man to prison and I demand a retrial.

I could go on and on about the similarities between us, even down to looks. I mean, look at the beard, look at the power of the man, look at the bald head ... cor fucking blimey, if that isn't insane then I don't know what is! Right now, Mick is living in Hartlepool, he's married and has a grown-up son called Mark – I've got a brother called Mark. Mick has one giant-sized LP collection and he used to buy and sell at record collectors' fairs – that's where he met Lord Sutch, but Mick's great interest is the legendary, now dead, Frank Zappa.

Now there was a fucking legend if ever there was one! Frank Zappa died as a result of prostate cancer at his Los Angeles home on 4 December 1993, shortly before his fifty-third birthday. Zappa was one of the most original and complex figures to have emerged from the rock scene.

Zappa said he didn't care how he was remembered after he died, can you believe that? We fight to live, we want our memories to live on and yet he said, 'It's not important to even be remembered, I mean, the people who worry about being remembered are guys like Reagan, Bush ... I don't care.' Is that insane or what? Can you figure this guy out? Anyway, Mick has one of the largest Frank Zappa collections, and all on audio tape.

You can grow up being a trouble-maker and then, before you know it, the next thing you're doing is listening to Frank Zappa whilst chilling out ... now that's the intelligent way out. What would a psychiatrist say about that? I can tell you what a psychiatrist said about me when I was 13 years old.

This was my first encounter with a psychiatrist. I can still see his fat, spineless face and hear the shit coming out of his mouth. I had to see him over my problems at school. In those days, it was rare to see one of those people, but it was my first time and the record lives on ... but truly what does it mean?

I learned at that early stage that these sorts of people are not from my planet; they think completely differently and live entirely differently, they may as well be from planet Zappa! They actually look down on the working class! They're above us all, but over the years I've also learned that 80 per cent of these prats can't even put their own lives in order; it's a fact. What right-minded people can sit down listening to a lunatic all day, every day, year in and year out with no side-effects?

Anyway, this prick was a lesson to me, one to remember. I seriously thought about punching a hole in his fat face. As he spoke, I had visions of serious violence. Within ten minutes, this mutant made me feel dehumanised. What was he? God? What can he tell me that my dad can't? I'll tell you – dog shit. I should have punched him! Why not? Cunt!

Nowadays, the shrinks won't see me unless I'm in chains or with a dozen screws in the room. All apart from my lovely Dr Ghosh. She's just lovely to listen to. She came to see me at Whitemoor Prison, funnily enough, to see if I was sane (as I needed a report to say I'm sane to authorise a trust fund). She made a joke of it. 'Charlie, it's the first time I've had to come out of an asylum to do a report saying that you're sane.' She's like that, a lovely lady. (OK, I'm sane and my trust fund is sorted.) If I had seen someone like Dr Ghosh thirty-plus years ago, maybe I'd not be like I am today!

I remember a shrink in Wandsworth Jail back in the '70s. Now he was a really evil fucker, loved to juice you up using the liquid cosh, fucking done me up like a zombie, he did! I went to see him to chin the cunt, but I was so fucked up I could barely lift my arms up! He had me good and proper sorted!

That Dr Falk at headquarters was, in my opinion, a nasty bit of work, too. In the '70s, he diagnosed me a psychopath. That label has stuck with me ever since! Well how am I supposed to get a decent job outside with 'PSYCHO' stamped all over my medical file? Would you employ me ... would you? Would you fuck! A label sticks to you like shit to a blanket. I'm branded, I'm a marked man over all them reports. Nasty fuckers ... it's enough to turn a man to crime; well, a man's got to make a living, hasn't he?

You only have to look at our most famous doctor at the moment – Dr Harold Shipman. Need I say more? I fucking hate them all. I call them vets! And that's an insult to vets! A very prominent doctor at Parkhurst Prison was one of the psychiatrists who certified me mad, but years later he had a breakdown and got caught in the local woods, naked, taking his dog for a walk. If you work in a pig farm, you smell of pigs; if you work in a jail, you smell of crime!

Just take my advice and stay away from psychiatrists – they're dangerous. And if you're 13 years old and sitting in front of one, do what I never did ... chin him, 'cos if you don't, you'll live to regret it. You talk to your mum and dad (they know you best), and keep your problems in the family. Live and die with them.

Prison is riddled with madness and sadness. A young guy comes in weak; he gets hooked on heroin or smack, he sells his watch, radio and even his clothes. Then his arse gets sold; he sucks his life away for a bag of smack! One lad in Full Sutton came up to me. 'Help me, Chas,' he said with tears in his eyes. I took him into my cell, sat him down and he poured his heart out. He owed money, he had nothing, he was afraid. I went to see the 'dealer' and sorted it, but you can't help, it just gets worse. Once hooked, they're lost souls.

He kept sucking cock and taking it up the arse. That's madness. The poor fucker was probably a nice lad when he came in, now he's a faceless lost soul, going out a very bitter and hateful person who will kill for drugs. The system created it! The public will suffer ... prison is madness, it creates what you fear – a nightmare! Well, it created me, didn't it? I wasn't born like I am! I had a lovely family; prison drove me over the edge! I'm not crying, I accept it, but the system never will.

Is Bronson mad? Let me ask you. How else can I be? I'm probably the maddest guy on two legs if the truth be known, but prison will never beat me. I'd sooner die today than allow it to! I once walked into a cell in Frankland Jail, some seven years ago, right into a party of eight cons (all heavies). I pulled out a glass bottle of pop; they all looked. I handed it to one and said, 'Go on, use it on me!'

'What?'

'Hit me, any of you, hit me, smash it over my crust!'

No one did, so I did it myself! All looked, no sound, I walked out in peace, pissing blood and laughing ... I felt free of madness. That's mad! Nobody knows why it happens or how. But mad people live with it, day in, day out and, to some, it's horror and pain, but to others it's pleasure. My only sadness that day was that they never done it! Violence can be a release, a pleasure, it's a form of being loved and wanted.

So if everything I've said is the definition of insanity, then the next thing is – how do you define an evil bastard? People can mix evil and insanity up, thinking both to be the one and self-same thing ... wrong! Let me tell you about evil. First, you smell it; second, you feel it; third, you taste it; and finally, you need to destroy it.

If evil lingers around you, it will rub off on you; it will cause stress, anxiety and a lot of mental anguish! Eyes – you can see evil in the eye of the beholder! Body! Talk! Stance! Walk! Posture! Evil oozes out!

Ever see Moors murderer Ian Brady? Study his photos, study Black, study Cannon, study Sutcliffe – study them all! Who says evil is not recognisable?

Look at them mad bastards who go around shooting groups of innocent people; one guy in the USA shot seven dead around Christmas and a further ten were killed by a sniper ... if that doesn't resemble Bob Maudsley, then what does? The crazed eyes, out-of-this-world caveman look! That's evil out of control!

Evil is there, out there and in your face! You have two choices — either run or fight! To run is to die a coward. To fight is to win. 'Pleasure' is destroying the evil bastards. Once I would have taken the biggest axe and used it on all of them. Now, though, I'm a little bit cleverer than that. If I was free, I would be fighting the MPs to change the law, to make it so you can check who is on the register and who isn't. You deserve that from me, and so do they!

I've met 'em all — anyone who's anyone. If I've not seen them then I've spoken to them from my cage window or through a pipe in the wall or through a door! Bear in mind, I'm a solitary man, but at times people see me being escorted through the jail, into the dentist or for exercise. They'll chime out, 'Hi, Chas.'

'Who's that?'

'It's me, Mad Joe.'

'Hi, Joe.' I don't know him, but it makes his day and that's how it is with me.

Nowadays, I'm even harder to see ... I'm a myth! Soon, I'm dead.

Insanity can be a heavy cross to bear; I mean, look at all those people in loony bins compared to those who are free and walking the streets – a tiny percentage are classed as mad. The incidence of mental problems is said to be rising, so what do they go and do? They cut the number of asylums by half! Whoever makes these decisions has to be a complete nutter!

2

BEDLAM

How did madness start as an industry, employing millions of people around the world? Probably back in the days of the Egyptians when people were being lobotomised with nothing more than a hand drill ... and being charged to have it done! Since then, the world of madness has become a lucrative business to be in.

But as far as the industry in England is concerned, we have to go as far back as 1375 when the religious priory of St Mary of Bethlem, in London, was seized by the Crown and used for lunatics from 1377.

Would you believe that, by 1403–04, it had just six insane patients and three who were sane! This old Bedlam was a small institution by today's standards. The asylum stood on a site underneath what is now Liverpool Street Station. By the time the seventeenth century had arrived, it had about 30 patients. The Moorfields Bedlam replaced this in 1676 and, soon after that, I became an inmate ... only kidding, but it seems that long ago it might as well have been built in readiness for me.

There are different categories of madmen, and different types of asylums! I know absolutely nothing about the asylums that house the madman who thinks he is an astronaut. Would you believe that 90 per cent of madmen are treated in outside clinics? They're considered non-criminal, pathetic cases. This book refers to the other 10 per cent of madmen – the criminally insane. Killers, arsonists, poisoners and rapists – violent men. Men who have completely flipped, fallen over the edge, had nervous breakdowns and are brain diseased.

I was first certified mad in Parkhurst Prison in December 1978. Three doctors diagnosed me as being a psychopath and paranoid – Dr Cooper, Parkhurst; Dr Tipmarsh, Broadmoor; and Dr Falk, Home Office. So my prison world turned into the asylum world! I witnessed insanity at its best. If I wasn't mad when I arrived, then I certainly was when I left years later. I'll start my story of madness by explaining the everyday existence of being locked up in the asylum.

Rooms are cells! There are bars and locks everywhere, electronic cameras, walls, fences, alarms! And lots of highly trained psychiatric nurses built like rugby players, ready for anything. Ready to pounce, restrain and stab in the hypodermic needle to put the madman to sleep. They ask questions later.

When a madman flips, he normally has twice the strength of a normal man. So the male nurses go in fast, before somebody's missing an eye or a throat. These nurses live on their wits. They watch for signs – eye movement, body language, aggression. They only have to think a madman's gonna flip and they pounce.

These asylums are run by the Departments of Health and Social Security. After all, they are hospitals, or supposed to be! I've met them all and they've all met me! I became the most destructive madman the asylums had ever known. I could never accept life in the asylum. I've lived in a cage, in a strip cell and in a strong box. I've been injected, beaten, tortured and strapped up in jackets, but I could never come to accept who I was or what I was ... or what they said I was. Why should I? How should I? I never would.

One madman sat next to me. He kept looking, staring, bulging eyes. I felt tense, uncomfortable and edgy. I started to think fast. Be prepared. No madman's gonna get a crack at me! He started shaking, mumbling to himself; he looked upset. Tears welled up in his eyes, and then he hit me with the biggest bombshell ever! 'You killed my mum,' he said.

'How the fuck did I kill your mum? What the fuck are you talking about? I've never killed a woman in my life,' I replied.

He reckoned I killed his mother up in Scotland in 1948! For one, I've never been to Scotland, and for two, I wasn't born until 1951!

But this madman could not accept this! In his mind, I killed his mother. I had to keep an eye on this one. If I gave him half a chance he would kill me. No matter what I said or what I did, this madman truly believed I was the man who'd killed his mum!

Later, I used to shout back, 'Yeah, yeah, yeah and you killed my Aunty Rose, you evil slag, and you dug her up and shagged her, you filthy beast.' You learn to laugh or you would go mad!

I investigated, and it turned out he'd been sent to Broadmoor for stabbing his mother to death in a frenzied attack!

Another madman tore out one of his testicles and slung it over the wall in the exercise yard. This, I would have said, was humanly impossible, but I was there, and it happened.

And the madness in the asylums just piles up as time ticks on. One madman stripped off and climbed up a wall. At the top he shouted, 'I can fly.' He flapped his arms, and away he went ... with two broken ankles. Insane, but true! Another madman stabbed a fellow inmate with a pair of scissors a dozen times, just to liven up the day. Another madman drank another madman's blood, whilst the other drank his blood. Another two madmen killed another inmate by cutting his throat, wrists and penis. Another madman stabbed himself with a needle in the eye. He lost the eye. Another madman attempted to cut his penis off with a razor blade. Another madman snatched a doctor's gold pen and swallowed it. Another madman punched his mother in the nose, on a visit. Another madman stuffed a spoon in another madman's ear. Another madman attempted to use a saw on a nurse's neck. I was there. Another madman kept running at walls, head-butting them. Another madman swallowed a box full of drawing pins. And how do I know all those things? Because I was there!

I've truly seen some sights that even I still find hard to believe, and I can tell it all because ... I was there.

And if you think that's enough weirdness, here's some examples of madness at its best:

- One lunatic in Rampton used to have bouts of hysteria, in which he would let out a scream, and run at a wall and dive head first ... He was given a crash helmet!
- A nurse kicked another nurse in the bollocks at Broadmoor and got the sack! The nurse he kicked deserved it. Well done, mate.
- One lunatic in Broadmoor used to flop his dick out on the dinner room table and smash it with the teapot! Why? He just did it, that's why.
- One lunatic in Ashworth used to drop his trousers in the garden and shit in the rose bushes. Why? 'Cos he liked to do it.
- A loon thought he was Frank Sinatra and every time

Frank came on TV or the radio the loon would go mad – 'Imposter!'

- A loony in Broadmoor picked up a TV set and hit another loony over the head with it. Why? 'Cos he was laughing!
- A loon made a model gallows out of matches; it took him ages, it looked so real! Later, he did actually hang himself.
- A loony stabbed another loony 12 times with a pair of scissors just to brighten up the day!
- A loony was found in the dormitory wearing a bra, suspenders, a wig and a very sore arse!
- A loony once buried his watch and rings in the gardens at Broadmoor then forgot where they were!
- A loon asked a nurse to ride around the exercise yard; he got so upset, he took a hostage!
- A flotilla of used condoms was often found in the soup! (I never ate it, ever.)
- A loon used to suck off three loons in one go. They called him Jaws!
- A game of bowls was banned as one ended up over someone's crust!
- A loony used to pay other loons in fags to rip his pubic hairs out!
- A loony fell in love with his budgie and applied to marry it!
- A loony bit through the TV wire and almost died!

PARANOID SCHIZOPHRENIA

This is the real McCoy! Dangerous and unpredictable. Schizophrenia is a mental illness and is treated with psychotropic drugs. Sufferers hear the 'voice', it tells them to attack! Nobody knows where the voice comes from, even the doctors are baffled. Maybe the voice doesn't exist, maybe it's the spirit, maybe it's in the mind, maybe it's Lucifer! Nobody knows. But the madman hears it, and the madman acts on it. Sometimes innocent people die because of that 'voice'. There is no cure, but the drugs help to stabilise the condition.

PSYCHOPATHIC

This is a disorder, not an illness. It's an untreatable personality disorder. But the asylums are full of psychopaths. Makes even me wonder!

PSYCHOTIC

Mental illness – voices, delusions, dangerous, unpredictable. Treated with strong tranquillisers.

HYSTERIA

Loss of control, unacceptable behaviour; insanity takes over!

PYROMANIA

Fire freaks – they get a buzz out of setting fire to buildings. They're dangerous, as one match can burn to death a lot of innocent people. Treatment: lock them away in asylums (with no matches).

DELUSIONS OF GRANDEUR

They imagine they're somebody else. I've met the Pope, Jesus, Hitler, Hercules, John Lennon – they're all alive in the asylums. Some will become violent if you don't believe who they are! These madmen bring a bit of character to the asylums. They brighten the place up.

EPILEPSY

In the years gone by, asylums were full of epileptics. It wasn't 'til the early 1950s that it was established by the medical journals as being a physical illness, and not mental. But sadly, even today, epileptics are still in asylums such as Rampton and Broadmoor. Obviously, they're the criminal element. But I've witnessed epileptics having fits and they've been treated as madman. It's a fact, sad but true.

So these asylums cater for every kind of insanity. But, bear in mind – we are all criminals ... in our own ways. My crime was armed robbery, but I was turned into a madman whilst serving a prison sentence. I became violent and difficult to control. I was created by a very brutal system which meets violence with violence. I became what I am today. I'll now die with the label 'mad dog'.

A doctor once told me in Broadmoor something I've never forgotten: 'We only take the best here, and you're the best.'

I often think about this, and what he said was true. And it doesn't just go for Broadmoor, it goes for any of the secure asylums. Once you've been certified criminally mad, it's never forgotten. How can they afford to forget – police, doctors, probation officers, social services, courts, prisons and, of course, not forgetting the public? Ask anybody – would you want an ex-madman living next door? It's difficult enough being an ex-convict. It's doubly hard for us 'madmen'. Believe it.

Nowadays, when the police come for me, it's with guns! One false move from me and I'm dead. They come for me with instructions to shoot. They know it; I know it. It's a miracle I'm still alive today. On their part, it's fear of the unknown.

They ask themselves: 'What will he do?' 'How will he react?' 'Will he go mad?' 'Will he bite?' 'Will he be armed?' They're pumped up with fear. Adrenalin pumping, fingers tense on the trigger, brains racing. And I'm cool as a cat! The name 'Charles Bronson' causes panic! The name 'Mickey Peterson' causes stress! The police all love to arrest me, as I'm the most exciting madman they will ever bring in! It's a fact. So here I am, years later, and I'm still the madman.

There is no escaping my past:

- I've left behind a trail of havoc, destruction and violence that will never be forgotten! The Home Office must really be fed up with my name. 'Oh no, not Bronson again.'
- I've destroyed TV sets, furniture, sinks, toilets, offices, cells and roofs!
- I've punched more prison officers than any convict I know!
- I've attempted to kill two madmen by strangulation!
- I've spent years and years in solitary confinement!
- I've taken more hostages than Saddam Hussein!
- I've attacked prison governors!
- I've been on eight prison roofs!
- I've cut a prison officer!

And all for what? All for a label of madness. I've achieved absolutely fuck all ... just a 'mad dog' tag.

Looking back at the years I spent in the asylums, I'm now convinced some of that insanity rubbed off on to me. And I'm also convinced my ending will be a police ambush. They will shoot me dead. It's a fact of life!

I'm actually lucky to be alive today. Way back on 25 February 1993, I had a dozen police marksmen aiming at my head – from my point of view, not a nice sight. Fortunately, I was with somebody, otherwise I believe they would have shot me dead. It's a fact of life, which I've come to accept!

I have received a raw deal just like Michael Peterson from Durham County in North Carolina, USA. Some would say I've dug my own grave. Some would say, 'Shoot the nutcase.' Say what you will, but I say, 'It takes two to tango.'

Mad people are very emotionally orientated! They have complex feelings, they're easily upset, but are also easy to please! Most mad people have lonely lives, as nobody understands them. So they become 'lost souls'. They dream a lot, go within their minds to search – some will turn strange and become dangerous. So a madman is created. His world becomes a mission. Bear in mind, every madman was once a lovely, innocent baby; every mother's little angel. Man was not born to be shot down like a 'mad dog'. All mad dogs end up in a pool of blood, or a cage for life. Either ending is a disaster; a waste of life. It wasn't worth being born!

DEAD EYES

I've watched the old men in the asylums. Men of 70, even 80, who have been locked away all their lives. I've even seen them die, go to sleep in a chair and never wake up. They arrived 40-odd years before in a straitjacket, and left in a body bag. They only ever knew one life – madness.

But when these madmen get to a certain stage, their eyes go dead. There is no more sunshine, no more to see, just memories in a cage. Forgotten men. They're just waiting to die.

There is a hell before they arrive. I've spoken to these old men. I've tried to understand them, but they're too far gone. Their eyes say it all. It's a bit like looking into a hole in the earth ... emptiness!

I've always said to myself, over and over, 'Don't end up this way.' Well, I've spent nearly two-and-a-half decades behind closed doors and nearly three decades behind bars – I'm still in a fucking cage! So I had better be careful. I don't want dead eyes – the bullet would be better.

I personally could never come to terms with my label of 'Criminally Insane'. Just because of my violent outbursts in prison, it doesn't mean to say I'm mad. Obviously I had become

a disruptive element within the penal system. Uncontrollable! Unpredictable! But that doesn't make me insane!

I'll go as far as admitting I had problems, severe psychological problems. The reason for this was that my prison life had become a war. I felt every day was a struggle, so violence was inevitable! It was the only way to get myself heard. One doctor once told me I was a victim of my own notoriety. Prison officers saw me as a threat, so they made my life hell. And, basically, that's what pushed me over the edge.

I survived every sort of punishment and, in the end, there was no more, only to be certified mad. The asylums really opened my eyes. They had a strange effect on my personality. As the years rolled by, would you believe, I became a more compassionate man. For example, in prison I would punch a con's face in if he had killed his wife or mother, but I soon realised they were very sick people. Asylums are full of tragic cases. Some of these guys killed their whole families while in a depressed state.

I've seen them live with the memory, year after year. Smashing their heads into walls, cutting their throats, screaming in their sleep. They live on in horror, in a 'drug haze'. Yeah, some of these old boys I've met in the asylums are tragic cases. They tell me if a man loses his roots, he also loses his soul. I believe this. I swear to God, the thought of me dying an old man in a madhouse just turns my blood cold! If this were my end, then I'd sooner die today.

A lot of these old boys have spent three-quarters of their life inside, so really it would be cruel to set them free. Imagine it! Fifty years in a lunatic asylum, living with dangerous killers, then at the age of 70 they free you! It just can't happen! There were times I was up on the roof protesting for better treatment and better conditions, when some of these old boys were shouting up to me from their cell windows, 'Come down, stop tearing our roof off.'

This used to confuse me, as in a prison cons would shout, 'Tear the place to bits.' But these old boys were in my heart. They had suffered more years than any men I knew. Obviously, they were mad or had been. One had killed two men with his bare hands. But that was long ago, before arthritis set in! These old boys were legends, historic, myths waiting to be born!

After a while, one learns to accept the madness. I was surrounded with it. Some of the madmen are really fun to be with, and I soon learned to relate to them. I soon became one of them. I ended up the maddest of the mad. There is no one madder than myself! Please believe it. But my madness is still a mystery. There is no cure, as there is no diagnosis. Over the years, I've been labelled all sorts. Nowadays, I just don't care; I've taken the Frank Zappa stance. I am who I am! Some love me, some loathe me, some respect me and some despise me. But after all that's been, I still love the insane, as they're exciting, dangerous and highly explosive! For me, mad dogs are gentlemen.

I end this chapter with a poem of mine:

Psychopathic Poet

Yeah, I put three bullets in his head.
If that's what the coppers said.

Yeah, I stabbed a man through the heart,
Twenty-five times with a poison dart.

Yeah, yeah, yeah, I've done it all.
I've lived my life behind this wall!

The girl I loved she passed away,
My blood ran cold that tragic day!

Soul deep I've tried to find,
Red-hot coals inside my mind!

Charles Bronson
Prison No. BT1314

3

CRAZY LITTLE THING CALLED INSANITY

Insanity is everyday life inside the asylum – screams, banging about, violence and pain, but mostly depression. We are all lost souls living from day to day. We, Category 'A' inmates are like chess pieces – they pick us up and move us where they choose to; we have no say in it!

I'll tell you what's insane – years back, sitting on a plastic pot and having a crap – full-grown men sitting on a potty – then, when the cell door is opened, walking to the recess to slop it away! At times, I've slung it all over a screw – not a pretty sight!

Everything is mad in jail, and it gets under your skin, it makes you sick. It drives me to the edge and pushes me over. I've been unstable ever since. My senses are now on turbo! I expect anything, like my door crashing open and shields smashing me up against the wall or smashing into me whilst I'm in bed. They then wrap me up, secure me in a body belt, put on the ankle straps and cart me away. It's happened so many times. It can still happen today, even as I write these words — it's my life!

Tension is no longer a coiled spring ready to pounce ... it's a way of life for me and it can cause hate and bitterness. I went through a period in which I hated; I was full of hate but I came out of that stage, I learned to ride it, I learned to juggle it. I'm now a connoisseur of madness. I play them at their own game. And that's all it is, a game!

We all have to play a part; the system knows it's only a game, a game of insanity. I smile and laugh now, I don't take it seriously any more 'cos the system loves to upset people! Nothing would please them more than to open my door and see me dead, hanging, or a cut-throat lying by my dead body. They haven't the bottle to kill me! They've had 30 years to do it, but I'm still here and they know I'm telling the truth! Truth hurts, see, truth is a weapon; kill me or drop me out! Leave me in my madness, I love my own space!

Insanity is prison life. It breeds violence and madness and really fucks you up. It made me what I am today — unpredictable. I'm a very confused man, but I have this power to help the insane. Mad people come to me, I attract them — like attracts like! They wave to me regularly, pure 22-carat nuts! But I love them all. My life is now madness; the madder the better for me.

I once had a thought, before I married my beautiful Saira, that I'd like to meet the maddest bitch on the planet, and I mean dangerously mad. I'd like to fuck her in a pit of scorpions, poisonous ones, or swim with her in shark-infested waters. Live dangerously — drive at 130mph the wrong way up the motorway at 3.00am and hope nothing is coming so we could laugh and cry together!

Another outlandish thought was to get two guns. One bullet in each ... spin the chamber ... she puts her gun into my ear, I put mine in hers. Click! Click! It's love. What girl could or would do that? Find her, if she exists! She's the one, pure mad. She doesn't smoke or do drugs but she kicks ass. She fights to live.

All aspects of life are insane, but this prison shit is the maddest! I'm now getting older, some say too old. 'Old Charlie's past his best.' 'Charlie should get out now and retire.' Who knows when the end will fucking come? Right now, I'm living on the edge. Madness is all around me; I smell it, I stink of it; I'm the ultimate madman: a poet, an artist, a sculptor, a writer, a fitness freak – I'm also a man of respect. Not bad for a madman, eh?

I've kept my morals and self-discipline, which is more than I can say for the system. The system is jealous of me. I'm caged up and they're fucking jealous of me. But am I jealous of them? The screws, the governors and the doctors – am I fuck! They're all puppets – 'Yes, sir, no, sir, three bags full, sir.' All for what? A wage, power or just to be evil. Whatever! They're all fucking insane. They're the same as me; the only difference is that I admit I'm mad – they never will. They sit on their fat lazy arses, scratching their fat lazy bellies. They fart away their lives. Oh well! That's the insane for you. Until they start to change, then how can I?

Insanity. Can anybody define it? Just what is it? Let me tell you, it's a terrible pain, or can be. Ronnie Kray once told me, 'It's a gift of life, if you keep it under control.' But my view is, it's a pain in the head. There are so many different forms of insanity, from the silly to the dangerous. Some mad people are quite harmless, loving and good-natured. Others are homicidal maniacs.

Me? Well, I guess I could be classed as unpredictable. Some would say the best thing for me is a .38 in the crust. Yes, I am, in fact, one of the insane and proud of it! My insanity has taken me on a journey through all three maximum-secure asylums in England, and at one time I was Britain's number one madman.

But right now I need to explain to you about insanity. I'm not a doctor or a poxy professor. I'm just a man who understands it, only 'cos I've lived among the mad for many years. I can smell it, taste it and feel it. Insanity hits me like a mallet over the head. And what is more, insanity cannot be cured. No mad person can be cured. They can be controlled, and then apparently get better, but the madness never goes away. You're born mad and you die mad!

We get urges, like some people want to stuff themselves with food or beer, or the reverse, they like to throw the food back up – it's all in the mind! We are addicted to madness and at times we lose the plot, just like a seizure. Believe me, it's never cured; we get older, slower and more mature, but the insanity lies deep within, it's a disease of the mind and it doesn't just affect the insane, it affects everybody around them – family, friends, nurses, everybody. Believe me, it's awesome! It's, at times, lethal and dangerous to the point of death. We get vibes, visions, voices and urges. We just go on a mission; some don't come back. It's a dead end. We exist but we do not live.

Some will be drugged up, with psychotropic tranquillisers, but that is only control. Some will be given electrotherapy – shocks to the brain, torture. Nothing works, nothing ever will. How can it?

I'm now gonna shock you with some true facts. I've mentioned some of these nutters already. Now it's time to meet them properly. Let me take you on a journey to hell!

• He sat in a chair, silent, shaking, depressed! On the edge, and then he jumped up and started to scream. He was still screaming as the white coats carried him off to the 'silent room'. He had stabbed himself in the eye with a needle! I can still hear his scream inside my head. That's insanity. He lost an eye, but that's not all he lost — his mind went with it!

• Another swallowed a pen, a whole pen. Could you swallow a pen? Who wants to swallow a pen?

• He was locked up safe for the night, but his mind was in agony! Insanity was back. He was crying out for help, but behind the door there was nobody to help or listen to him. They found him swinging off the bars at 6.00am in the morning. He was 22 years old.

• The pyromaniac felt the urge coming on. So he set fire to the dustbin whilst he was pulling himself off watching the flames. The nurses put it out, then locked him up in seclusion. It was funny to see; he was still watching while they carried him off. Insanity at its best! Violence out of control, that's what it is.

• One guy, who climbed a building, flapped his arms to fly, and when he landed he broke both his ankles. Something inside him told him he could fly. The insanity came back. It never really went away, it's always there. It's there until you die. It just goes to sleep at times, but believe me, it wakes up and starts to scream!

• He sat in the corner of the cell looking at his hands. They looked deformed, old, tired and worn. He punched himself in the face, again and again. He began to laugh as he pounded into his ugliness. When the door unlocked, he steamed into the white coats. It took ten to restrain him. Insanity is beyond reality. Don't even try to work it out. That's insanity!

• He walked around the yard, hunched up like an old man. Hands in his pockets, eyes on the floor, nobody took a lot of notice. He had been walking around for 25 years, no trouble. Why should he be any trouble? It was just another day, until he jumped on another madman and bit his throat out. That's insanity! It was bubbling up inside him all the time! Nobody ever knew why, or how it got there. So what good are the

doctors and nurses and the drugs and the therapy? I'll tell you
– no good. Insanity is incurable and you'd better believe it!

• He put his cock on the table and hit it with a large, square
PP9 battery in a sock. Anyone else would have screamed. He
does it for fun, pain and pleasure. You should see the size of it!
Awesome! He must have hit it a million times. There is no more
pain. Tell a doctor that. How does he cure that? He can't. That's
insanity; pain is insanity!

• She sat crying in her room, in the asylum, alone, depressed.
She began to peel off the flakes of paint on the wall. Do you
know how sharp these flakes of paint are? Sharp enough to cut
a wrist and pull on the tendon and artery. They found her in a
pool of blood the next day. Took her out in a body bag; 26 years
old, a pretty little thing. That's insanity!

• He never did like the loon with the funny eyes; it was his
eyes he never liked, so he stabbed him ... 28 times. The loon
never once said a word to him.

• Another one got stabbed in the ear; it pierced his brain,
cabbaged for life. He's in a chair, shits his pants. What a way to
end up. He was 32 years old. That's insanity!

• The gay psycho loved a bit of fresh meat. The new loon was
only 21, with a lovely tight arse. The psycho left him in a heap
in his cell with a bleeding arse. The lad got eight stitches and a
scarred brain.

• What about the guy who ripped out his testicle? Why? No
one knows, no one ever will know! They can guess, they can
pretend to know, but they never will know!

• Then there were two madmen who took a fellow madman
hostage. (Durham) Dead man. They took half his brain out, cut
his bollocks off.

• He hated his face so much he smashed it to bits with a
bottle of Ribena ... 850 stitches. Now he loves it!

• He had a toothache, 'bad'; it took him all night to cure it.

He tore out all his teeth! 'PAIN!' Then pain free. That's insanity!

• A man, 38, spent 15 years of his life in the asylum. He picked up the razor and began to cut. The screams could be heard all over the asylum, but why did do it? He had his cock in his hand as the white coats rushed in! Insanity at its best!

Yeah, I've met them all! Hey, I'll tell you who's mad – Chris Brand. We call him Brandy, and he's one sad bastard. He killed a con in Norwich Jail 20 years back; he was only 20 years old at the time and he drowned this old lag in the bath. Brandy gets bad bouts of madness during which he does mad things like sticking razor blades up his arse! Ouch! Sets fire to his hair, cuts himself up. He is a sad case.

Last I heard he took an overdose ... and survived. How many fucking lives has this guy got, I ask? But he's a game fucker; he once cut big Fred Lowe down his face. Fred killed two cons in '93. If he gets a hold of Brandy, Fred's 18st, Brandy's 10st! Not good odds, is it? But Brandy never runs away from anybody. He once said to me, 'Chas, do you know why I'm not scared of anybody?'

'No, why?' I replied.

'Because one day I've got to die and the truth is the sooner the better!'

Brandy will die inside and, no doubt, violently. What a fucking sad world. Insanity drove him mad!

I'll tell you who's also lost the plot – Dougie Wakefield. I met Dougie in Armley Prison in Leeds back in 1975. In the '70s and '80s Doug had the label as Britain's most violent man. He was a Yorkshireman, having been sentenced to life for stabbing his uncle with a garden fork. The poor bastard had more perforations in him than a tea bag when he finished with him.

Dougie just lost his mind in the '70s. I don't think he knew what day or month it was; he took a screw hostage in Long Lartin and demanded a cat! Why a cat? Fuck knows! Then he half-strangled another screw, then he killed Brian Peak in Parkhurst. Brian was the wing barber, and often trimmed my tash for me!

Dougie got another life on top. Broadmoor refused to accept him and he spent years in solitary; two years of that was spent in the box in Albany. That's where he started to deteriorate mentally, so they moved him to the hospital wing in Parkhurst. Whilst there, a little Jock stuffed a coffee jar into the face of the Yorkshire Ripper, and ripped him right up. Jock Costello got ten years on top for that attack. He should have got a medal.

The Ripper was right chopped up; 100 stitches, he was a beauty. But Dougie made a statement to the pigs that it was his coffee jar and he gave it to Jock, which helped to convict him, so Dougie lost his good name. All his years of suffering finally took away his morals. You don't fucking make statements to pigs. Full stop.

I lost touch with him for some years, then in the early '90s I bumped into him up in Full Sutton Prison – he was still very strange. I noticed his walk, it was pathetic, 15st and wiggling his fat arse, and he seemed to talk in a high-pitched voice. Twenty-plus years had turned him into a fucking lunatic.

Then in the mid '90s, I was blown away, I opened the *Guardian* newspaper and there he was, looking at me. PRISONER WANTS A SEX CHANGE. After 30 years of being caged up, he had finally lost his mind; he believed he was a woman trapped in a man's body. Dougie Wakefield was insane, he was still 15 fucking stone and looked like a rugby player. Who the fuck's he gonna hitch up with? The Elephant Man? What man would date him? Fuck me, your life would be at stake! Still, the facts are simple; Doug lost it over the Ripper attack in the '80s at Parkhurst. He should not have done that.

Ask Jock Costello what he thinks. I had a lot of respect for Dougie up until then, as he was a legend! Fearless! I wonder where he is now. Gotta be an asylum, surely ... and I can't see it being Holloway women's prison, can you?

Having mentioned the Ripper, it's probably a good time to talk a bit about the attacks on him. The first happened on 10 January 1983 in Parkhurst, two years after his trial in 1981. The Ripper's attacker, James 'Jock' Costello, 35, from Glasgow, had the right qualifications for the job – 28 court appearances between 1963 and 1980, nine of them in relation to violence, and 15 appearances resulting in prison sentences. He had been convicted in 1980 for possessing a firearm with the intent to endanger life, possessing a firearm with intent to resist arrest and possessing a firearm without a certificate. He had received a ten-year sentence. He had been diagnosed as mentally ill at Parkhurst, and was awaiting transfer to Broadmoor.

The attack took place while Sutcliffe, the Ripper, was getting water in a plastic bowl. Jock Costello entered the recess and, as Sutcliffe turned to leave, he smashed him twice on the left side of his face with a broken coffee jar. Sutcliffe, the lucky bastard, managed to push him away, but by this time he had four nice wounds requiring a lot of stitches. One deep cut ran five inches from near his mouth to his neck, leaving a nice Mars bar, and another was $2^1/_5$in long, running from his left eye to his ear. He also had two smaller cuts on the eyelid and below the eye. The Ripper had lost about a pint of blood and had gone into a mild state of shock. He required an operation to repair superficial muscle damage. So you see, these attacks on monsters are well worth it ... it gets the desired result and leaves them with a label.

The Home Office doc and a visiting professor soon sectioned the Ripper off to Broadmoor under the Mental Health Act. In September 1982, my old friend, the prison medical officer Dr David Cooper, and a consultant forensic scientist, Professor John Gunn, both recommended that Sutcliffe should be transferred to a top-security mental hospital under Section 72 of the Mental Health Act. Section 72 states that the transfer to a mental hospital cannot be made without the approval of the

Home Secretary. In December 1982, the Home Secretary, William Whitelaw, rejected the transfer, saying that Sutcliffe would remain at Parkhurst in the public interest. Good on Willie Whitelaw to make this move; the Ripper was done good style by Willie's insistence that he stayed at Parkhurst.

The new Home Secretary, Leon Brittan, finally transferred Sutcliffe to Broadmoor on 27 March 1984. Now bear in mind that Jock Costello, the man responsible for the Ripper needing stitches in his face, has already been transferred to Broadmoor ... good on you, Leon – method in your madness! Get Jock to Broadmoor first and then send the Ripper on to him.

When Jock Costello was asked what had happened, he said that Sutcliffe had attacked him. Sutcliffe said, 'As I was turning the tap off I became aware of someone else in the recess. I didn't pay particular attention to who it was. I took about two strides, that's all, and all of a sudden I was the subject of a particularly nasty, unprovoked attack. The first thing I was aware of was a glinting coming from a glass container. I saw it glinting just before it hit my face. That was the first I saw of it when a person used it to cause severe damage.'

The Ripper pointed to the left side of his face. 'It hit me there. He had time to smash into my face twice before I could do anything. I just put my arms out. Before I held him at arm's length, the glass smashed on the floor. I quickly put the bowl in the sink and stuck my arm out to keep him away from me. Blood was coming from his hand and then some hospital officers came running in. The only thing I noticed was when it was practically in my face. There was only a thousandth of a second before it smashed into my face. There was no chance to avoid it or anything.'

Yeah, just the same sort of chance he gave all those innocent women when he disembowelled them.

Costello was committed for trial at Newport Crown Court and

was granted legal aid. The magistrates also rejected a request for the trial to be held at Winchester Crown Court. James Costello, just as I had in my last trial, had dismissed all his lawyers and was defending himself.

Would you believe that the prosecutor, Christopher Leigh, told the jury to put anything they knew about Peter Sutcliffe from their minds? Is he for fucking real! Sutcliffe spent over two hours in the witness box swearing Costello's life away; he might as well have brought a packed lunch.

When Jock Costello questioned the Ripper – several times they had a verbal ding-dong – the Ripper admitted that he had become 'a cell recluse', and didn't want to mix with other prisoners.

Jock claimed the Ripper attacked him after a confrontation between the two of them when Jock said the Ripper had 'censored' an article in the *Sun* newspaper about the January prison siege at Parkhurst. The Ripper admitted that he had blotted out an article about vice and prostitutes in the *Sun* newspaper with his artist's paint, and occasionally cut out libellous comments before passing it on to other cons.

During his testimony, the Ripper said to Jock, 'I am being generous answering these questions, because you need all the help you can get from psychiatrists, not from the courts.' After all that, the judge ordered a retrial. He wouldn't give a reason; now that's what I call insanity!

The evidence was again presented to the new jury. Jock Costello and the Ripper again clashed. When Costello suggested that Sutcliffe had attacked him, Sutcliffe replied, 'I didn't, and you know it. There was no question of any argument or fight.'

Jock asked, 'Have you ever thought you heard me say I was going to kill you?'

'Yes, at the time of the incident. But I didn't put it in my statement to the police because I could not swear to it.'

Jock asked, 'Do the voices tell you to attack people?'

'You won't raise that with me. You are getting into something you can't understand.'

Dr Cooper agreed that the Ripper was mentally ill at the time of the attack.

Jock asked, 'Would his mental illness make him likely to attack someone?'

Dr Cooper replied, 'Women,' and said it would be unlikely that the Ripper would ever attack a man.

The Ripper was becoming braver when he started giving Jock the lip. 'I answer questions like that to qualified people, not idiots like you.'

Jock responded, 'You are the one that has got the scar.'

The jury found Jock Costello guilty, by a ten to two margin, of wounding the Ripper with intent to cause him grievous bodily harm. I hope if you were one of the jurors that you never have to see any member of your family on the mortuary slab after someone like the Ripper has finished with them. Jock Costello was sentenced to a further five years. Judge Lewis McCreery said to Jock, 'You inflicted appalling injuries on Sutcliffe. You are one of the most dangerous and evil men it has ever been my misfortune to encounter.' What about the Ripper? Wasn't *he* one of the most evil and dangerous men that Judge Lewis McCreery has had the misfortune to encounter?

Jock told the judge, 'I don't understand how any man can get sentenced for using too much violence against a guy who has killed 13 people and had me by the throat. I know I am a violent man. I was not well at the time. I was on my way to Broadmoor.'

In 1996, Jock told the *Daily Record*, 'We were both in the Parkhurst psychiatric wing. I was doing 22 years for carrying a gun and resisting arrest. Peter Sutcliffe was always swaggering about with his minder, a nutter called Wakefield. So I got my chive and done him when his minder was slopping out. I remember Sutcliffe roaring like a wounded animal.

'My original diagnosis at Broadmoor was that I was a psychopath. The consultant read this out in court and the newspapers took it up, which was degrading. I felt Sutcliffe was a psycho, but not I. I hadn't slaughtered all those women. But then I was re-diagnosed paranoid schizophrenic when I admitted hearing voices.'

Paul Wilson carried out attack number two on the Ripper in Broadmoor on 23 February 1996. Paul, a big guy, was a blagger who had been diagnosed as mentally ill; he tried to strangle Sutcliffe. On Henley Ward on a Friday night, Paul knocked on the Ripper's door and asked whether he could borrow a video. The flex from a pair of stereo headphones was the tool Paul used to try and strangle the Ripper.

The battle was on, but the Ripper had managed to scream for help. Two other murderers – Kenneth Erskine, the Stockwell Strangler, and Jamie Devitt – rats that they are, ran to help the Ripper. Nurses then took Paul to an isolation unit – probably the plastic room! Like me, Paul has a deep hatred of monsters, and told the staff that he resented being locked up with them. Although I wasn't at Broadmoor, news travels fast in the system so all the details are 100 per cent reliable.

The staff had been told not to talk about it. Broadmoor had not called the police in to investigate. Broadmoor's general manager, Alan Franey, said, 'You know I cannot and will not comment on any incident which involves one of my patients, especially one who is of such high profile. It is hospital policy not to refer to individual patients and I have to respect that confidentiality.'

The police said, 'We are surprised we were not asked to investigate but Broadmoor appears to be a law unto itself.' Although the police later investigated the attack, the Ripper did not press charges.

Attack number three on the Ripper came on 10 March 1997,

when Ian Kay stabbed him in the eyes with a Parker rollerball pen. I think we'll rename Kay 'Rollerball Kay'!

Rollerball Kay had been jailed for eight years in December 1991 for nearly killing a shop assistant and for carrying out a series of 16 robberies on stores in London.

Within two hours of Rollerball Kay being released on home leave from prison, he had robbed a post office. He was again given home leave in August 1994 and failed to return. Between August and November of that year, he later admitted to seven robberies, a theft and an attempted theft, all on Woolworth's.

In November 1994, Kay was charged with the murder of Woolworth's have-a-go-hero assistant manager John Penfold. Kay had stabbed the assistant manager through the heart with a kitchen knife before grabbing two 50p coins from the till, which he dropped as he ran to a nearby getaway car.

Psychiatrists said Kay was suffering from an abnormal personality disorder, and it was argued at his trial that he was unable to control his violent impulses. His plea of manslaughter on the grounds of diminished responsibility was dismissed and Kay was jailed for a minimum of 22 years in 1995. Later, after showing signs of mental illness, Kay was transferred to Broadmoor.

There are a number of stories as to how the Ripper was attacked. One is that he had been sitting in his room in Henley Ward when Rollerball Kay burst in and, before staff could reach them, an argument had broken out. After a scuffle, the Ripper was penned in both eyes. It was believed that Rollerball Kay was padded up a couple of doors away from the Ripper and that he objected to being so close to one of Britain's most notorious monsters. Let that be a warning to all the other monsters!

Rollerball Kay had made a couple of attacks on patients in the months leading up to penning the Ripper in his eyes ... practice makes perfect! I have to wear special glasses with darkened lenses to shield my eyes from bright lights; all the years of being in artificial light has fucked my eyes — now maybe the Ripper knows what it's like to have bad eyes.

The Ripper was taken to the specialist eye unit at Frimley Park Hospital, near Camberley, Surrey. The following day he was again taken to Frimley Park Hospital where the eye specialists gave him the good news — 'We can't save the sight in your left eye,' while his right eye was likely to have impaired vision.

Thames Valley Police charged Rollerball Kay with attempted murder. On 27 January 1998, Kay was in Reading Crown Court, where he admitted the charge of attempting to murder the Yorkshire Ripper. How can a man who is in a mental health establishment be prosecuted and taken to court when he's been declared mental? Suddenly a man is sane enough to stand trial!

The Ripper was meant to be murdered by having his throat slit open with a razor blade embedded in the end of a toothbrush, but staff could not find the blade. Rollerball Kay told police, 'I was going to ask for an envelope, walk into the room and cut his jugular vein on both sides and wait there until he was dead. Killing has always been in my mind, ever since I've been here [Broadmoor]. In hindsight, I should have straddled him and strangled him with my bare hands.'

As well as the pen attack, Rollerball Kay had gone into the Ripper's room with a piece of electrical flex, intending to strangle him. Rollerball Kay said, 'I shut his door and attacked him. I started to stab him in the eyes and throttle him. My objective was to kill him, and I tried to do it as best as I could. I could not be bothered to use the flex in the end. I should have kneed him in the face a few times, straddled him across his body and throttled him with my bare hands.' Too fucking right.

Now this is insanity at its best. Kay was asked why he had tried to kill the Ripper and he said, 'Because it was the Devil's work ... God had told him to kill 13 women, and I say the Devil told me to kill him because of that.'

Mr Justice Keene, sentencing Rollerball Kay to be detained without restriction of time under section 37 of the Mental Health Act 1983, told him, 'You admitted your intention to kill him. It must cause some public concern that you were able to carry out such an attack. You are clearly a very dangerous man, indeed. I'm satisfied you are suffering from a psychiatric disorder and that you ought to be detained in a hospital for medical treatment.'

Now I know I've had one or two bad words to say about old Jack Straw, the former Home Secretary, but this time I praise him, 'cos he refused to move the Ripper from Broadmoor when the Ripper's family requested he be moved to Ashworth Special Hospital. The appeal to the Home Secretary was turned down. You know, I'm beginning to see method in all this madness.

Prisons are full of strange people. I met a real transsexual in Hull who had real tits and was waiting for the op! Nice legs, firm arse, she/he did stir my loins, I must admit. But I have to say now ... I just couldn't — could you? Makes me feel ill. Personally, I see them as freaks, fucking freaky people. But I also feel sad for them, as it's not their fault; they should be shot, put them out of their misery!

I've learned to understand it. I can smell it coming! It's an inner sense, it's no secret; I love mad people, they're unique.

Insanity comes in many forms, as we've seen — sexual psycho, depressive, schizoid, psychosis. Whatever, it can't be cured; well, it can ... with a bullet. They shoot a mad dog, so why not a madman? That's the cure! But they don't want to shoot us, they just cage us for ever, use us as guinea pigs. See how long it takes us to crack!

So what the fuck was I doing in these asylums? I'll tell you the truth, I was lost. I fell over the edge ... or was I pushed? I was dangerous, violent and unstable. Yeah, I was insane, it's always there, deep, sleeping, breathing, living, it's a hell within! And believe me now when I say, at times, it's a comfort to have. It can save your life or end it. Some give up and kill themselves. They can't live with it and they can't live without it!

I lived with the screams; I cried and laughed with my fellow madmen until I felt the pain. Mental pain is second to none! Your eyes begin to see things a normal person doesn't see. Mad people pick up vibes, voices and senses of smell. Mad people throw off a musky smell ... or is it fear?

Do you know what it's like to be certified insane? Shall I tell you? It's crazy ... you wake up with a strangeness and you're a lunatic. On paper, you're a danger to society. But it's not until you awake in the asylum that it hits you – BANG! The eyes, the cameras, the white coats, the screams, the stench, the madness and the emptiness. Old men with white beards, then you know the truth. Your room, the chamber pot, the door, the coldness, the damp, the stillness. That fucking smelly, piss-stained bed. The routine and the drugs. God, what's a guy done to deserve this?

Filth like the Yorkshire Ripper for a neighbour! Paedophiles, granny killers, rapists and arsonists, they're all there, like the big fat sado-masochist homosexual! One up his arse, two in his mouth and another bashing him with a stick. Even today, the fat pig still loves it. A .38 in the nuts would do him better, or a sawn-off up his arse. I could do that all day long!

Some need to be taken off our planet, permanently. Well, they're a disgrace to the human race. Me, I'm only gutted the pigs never shot me years ago. It would have saved the 30 years of pain, 'cos that's how long I've been caged up.

Let me tell you about true madness! You start to feel

untouchable, your power is awesome! The strength of ten men, you're invincible ... so you think!

They run away from you. Watch them run. Shout. You're the fear in their eyes! Then you're left alone, in the silence of madness. The war with yourself begins. The siege of insanity – you can't win. You never could. You're just digging your hole, and the crazy thing is, you're helpless and nothing can stop it. Paranoia sets in, psychosis takes over; fear is non-existent, only death lingers, sanity is no more. Welcome to madness.

Shall I tell you the one sure thing that can and does help control insanity? Love. I'm not saying it cures it, but it helps to humanise it. A cuddle, a touch of kindness, the human touch, a whisper, a long friendship – it helps.

Take my mum. I'd not even swear in front of her – doesn't that prove my point? If I was depressed and feeling dangerous and my door opened and my mum walked in, I would be cured. When she left, I would be dangerous again.

In my view, prisons and asylums are the insanity. They push and squeeze a man empty. Dry him of all feelings. Destroy the love and fill you with hate. Don't just believe my words. The proof is behind every door of broken dreams ... I rest my case!

I'm often asked, who's the most dangerous man I've ever met in the asylums? Well, I'll tell you ... the psychiatrists; they're lethal! They can kill us legally, pump us with psychotropic drugs, destroy us, make us dribble at the mouth and make us fall to our knees and make us cry in pain – yeah, they're evil! The only humane one I've ever met has been Dr Ghosh, she's lovely. I'd let her share a tin of pineapples with me any time; she is a wonderful human being with feelings and kindness. Like most Asians, Dr Ghosh is very sincere and warm-natured.

Insanity is in your blood, in your heart and in your being right up 'til the angels come to kidnap you.

Take a prison cell. They lock a man up in it 23 hours out of a 24-hour day, month after month, year after year – four walls, a door and just emptiness. No pets, no colour and no stimulation. After so long, the man becomes grey in colour. The skin turns grey with the lack of air; he looks old and haggard, no sparkle in his eyes, just black holes. He talks to himself; he laughs, he forgets and he cries ... he becomes depressed. He's alone, he curls up in the foetal position, sucking his thumb; he goes to sleep with a smile and wakes with a smile. The madness sets in. They drove him mad – he loses touch with reality.

The world has passed him by; he survives from one meal to the next, as tomorrow they may throw it on him or piss on it or maybe they won't give him any at all. He complains, but who listens? 'Yes, sir, we gave it to him but he refused it.' Or, 'Yes, sir, we gave it to him but he slung it all over us.' They lie; they are determined to drive him mad. Why? Because he's dangerous. He could attack, even kill; they fear him so they have to keep control. They may even kill him and say he's done it himself.

I'll tell you what's insane – Graham Young, Britain's number one poisoner. He was just 14 years old when he was sent to Broadmoor for attempting to wipe out his family. He managed to kill two of them. So while in Broadmoor, what did they let him do? Guess! You never will. They gave him a job as tea boy and, yes, he was in his element ... several of the staff started feeling sick. He was at it again. That's insane – only a madman would give a poisoner a job as tea boy.

Graham spent years in the asylum, then, after his release, he got a job in a factory and out came the poison again. This time he killed a workmate. He was lifed off, and later died in Parkhurst. I met the guy. I felt sad for him; he was a sick man, a dangerous fucker, but mentally sick. He was also a great chess player.

Another notorious lunatic was Nobby Clarke, a dear friend of mine. Nobby was an old war hero. After the war he could not get out of the violence so he killed a guy and got life. Whilst serving his life, he stabbed a Greek guy in the bathhouse in Parkhurst, and was sent to Broadmoor. Nobby was having none of that, and was later charged with murdering a lunatic, but he was acquitted and was sent back to Parkhurst. Nobby was a great character, a true madman at heart. I loved Nobby. Pure danger. They found him dead in his bed in the hospital wing with the book *The Godfather* on his chest. Nobby once told me, 'Don't fight the system unless you're prepared to die.' He fought the system all the way like a true madman should ... respect!

The mind of a madman is quite unique, complicated, erratic and even amazing. That's why I put my brain up for auction! The winning bidder was Andy Jones of the Crime Through Time museum, in Newent, Gloucestershire. Andy bid £2,000, and do you know why I want him to have it? Because Ronnie Kray's brain was stolen out of his head — after he died, of course, although some might say it was stolen years before he died. It took six months for the authorities to hand it back and, even then, how do we know it was his brain?

No, I don't want some Home Office pathologist sitting with a stick prodding my brain after I'm gone; mark that down as my legal request. Andy Jones gets my brain unless I say (in writing) otherwise!

Many geniuses were insane; it's a thin borderline. Hitler almost ruled the world; some say he was insane. Doesn't that prove my point? Madmen like Hitler are dangerous; it's their unpredictability. It's the despair that pushes a man over the edge, and then he becomes a madman — pain, mental agony, the wanting and waiting to be free.

To smell a flower, to see the sky, to lie on the grass, to have some woman's touch, to love, to possess things, to smile, to live normally, a madman forgets all this, he always sees blackness.

Sure enough, in his subconscious mind he sees rainbows, but the madness gives off a cloud of hopelessness. Nobody trusts him, yet is he a threat to humanity?

I've met all the best loons; the ones who just flip and kill five or six or ten people amaze me. Michael Ryan – responsible for the Hungerford Massacre – his classic words before he shot his own brains out were, 'I wish I had stayed in bed.' He wasted 14 innocent people including his mum, and he wished he had stayed in bed. Doesn't it amaze you?

Why did he do it? How? What reason? I'll tell you – insanity. It's in us all. A small problem can trigger it off, and then you are capable of the most evil acts. Thankfully, most of us never lose a grip on reality, but for those who do – believe me, it's a dream.

From the psychotic who cut his mum's head off to the schizoid who shot a man walking a dog, thinking he was the devil, they're both insane.

Senility – isn't that a form of insanity? And we all face it if we live long enough. You're gonna get to the stage where you forget if you had a shit, then it's too late ... your pants are full up! You babble like a baby, you forget your own name – that's insanity and it's gonna happen; your brain seizes up and you become a cabbage.

Insanity – most run from it, as they fear it. What about epilepsy. If you see a man in a fit, what do you do? He's frothing at the mouth, rolling about on the floor, his face is turning blue and he pisses himself. You'd probably walk by 'cos you're afraid he's a druggy or an alcoholic. You might think he's a rabid madman, but he is neither. Epilepsy is not insanity, but to you it looks mad; if it's not the norm, then it's dangerous to you. You fear what you don't know. Nobody is blaming you; it's only a natural reaction to walk away. It may be contagious, that's your immediate fear.

Some mad people will smash their skulls against a wall, so

because of that, after being sedated, they're put in a restraint and placed in a padded room. Why do they smash their heads off the wall. Probably because they want to smash your head against the wall instead, but they can't get to you so they do it to their own head. Have you thought it could be to take away their mental pain? By smashing their head it becomes a physical pain, which in turn acts as a distraction and helps take away the mental pain. That's my theory.

Pain is a lot to do with madness, as it's an inward pain, like a guilt-ridden depression that comes and goes. Some depressions are a killer and will drive you to suicide, a sense of hopelessness. You lose the fight, you let it conquer you, you let it become the master and you crack. You need to escape yourself so you have no choice but to die. I've seen it too many times, and believe me it's a terrible feeling of despair. They die, but the death never goes away for those left behind.

Take a hanging suicide. It's not as simple as you might think. The people who have to cut them down and attempt to save them have to live with that for ever. The face, the horror, that protruding tongue, those bulging eyes, the smell of shit and the stink of piss. That final zip of the body bag shuts the despair of it all away! Then the smell of death lingers on for days, weeks after. The atmosphere, the pain ... why? 'Could I have helped?' 'Was it me?' People are left traumatised. I've been there, believe it, it's a form of madness for us all.

Psychopaths? Yes, it's insanity, but it's the coldest form of insanity. They are heartless and soulless. Dangerous beyond your wildest imagination, they are the madmen nobody wants. Doctors fear them. Asylums don't want them. So many must live in prisons under maximum-security conditions, mostly in isolation.

So what causes such men to act so violently? A brutal childhood or are they just basically evil beyond help? How can a man put a gun to someone's head and say, 'Bye, bye,' and blow someone's brains out, laugh and walk away to enjoy a bag of fish and chips?

How can a man pick up a baby and throw it out of a twenty-fourth-floor window? How can a man knife to death three old-age pensioners at a bingo hall and steal their pensions? How can a 19-year-old man and a 21-year-old woman mug and kill a pensioner for her fish supper? Yet they do and they get a laugh out of it. Not all psychos are like this ... some are just totally evil.

I know one who is an armed robber and a contract killer; he would shoot his own granny if the price was right. Be thankful those types are a rare breed, but they do exist. They live out there on the streets; they are killing machines. Professional psychos.

So what turns a man into an insanity machine? What makes predators of men? They are motivated by one thing – *insanity*! And I'll tell you what's insane – Broadmoor doctors, they're all nuts. They try to rehabilitate people like the Ripper, but what for? Rehabilitate him for what? The cunt will die inside. There is nothing to rehabilitate him for. Why not just kill him now and get his brain out on the laboratory table. Why rehabilitate a monster who will never see the light again?

I'll tell you what's insane, Sir David Ramsbotham's (the former Prisons Inspector) report on HMP Woodhill's CSC unit, which condemned it as 'barbaric' and 'inhuman', but there are still 30 of them living in it. So what good are reports?

I'll tell you what's mad – letting the nonces in HMP Whitemoor work in the kitchens and giving them the best jobs. Why?

I'll tell you what's insane – making documentaries of monsters and letting them speak, but they will not allow me to speak. Why can't I speak? What about all this? Isn't it all mad? Am I insane? Well, I am a problem; I'm a serial hostage-taker, the only one in Britain. Lots say I'm mad, but am I? It's so easy to wrap a guy up and demand something, but it's not as easy to release him. A siege is madness; the longer it goes on, the madder it gets. A gun would solve the problem.

I believe the negotiations are mad; they want blood and they want a bad end so they can all get sick leave, because they've been traumatised. 'Oh, that nasty Bronson has upset me, my nerves have gone. I need £50,000 compensation and six months on the sick ... I may even write a book!' They're all mad, seekers of sympathy; I call them 'maggots of madness'; I've more respect for the hostage.

I'm often asked, 'Charlie, did any of them hostages fill their pants?' Yes, several, and it's not nice for me to smell it. I hate the smell of shit! How do those sewer workers put up with it? In fact, how do the queers put up with a shitty dick? It sort of makes me feel ill. Still, each to their own, I say!

Now where was I? Oh yeah, sieges. It's dangerous and exciting and it's actually a buzz. I'm often asked why do I do it. Simple ... I like to cause their insane system some problems. They deserve to be destroyed. I've got a pathological hatred for the plums up in Prison Service headquarters, and I give them problems. Or, I should say, did give them problems, as I'm now retired from sieges. In fact, I'm now a pacifist. I'm a peace-dweller! I'm on a mission of love. Well, 'til some cunt upsets me!

LEVELS OF INSANITY

1. Simple — mostly sad people who long to be wanted and loved so they cause havoc for a bit of attention. They're treated with tranquillisers; a lot of fucking tranquillisers! 'Johnny, be good and you can watch TV.' 'Now pop this pill in your mouth.' 'Did you make your bed, tidy your room? Good boy.' You need patience for Johnny — time and lots of support. He can be cured with love and kindness.

2. Very disturbed — you need to be cautious. These types

can snap and become a problem; they're unpredictable and totally irrational. They ooze danger; red light, be prepared. Try to pacify them, try to get into their mind and convince them it's safe. Get their confidence, build up a positive relationship and hope you've cracked it. If it can't be resolved, then just inject.

3. Totally dangerous – would you step into a lion's den without protection or a big fuck-off gun? Look, let me tell you ... you can't get through to this sort; once the fuse is lit, run. Come back later when the storm has passed.

There are killers and *killers* and I've met them all. Every type of killer on the planet, and I've met them – sick bastards, sad bastards and pure evil bastards. To most people, a killer is a killer, but it's not so. I've met guys who kill for love; they kill once and part of them dies, too. It's emotions; they can't handle it and they crack and kill. Most killers are domestic cases; they're sad people, broken men, believe it!

A guy comes home early, unexpectedly, and finds the milkman right up his wife's arse ... what's he supposed to do, order a few yoghurts? Nah, he goes insane, he can't help it. The bitch fucks his world up and he goes to prison for life and she goes to hell, and the milkman ... well, he loses his bollocks. That's life – tragic!

But the sickos, the psychos, the predators are a different breed; believe it, unique specimens, cold and cruel. No remorse just a regret of not killing any witnesses. They rot in jail! Thirty or forty years and then they leave in body bags. Killers like Dennis Nilsen (the UK's version of the USA's Jeffrey Dahmer), Sutcliffe, Ireland, Hutchinson and Miller, they're just never gonna walk the streets again! You'd better pray they don't and hundreds like them.

Fear of the unknown – we all have to fear something or

someone, all of us. It's no good saying you're fearless, 'cos you're a liar, OK. Fear is personal, but it's still there. Subconsciously, most madmen fear themselves. Some people are terrified of moths. Can you imagine a great big pansy of a man running away from a moth, but to him it may as well be a two-ton rhino!

What do I fear? I fear my unpredictability and all around me fear it, too. Each day, I am unlocked by never less than six guards. Nobody knows what I'll do ... I don't even know! I can smile one second and then explode the next, it doesn't take much to set me off. Sure, I'm not as bad now as I once was. Age and maturity — I seem more in control as time goes by. Maybe I'm cured ... whatever, I'm still in max secure, still in solitary, so the system seems to think I'm still a danger man.

4

MAD AS
A HATTER

I'll tell you who is mad – Bert. I met Bert outside in the late '60s or early '70s and I've never forgotten him. Bert was a good 20 years older than me, so he must be at least 70 by now. I met him in my local pub, and we got chatting. I sold him a gold watch and he invited me to his house.

We went back for a drink and to collect my payment for the watch. Well, to say I was shocked is an understatement. I've never forgotten it and never will. As soon as his flat door opened, a strange smell hit me, like a farmyard smell, a strawy smell, then I saw it ... a fucking pig! He had a big pig in his flat, and I mean big; I'd say twice as big as a dog. But that wasn't it ... this pig had stockings on, black fishnets on each leg. Well it didn't take Einstein to work it out!

'Take no notice of Gladys,' Bert said. He paid me and I fucked off lively.

Days later, my pal John and I went round. He hadn't believed me! I banged on the door.

'Who is it? Bert said.

'It's me, I've got another watch, if you're interested?' I had — a nice Seiko.

He opened up and I said, 'This is John, my pal, he's safe.'

'Come in, lads,' Bert said.

The fucking pig was lying on the sofa, still with the stockings on and it looked tired! John looked at me and said, 'Fucking hell's bells.'

Bert shouted at the pig, 'Gladys, get off the sofa, let the lads sit down.'

I've never forgotten it!

Some time later, I bumped into Bert again, this time in a club and he was well pissed! So I pulled him over, saying, 'Hey ... Bert, how's Gladys?'

'Oh, she's OK,' he replied.

'Hey, do you really give her one, Bert, do you, do you shag it?'

He got nasty. 'Don't talk about my wife like that.'

I had to chin him; I had to, as he was getting very aggressive. But in a strange way, I felt very confused over it; it obviously was a serious bestiality case, but Bert had totally lost the fucking plot!

I often used to wonder, years later in my solitary, locked in the padded rooms, strip cells, when I was naked and in a canvas restraint suit and in drug-induced states, what the fuck I was doing in the asylum when people like Bert are still out there? Sometimes I used to laugh myself into oblivion thinking whether he had had any little piglets. The world is a sad fucking place! In and out, nobody is safe from madness, nobody, not even Gladys — the poor pig!

Something else that's fucking mental — porridge. Ask anybody in the street to give you another word for prison, and they will say, 'Porridge'. Porridge is 'bird'. Well, it was. Now I have to buy my own porridge oats, as jails are now full of fairies, corn flakes and rice crispies. It's gone silly, soft ... we want porridge. My wage is £2.50 a week and for 39p I get a bag of Happy Shopper porridge oats and make my own. I sprinkle brown sugar on it with some raisins for porridge. I'm the original 'Birdman', stuff your corn flakes!

I'm usually on a riot shield unlock, which means every time my door unlocks a MUFTI – Minimum Use of Force and Tactical Intervention – team rush in with sticks, all wearing protective gear. They're all big lumps and complete wankers. They stand there glaring into my face from below their helmets. In a one-to-one fight I'd smash their noses into the back of their skulls, then rip their limbs off.

I remember an incident that took place on 4 August 2000 in HMP Whitemoor when I was being brought in from the exercise yard by the MUFTI team. I spotted the deputy governor, Mr Pritchard.

'Gov,' I shouted. He came over. I've known him for 20 or so years; he's of old stock with old type morals. He treats men as men and boys as boys.

'Gov, four weeks I've been on this MUFTI unlock; it's madness, can I talk with you?'

Now what he did just blew a hole in the whole system! 'OK, Bronson,' he said, and with that he ordered the MUFTI squad to take me to the seg adjudication room; he followed me in, then he did something insane. 'OK, lads, leave us alone,' he said.

So there's just him and me sat in there; it went through my mind to do something, but how can you abuse such trust? I just couldn't. I admired and respected him. We spoke for 15 minutes; he listened, I listened ... a lot of sense. He told me that it was Prison Service headquarters that were responsible for the riot unlock, but he told me he wanted to get me off it. 'Basically, Charlie, every fucker is terrified of you,' he said.

So here's a man in his fifties, been in the game for more than

30 years, sitting here with me and all the MUFTI are fighting to get past each other and staring in through the door with mad eyes! You could read the screws' faces; they would have loved me to attack this man just to say, 'Bronson's a beast.' No, I'd not attack the gov ... so I did the opposite; I shook his hand and said, 'Thank you!'

All the cons in the seg – Tony Crabb, Timmy Berry, Stevie Miller (Caveman), Johnny Allen – were all in shock even to see such madness. I walked back to my cell with the MUFTI like I was dreaming. I'm still dazed over it! Some will say the governor is a fucking idiot; some may say he's a mug. But I say he's a man amongst men. He spoke some truths I never liked, but truth is truth, we all have to face it. I'd sooner have truth that hurts me than lies that kill me.

My life continues on a MUFTI; I don't know what headquarters will make of Governor Pritchard's madness; maybe he will be in trouble, but as I've said from the word go, why send in a riot team to feed me when one female guard could do it and be safe?

I spit at bullies! These prats are just clowns who are actually mugging themselves off big time, so the question is, if the governor can do that, why am I still on a MUFTI unlock? I'll tell you why – 'cos they now fear I'll retaliate against the way they've treated me. This scum cause the problems and now they are not prepared to put it right. This way does not work every day, so at times I slag them. How can I do anything else with riot shields and aggression in my face? These maggots could not intimidate a sausage; they're complete clowns trying to be ring masters, but I learned one major thing because of Governor Pritchard – there are still some of the old school about, men with good morals and bottle.

You younger governors should take stock of all this and have some backbone to stand up against the screws, 'cos believe me, they have too much power in these segs! You have to stamp out all the madness! Insanity cannot prevail ... or can it? Was Governor Pritchard mad as a hatter to sit alone with me in that room? Only he knows, but he was certainly a brave Mad Hatter at that!

Sex — it does happen. It happened in the forces; you put 10 women on a ship with 500 sailors and tell me it doesn't happen! Now put 10 women on a prison wing with 400 cons! Tell me there's no chemistry; they smell us and we smell them. With me, it's difficult, as I'm forever in solitary, but I know someone who has had a blow-job off a woman screw. Not a month goes by when you don't read of some scandal in our jails. Check the library newspaper archives, go back five years; I'll bet you'd see loads of woman screws falling in love with cons!

Fuck me, you even get male screws falling in love with cons, gay screws, plenty of them about! They usually fight to get the reception jobs so they can check out all the naked bodies as they come in. 'Bend over, son' — they love it. See their eyes light up when a nice 18-year-old lad comes in with a nice firm arse. 'Bend over, lad, ooooh, that's nice!' Of course it goes on and always will.

The closest I ever got to a sexual relationship was in Belmarsh and I'll not say her name even though she was later dismissed. But I was very attracted to her; she was my cup of tea and apple pie in one helping. Often, she stroked my leg, or touched my face! Once, I felt her bum, it was lovely.

She was at my door once talking through the spy hole when I got a big hard-on, I couldn't help it. I told her straight, 'Fuck me! Look at this!' I whipped it out so she could see it!

'Bloody hell,' she said. 'It's a beauty.'

Talk about madness. Me standing there with my kecks down around my ankles holding a big stiffy with a woman screw watching me!

'Go on ...' she said, 'give it a pull for me, Chas.'

'I bet you say that to all the boys,' I said.

'No I bloody don't,' she replied.

God, I wished she could have come in ... I was just in the mood! These places are fucking cruel!

'How long is it, Chas ... it looks a good six inches,' she said.

'Bollocks, it's bigger than that!' I got my ruler and measured it in front of her. '7^1/$_4$in!'

'What's the girth, Chas? Eh ... how thick?'

'I don't know ... a good mouthful!'

This went on for a good 20 minutes. Then a fucking supply screw arrived and she vanished and left me all frustrated; that's the closest I ever got! But I did like her, and she knew it.

Nowadays, we get a lot of women screws, so it's a sweeter smell. At times, too sweet. Remember, us lags go years without a smell of fanny and then it's there in our faces. Some give a nice wiggle, a smile; it's only natural we are all affected by such femininity, isn't it?

I remember a nice one in the very late '80s in Leicester seg unit. She was on nights – blonde, blue eyes, beautiful teeth and very fanciable. I was working out doing my sit-ups; it must have been about 9.00pm. My spy hole went. I knew it, but I carried on, then I noticed this lovely face looking down on me. 'You OK in there, Charlie?'

'Yeah, who's that?'

'Only checking on you.'

I went to the door. She looked like the one in Buck's Fizz, the nice one. Well, they're both nice, but the nicer one of the two. I stood at the door in my Y-fronts, as I like to feel secure. I don't like my balls swinging about. I'm a secure sort of guy.

'Hey, you on nights then?' I asked her.

'Yeah,' she replied.

'Fancy coming in for a work-out?'

She smiled and said, 'No chance.'

'Would ya if you could?'

'Maybe,' she replied.

'Maybe or not?' I asked.

'Yeah ... I'd give you a run for your money,' she said.

She was fucking gorgeous. Isn't prison a bitch? She fucked off and left me feeling all horny. Well, I'm only human. I knew she would be back every hour, so what I did was this. I had a string vest, sorted myself out and waited by the door in the dark for the 10 o'clock check. In Leicester Prison, we had our own light in the cell. There is a night-light outside; there, they can turn it on or off.

I was naked down below, and semi-hard, too. Don't get the wrong idea that I'm some sort of sick pervo. It was only for a laugh.

'Fuck me, here she comes.' I hear the steps. I rushed into the middle of my cell, and started dancing like that Travolta geezer. As I whizzed about, my dick was all over the place.

'Yahooooooooooo! Yeheeeeeeeeeee!' The light went on. 'Yehoo, whizzz, yeheeeee.'

'Bronson, grow up!' Fuck me, it was a geezer screw. 'Grow up,' and he slammed the eye flap shut.

I rushed up to the door and shouted, 'You dirty fucking Peeping Tom, you're a faggot, you are. Go on, fuck off and play with your marbles.'

Talk about a creep. Fucking poofs all over the place. Story of my life this is! Anyway, the Buck's Fizz chick later got suspended over an alleged carry-on with a con on the wing. See how I always lose out. Days later, I got the arse ache with that piss-hole so I staged a rooftop protest. Fucking pissed it down all day it did. I was glad to call it off.

But my greatest love in prison is Bertha, my medicine ball. I broke a world record for medicine ball sit-ups with her; a 14 pounder and real leather, I loved her! But the cunts don't allow me her no more. I'm allowed fuck all.

Pain can and often does become a pleasure, a way of life. It was years later I realised I enjoyed a good whipping. I love to be whipped across my back; it's not a sexual thing, it's more a test of my own ability to survive the sting, the shock and the pain – it sets me on fire!

On the Hull special unit, big 20st Fred Lowe, a double con killer, used to whip me with the weightlifting belt and the skipping rope. I would hold on to the punchbag, and big Fred would lash me big time; at times, my back would bleed and other times I'd be so fucked up I'd not be able to breathe, but it was my way of testing myself. Fred probably enjoyed it as he's a raving psycho, a sadistic evil bastard! I'd just say to him, 'OK, Fred, let's have a session.' His face would light up; it was his highlight of the week to smash Bronson up and to draw blood.

Once, we were caught in the act when one of the female civilian education workers saw us through the gym window. She got the screws ... they were all in shock! I was later called into the office, but what could they do, what rule had been broken? Again, it's madness that can't be explained; after all, it's my back and Fred was only doing what I asked. If he'd refused I'd have probably smashed his fat ugly face in, the cowardly bastard! But I must say, he was a good whipper!

So was one girl I met back in '87. I had just got out of jail after 14 years inside, although I was soon rushed back in after 69 days of freedom. I was a mucked-up guy, but she helped me a lot over a few bad weeks. At first when I said, 'Give me a fucking good whipping,' I think it did shake her up a bit, but in the end she loved it! We only lasted a few weeks but she helped me so much.

I soon came back to jail on another robbery charge, but my time with her is nothing but sweet memories. I'll always respect her and I loved her family, who are all salt of the earth. I took her daughter to one of my unlicensed fights; she was only 15 years old but she loved it and she made a few quid by helping out with the seating and so on. My manager looked after her.

I just love the look on the faces of kids when you surprise them! That look is priceless; money can't buy a kid's love. They either love you or hate you. I've got this thing with kids, I show them respect, treat them as adults and they seem to believe in me. Some will say, 'Fancy taking a 15-year-old girl to a fight!' But I say, 'Fuck you, so what?' It was a one-off experience for her and she was safe with my East London friends. They all spoiled her rotten, got her presents and treated her like a princess. She will always remember that occasion; and she saw me win! She will now be at least 30 years old, but I bet she's never had a better occasion, and some of the crowd were 'infamous villains' – top underworld characters. Even Charlie Kray was there! So that young girl met the 'real faces' and she was safe and respected.

I was once photographed in the nude with a pair of crotchless panties over my head, holding a pump-action 12-bore sawn-off whilst standing there with a big hard-on! I've always dreaded seeing that snap in the *News of the World* or the *Sunday Sport*. God, how I've prayed not to see that; you can tell it's me as my tash is sticking out of the panties and you can see my tattoos; it's me all right. I wonder what she did with it? A nice shooter, though. I do love a gun; something about a gun that sends me to heaven, the feel of it and the power it holds. I love a nice piece; it's better than sex!

There was a screw who worked in Durham Jail; he got lifed off about ten years ago for killing his wife; he cut her up and put her body in the freezer. He's now a cleaner, in the block, in Frankland Jail. One day, he's locking us up and the next he's being locked up himself; it really is a fucking crazy life we live and, do you know what ... it gets madder.

I remember years ago the case of the copper who was a regular outside 10 Downing Street. He got nicked over killing a prostitute. He took her home, cut her up and took her body out to Epping Forest in bin bags. Do you know, he was only convicted of manslaughter and was sentenced to a paltry seven years? Seven fucking years! It was premeditated murder, what else could it have been, and all he got was poxy manslaughter, what a joke! Lots of cases flood back to me where the law is a joke. How can you get seven years for taking a woman home and chopping her up and taking her out in bags? Still, he was a 'pig' ... probably suffering from stress!

Every long-term jail or asylum has a birdman; Hull unit was no exception and our birdman was Eddie Slater. Ed's a little Scottish geezer serving life; he's only 10st, but he can bench press 20st, he is one powerful little fucker and a nice chap. I've not seen him for years. Last I heard, he was up in Frankland when his father died, and headquarters refused to allow him to go to the funeral ... that about sums that lot up, doesn't it!

In Hull unit, Eddie was given two cells, one to sleep in and one for his birds, so it was like an aviary. He spent most of his day looking after the budgerigars and he had a few pigeons, too. One day, he was on a visit when big Tony McCulloch got a cardboard box and put the birds in it and put the box under Ed's bed. (We did all our own cooking on that wing.) So Tony got a load of chicken giblets, and Tony draped them all over the perches and around the cage!

Can you imagine it, when Ed came off his visit and checked his birds! Talk about funny! But looking back, it's a wonder Eddie never destroyed the cunt, as once he took Durham's roof off over a plate of cold chips.

Prison is full of fun and games, like the time I put a dead mouse in the soup at Brixton, and another time I slipped a pigeon I'd caught in the exercise yard into my mate's piss pot!

That was Tommy Tegstowe ... he nearly had a stroke! Well, imagine it, getting up in the night to have a pee, you pick your piss pot up and out flaps a pigeon.

And jokes don't get much crazier than when I once robbed a place with a banana in a bag! You should have seen them dive on the floor! I walked out eating the banana with the load of notes in the bag. That's insanity – life is insanity! Like the time I climbed Liverpool Jail's roof – five floors up. I squeezed down on the centre, where I kicked in a hole and shit through it. It fell 60ft and splattered on the floor!

'You dirty bastard,' the screw screamed up at me.

'That's all you're worth to me, you lot, you're all shit, you're all insane,' I shouted back.

The birdman wasn't unique by any means. Ninety nine per cent of mad people love animals. Why? Simple – they can relate to them. They have so much in common. Treat a dog well and he's your best friend. A dog will die for its master. So will a madman. Always remember that. Kindness goes a long way.

I know of madmen who have fallen in love with their pets. One I know of used to live alone in a cottage with a big St Bernard bitch. He used to sleep with it ... the dog was dressed up in panties and suspenders and he'd be kissing and fucking it all night! To some that would be horrific, if not evil, but that's love. Maybe the bitch loved him, too; it sure would have bitten him if it didn't. He told me this in Broadmoor; he actually cut his own throat when he got locked away, as he was broken-hearted over having to be separated from the bitch. He survived, but he lives in severe depression. Most people can't imagine how that madman ticks; to him, that bitch was better looking than any Page Three model.

I asked him whether he had a '69' with it. To my amazement, he replied, 'Yes, Charlie, regular.' That blew me away, but that's madness. This was a level of depravity I do not support;

obviously, it's bestiality in the medic books, but to him it's normal. I'm mad, but that to me is fucking sick! A bullet would cure it ... or did the bitch lead him on? In his own mind, she probably spoke to him or sent telepathic messages.

It was in the early nineties; I had a visit from an admirer. She had travelled all the way from Luton to see me. My visits at this time were in the seg unit. As usual, she was pissed. I fucking hate birds who get pissed, as they become very emotional. But what she did on this day blew me away! A day I'll never forget.

I sat with my back to the screws, with this bird feet away on the next chair. The table was at the side.

If my name is not Bronson ... she opened her legs wide! She had no panties on ... it was winking at me! Now I'm only flesh and blood, aren't I? There it was, looking at me on a plate. A real fanny! I could smell it ... I touched it ... I pulled it open! It looked like a freshly sliced melon, one of those honeydew ones. I turned around to see the screws; our eyes met. As I turned back to look at her, she was getting my dick out (which was difficult, as it was so hard). How the fuck we did it still blows me away today. I just had to get into that snatch. She wanted it so bad, but her crazy mind — the lunatic went down on it, slurping away.

I turned to see the screws. One got up, said something to the others about a cup of tea and fucked off. It was now or never. I grabbed her and spun her round so she was sitting on me. In seconds, I was inside her! She was bouncing about like a fucking good 'un, laughing, 'Fuck me ...' I lost it. I was also laughing.

One screw could never stop it. I looked around at him; he was red, only a young screw, too. If this girl wasn't mad that day, then neither was I. It just had no sanity to it. It's a wonder I never blew the top of her head off when I shot my load.

When she was back in her own seat, she was sitting there

wiping herself with tissues as I watched. Blow me, if I didn't go and get hard again! We went for round two, this time with two screws on duty. Nowadays, I normally have seven screws. Wonder why?

Yeah, that was pure madness at its best! The girl won't mind me saying this, as she loves a laugh. She almost got me shot up once outside, but that's how crazy the bitch is. There is only one like her! Hey ... it really was like a fresh sliced honeydew melon.

I'm also reminded of the time I smashed off a light switch and fittings in a box. Big deal, you say, simple. Well, you try it while secured in a body belt. Yeah, a bit difficult. I head-butted the fitting 40 or 50 times. Don't try that at home – it cuts your head and gives you a terrible headache. Once I saw it start to buckle and the screws holding it together start to pop, I knew I had it; a few more nuts, crash, crash. Surprising how much blood's in your skull. Makes a terrible mess on the wall.

Then I got my teeth on the steel fittings and tore them off the wall. Live wires may give you a nasty shock, but I'm a bit of a gambler myself. Hell ... I actually put my tongue on the wires. Just to test. I then lay on the floor and grabbed the light fitting and attempted to use it to cut through the belt. I gnawed the evil belt off.

Of course, the screws came in while I was at it. Guess what for! Yeah ... to take the belt off! You should have seen their faces when they saw the fitting ripped off, and the belt half sliced through and, of course, the blood all over the floor and me. 'Erm ... all right, boys ... lovely day for a spot of golf.'

Prisons and asylums are strange places. They affect us all differently, even the screws. A lot of the screws die early on in their careers. A good percentage end up divorced. Many have breakdowns, many hit the booze, and many more end up on tranquillisers. It's a known fact. Well, the ones who unlock me do, that's a fact. Imagine your postman or milkman coming to your door and always thinking that you're there to smash their face in, or throw a pot of shit over them!

It was 1987, Gartree Prison seg block. A con came down who is a known transvestite, a funny little geezer. He was obviously a faggot, but a funny one at that, a right character. He called himself Petal; so I thought I'd have a laugh.

'Petal,' I shouted out of the window.

'Hi, Charlie,' he said in his tart's voice.

'Hey ... when you slop out, come to my spy hole and have a peep at what I've got for you,' I said.

'What is it, Charlie?' Petal replied.

'Oh ... just a little surprise, Petal,' I said in a calm voice.

So there I was waiting for him to slop out. At this time there were no cell toilets. Slopping out was one at a time. I judged by the doors opening and shutting when it was time for Petal to slop out. So I planned it carefully. I stripped off and got on the chair, and started jumping up and down with my dick in my hand, shouting, 'Happy birthday, Petal.' The spy hole went. I clocked the eye. 'He, he, ha, ha, he, he, he, he! Happy birthday, Petal,' I was shouting as I was jumping up and down. The eye just stared. I was starting to get angry. He shut it, laughed and fucked off, as it was only a joke. Then I heard, 'Bronson, how many letters do you want?' It was a fucking screw!

When I slopped out, I told the screws, 'Don't ever creep up like that again.' Petal laughed his arse off over that. It took me a good month to forget that one.

1976 was a hot summer in Parkhurst Hospital wing. I remember those summers when days were beautiful, not like summer is today. In the 1970s there were great summers! On the Isle of Wight, the weather was fantastic. I had a brainwave. I got a straw and jumped in the pond, a lovely pond that Frank

Mitchell made in the '60s, and I lay in the pond and breathed through the straw. Why? Well, I was gonna escape! I had a plan – as insane as it was, it was a plan. It could work, I thought to myself. As I lay in that pond, I could feel the fish bumping into my body, like they were sniffing me, wondering who and what I was. A minute in such an environment feels like an hour.

The plan was simple. Lie under water. When all the cons go back into the wing, I'll jump out. I would climb a pipe and get on the roof, over the other side and maybe wrap a screw up. Then go home for a cup of tea and a slice of apple pie with my mum, Eira.

So I sat up, wiped all the slime and fish shit off my face, only to see 20 or so screws all looking at me! 'Err, I must have fell in ... fainted.'

'Yeah, Charlie, sure ... 25 minutes you was under water.'

The van shot off ... with me in it to another prison! Oh well ... it could have worked. If you don't try, then you'll never know.

5

BEHIND THE WALL OF HELL

The number of suicides in jail has risen to a record level, and the Christmas period usually sees an increase in such self-inflicted deaths.

Many inmates who kill themselves are held at local prisons, which often suffer from overcrowding. These prisons house inmates on remand and immediately after sentence. The majority of suicide victims in prison are remand prisoners awaiting trial.

Manchester Prison had seven suicides in 1999, the worst record, compared with five at Leeds and four at both Brixton and Leicester.

The director of the Howard League, Frances Crook, said, 'Despite the best efforts of many prison staff, the prison experience continues to prove unbearable for many who are sent there.' Ms Crook went on to say that the prison system was failing to provide decent, humane care.

The Director General of the Prison Service, Martin Narey,

said he was 'deeply concerned' about the rise in suicides and pledged that reversing it was the 'top priority' for prisons. Key areas for improvement include screening inmates quickly to identify those at risk as soon as they come into prison, when many suicides happen, and devoting more resources to relieving the pressure on local prisons.

Mr Narey has also ordered the end of the use of bare strip cells as holding rooms for suicidal inmates. He added that a large number of people coming into prison already had a lot of problems, including mental disorders.

Sir David Ramsbotham, when he was the Prisons Inspector, said the number of suicides was due to a management failure to implement the correct measures.

'The guts of this problem is prison service management, which is not managing the suicide problem in a proper way with people responsible [for it] up and down the system. In my view, area managers should be responsible for checking that suicide procedures are really being conducted properly. What is more, I would also make them sign a certificate to say that they have done so – so that they can be held accountable.' Too right, mate, too right!

Privately run Doncaster Prison was awarded a Charter Mark by the then Home Secretary, Jack Straw, when it had the worst suicide record in England and Wales!

And someone who's managed to add a couple of extra victims to the statistics is big fat Fred Lowe – what a nutter! He killed two cons, one in Gartree Prison and one in Long Lartin. The one in Gartree he did with a pair of scissors; he just lost the plot and went mad. Covered in blood, he walked out of the con's cell and shouted, 'One off.' But if the truth were known, Fred Lowe is a fucking cowardly piece of filth. He refused to come to my trial to give evidence for me; he tells people he couldn't, but it's shit, he refused to come. Now here's a guy who's never going to get out and he's too frightened to come to court to help me, but he's all right with killing cons! Why kill his fellow cons?

It's a fact of life that most con killers are bullies; they take their frustrations out on them 'cos it's too much for them to do a screw.

I cried when young Tommy Hole hanged himself on M-Wing in Parkhurst. Old Tom, his dad, was the one to find him. Imagine that, a father walking into his son's cell to find him hanging off the bars. Tommy was serving nine years. Old Tom was serving 24 years for blags, a true East End family, loyal as they come, from Canning Town. Salt of the earth people! Let me tell you now, I have seen it all; I have felt the coldness and emptiness. But this tragedy had to be one of the coldest days of my life; it had a bad effect on my mind.

The day it happened I was in the box. I'd chinned a screw a couple of days before. But when I came out of that box, I could smell the depression in that jail; every con in Parkhurst was on a low, it was a sad occasion. Old Tom actually went mad and was later sent to Rampton. He could not get his son out of his mind. That same day, they were to have a visit together with their family. Imagine Tom having to go on that visit to say, 'Young Tom's dead.' This is the reality of life in jail — it's madness! Why did he do it? He had just 18 months left to serve; he was fit, strong and he had a wife and kids, why top himself? Who knows why ... it does your head in trying to think why.

In later years, Tommy got out and remarried. He fought his way back out of the coldness and was doing well, then ... Bang! Some cunt blew a hole in his head in a crowded pub! But I knew Tom well and that's how he would have wanted to go. Personally, I don't think he ever got over young Tom, three-quarters of him died with his son that cold day in Parkhurst.

Barry Rundean was another sad suicide; we all cried — hardcore men just in shock. Why? A top-class man can't just top himself for no reason! Barry cut his throat and wrists, bled to death in his cell in Long Lartin. He was a fit man in his late 20s; a lifer, we all loved him to bits, a number-one guy. I used to train with him; nobody could do sit-ups like that man did. Fucking awesome! I can't work it out, I never could, but it blows a hole right through me, it's madness.

Dessy Cunningham was another one. Hanged himself in Whitemoor, a good blagger, a top villain. He spent a good ten years fighting this piss-hole of a system; a lot of those years were spent in solitary, but he survived it all. Then he has a year left to go and he dies! When cunts like Fred West do it we have a party, but when our own do it, then it fucking hurts. We don't stop hurting; it lingers on and on and on; it's for real.

You'd be amazed at the number of murders in jail over the last 30 years. Most of them are just heated moments that get out of hand; a blade goes in and lights switch off ... permanently! But any con thinking about it, I'd advise them not to 'cos you'll be looking at 30 years. You may kill him, but you'll be killing yourself at the same time; con killers rarely get released. I don't know of any who got out in the last 30 years ... oh, sorry, some did, in a body bag!

Barry Prosser may not mean a lot to people in the free world, other than to his family; neither will George Wilkinson or Michael Martin, and all the other poor souls who died in custody, in 'mysterious' circumstances. Go and research prison deaths in the last 30 years; who says there is no death sentence?

They may not hang us but they choke us, punch and kick us to death, drug us, suffocate us. Let's take Barry Prosser, a big man, 6ft 3in tall and 17st; he wasn't a real criminal, more a disturbed giant than anything else. His body was a mass of bruises his spleen had been completely ruptured, and he was found dead in a hospital cell in Winston Green.

A doctor's report actually said he did it himself! Come on, let's get real here; it's gone on since the beginning of time. At times, a crowd of screws just lose control, bash us a little too hard; one may squeeze the neck just that little bit too much or crush a skull off a wall just once too often and it's all over. But is it? Why is it few or none get life for murder; how do they escape it? Simple! The system covers for such atrocities, and they all stick together.

'Prosser was mad ... he just threw himself off the walls ... he was suicidal ...' What a fucking load of shit! Wake up and smell the shit! 'Cos Joe Public is eating shit, fed by shit people! The system is corrupt and rotten right through, but only guys like me remember the Barry Prossers of the world. I can't forget it. It's like with you sane people outside: you remember John Lennon or JFK; it sticks in your mind. But every time I'm jumped on and taken to the box and bashed up, I see Barry Prosser in my head. I picture George Wilkinson. I feel the ghosts of shame.

Vince Powell was one dangerous fucker. In the '70s at Parkhurst, he was on the garden party and he buried a shovel in another con's skull; rumour had it that it was over a half ounce of tobacco. To kill a man for half an ounce of 'bacca' is just beyond belief, but that's prison madness! They moved Powell to Winchester to await trial; weeks later, a screw opened his door to let him out for exercise and he was hanging; many say he didn't do it, one of many iffy suicides.

Billy Kringle was one of the maddest cons I ever came across. Billy shot a cop in the '70s; he was on home leave at the time, shot him six times. He always claimed it was a hair-trigger, funny that ... six times! Anyway, Billy actually escaped off the special unit in Parkhurst, but sadly they got him four hours later in the woods.

I last saw Billy up in Full Sutton; by then he had done a good 25 years, but it wasn't the same old Billy. He seemed distant, like he was in a dream. One day, he just said out of the blue, 'Chas, do you believe in little people?'

'What? Little people? What, midgets?'

'No,' he said, 'the little elves!'

I looked at him and saw madness all over his face.

'I've seen one, Chas, an elf!'

'I'll see you later, Bill,' I said.

Phew! It was soon after that he was found dead in his cell. His heart gave up on him. Insanity drove him mad! It's never nice to see, but it's worse watching the body bag come. Sad. I wonder if the little people have body bags?

They reckon that two-fifths of women prisoners and a fifth of male prisoners in England and Wales have attempted suicide, according to official statistics. Now I'm not one for rattling off facts and figures, but these figures aren't from me, they're from what you call the Office for National Statistics (ONS). Now it doesn't take a brain surgeon to work out that suicide rates in prison are on the increase, especially when the prison population is rising. Naturally, there is a strong link between social deprivation, mental ill health and imprisonment. Another survey also found that prisoners in England and Wales have very high rates of mental illness, substance misuse and personality disorder – see, I told you we were all mad!

Do you know that all these fancy groups like MIND, NACRO and the Howard League for Penal Reform were all written to a few years ago on my behalf asking for help? What a waste of time they all are and you lot keep sending them money ... Are you mad? Send the money to me instead!

A few years back, in December 2000, the Dangerous and Severe Personality Disorder Act was passed through the British government to become law in England and Wales. Sounds OK, but do you know what it means? 'A small group of people who are very seriously disordered and who pose a very high risk to the public.' This group are 'dangerous, severely personality disordered people' (DSPD), meaning that an order could be obtained for the indefinite detention in a specialist unit for DSPD. Do you know what it will mean? It will mean that prisons and asylums will become full of psychopaths – you will see the murder and suicide rate rise if this happens. Like I said, you cannot ever cure madness; tame it, yes, but never cure it.

You'll be amazed how many murders are committed in our prisons and asylums. Just to put you in the picture, 28 cons have been murdered in the prison system in the last 12 years, and that's not counting asylums. I personally know of at least 20 murders in which cons have killed fellow cons. Why did they do it? Hate, jealousy, anger, madness ... call it what you will, but people die over madness.

When Fred Lowe killed his first con in Long Lartin, he did it because he was serving life for a robbery and violence. He made it clear to the authorities, 'I'm not serving life for fuck all.' So he got some scissors and hacked a con. He stabbed him 58 times. He was a human teabag.

When Bob Maudsley killed two cons in one day he ate part of the brains from one of the cons. Why? When Doug Wakefield killed Brian Peak in Parkhurst, he first garrotted him with a bootlace and, when he was dead, he set about stabbing him. No need, as he was dead.

When Danny Blanchflower killed the works screw he used a hammer. He battered in the man's skull so badly he was unrecognisable. This is what prison madness is all about! It's out of control. Some of those murdered were nothing less than liberties. They picked on the weak.

My question is ... why have they all killed cons (apart from an isolated incident with a works screw), why not the screws or the governors or the sadistic doctors? Why do they go for the soft option – their own kind? Are they killing themselves by killing another con? Or is it war? Are cons at war with cons? The answer is an emphatic YES!

We fucking despise paedophiles, rapists and grasses. Dirty scum! We don't want to live with shit. So, at times, there are bodies, but half of these murders are totally unnecessary. Some of those dead men were diamonds, never deserving to die.

Maidstone – Kessen killed a fellow con. Bashed in his skull with a bed leg. (A lovers' tiff.) God, you've gotta see it to believe it. Killers. Would-be killers watching the prison yards, searching for a victim. 'Who can I kill today?' Just like nutters in the street betting their friends that they can knock this one or that one out with one punch.

It's fucking madness at its very best. Some of these killers are 10st, soaking wet, but with a 7in piece of Sheffield steel they are ruthless. And when it's pushed into the back of a 20st giant, it's over. You can't always survive such an attack. Some do – I did myself – many others have, but most go out in body bags.

Prison killers are totally cold and ruthless. I must add that the odd few had no choice but to kill. It's kill or be killed. But when a big strong guy goes into a weaker guy and kills him just for the sake of it, I call it out of order. When a con stabbed another over a pork chop, I call that fucking insanity, senseless. When Bob ate the brain, I call that crazy. Fuck me, the food ain't that bad. When Cheeseman and Maudsley killed Alan Francis in Broadmoor, I call that a cowardly act of

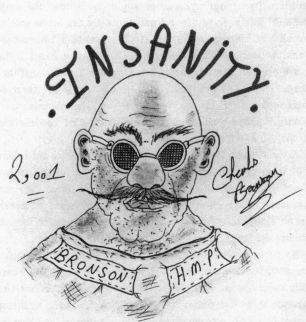

senselessness. But if it's a paedophile or grass, I say well done, kill some more of them.

I almost joined those killers twice — once in Rampton, and once in Broadmoor. When I was in Rampton, I did actually kill him by strangling him, but would you believe, the screws brought him back to life; he was clinically dead. The shit had raped and killed a young kid, so they saved a monster. But looking back on it I'd sooner blind the fucker than kill him. Let them live on in darkness. Imagine living in the asylum or prison 'blind'. At that time, though, I was heavily medicated and, looking back on it, I wasn't in control of myself.

Who's gonna bash in your skull in an asylum? You just don't know. Now that's worse than death. It's a living hell. Insanity at its very best. Don't kill them, blind them. Snap their spine, put them in a chair. Let them wheel around the jail in total blackness. We could jump out and punch them as they pass. Throw soaking balls at them, darts. We could create games with them. That would lend a purpose to life. To keep us amused. Killing the scum is too good.

So what causes men to become violent? I'll tell you — boredom, silly rules, muggy screws and pathetic governors. What else can we do? Swallow it, wipe our mouths out? You have to fight for your rights, not sit back and take it. If some mug outside tried to mug me off, I'd put him in his place, not in a hole, just simple guidance. I've learned the hard way. When screws treat me decent, I act decent. Treat me bad and I'm badder than them.

Violence leads to madness; it fills you with crazy thoughts. You sleep it, eat it and shit it. You become a time-bomb. They push you a bit more — you blow up. They beat you and you survive. You get strong and you blow again. So how long can a man live this way? I'll tell you ... until he dies, if need be. It becomes a way of life, but I don't remember it. Why? Simple ...

it's painful; it's empty and alone. Your cell becomes a hole in the earth, it sucks you in. You drown in your own bitterness; it's not right to live this way.

The door opens to feed you. It's fear, all eyes on you. One little movement and ... BANG! They're on you, bending you over; fear causes them to do this. They're afraid of losing an eye and if they put their faces near you they may never see their kids again, simple as that. Who the fuck wants to live like that? If they crept in ten-handed in the night, silently, what's to say they're not going to kill you? (Make it look like suicide.) And I'll tell you what — they can do it. You'd better believe it!

Prison madness is much the same. Insanity is plentiful in prisons. These days with the drug culture there's not a lot of difference, as a lot of convicts make themselves psychotic and paranoid. Many end up killers, all over petty and minor problems. Where men would once squabble, fight and kill over a half ounce of bacca they now do the same over a gram of white powder or a bag of brown.

And what are the signs of killer madness? Insanity hits home differently. In the max-security asylum, you mostly see dangerous behaviour, very over the top and usually violent. You learn to watch it and say nothing. You allow them space. You allow their moment of madness to pass them by. They feel relieved by what they do. It's a sense of relief, like a shit; you have to do it. Once you do it you feel better for it.

Sadly, most madmen do things that harm them or others, such as the loony who enjoys strangling; it's his buzz. He gets depressed when in seclusion, as he can't strangle anybody, so in the end he hangs himself in turmoil. Their brains can't handle it. He wants so badly to kill, but they will not let him, so he has to kill himself.

Insanity is a very lonely and empty existence — it's painfully true. They may laugh and smile, and skip and dance, but behind all the faces there is hollowness like a bottomless pit. The living dead; depression is a terrible illness, so is psychosis, the mentally inflicted beyond cure.

'Charlie ... Please kill me.' Until you've had a lunatic beg you to waste him, you can't ever understand madness. 'Strangle me, Charlie ... Please, hit me with the mop bucket ... Stab me in the ear with that pen ... Just kill me, put me out of my misery.' Until you witness madness, hear it and smell it, you'll never understand. Some will recycle their own body waste, eating their own shit and drinking their piss – you might not believe it, but it's true. Years of this can rub off on the sane.

It's why a lot of psychiatric nurses have breakdowns and broken marriages. It's obvious why – they're wrecks. How would you cope with a job in which someone could attack you or even kill you, maybe rape you, maybe even put you in a wheelchair for the rest of your life? What a fucking job! Could you do it? Would you want to? You may as well be a lion-tamer ... better wages.

Insanity is beyond any comparison, it's unique. An old madman sat next to me in Broadmoor. He had been there for nearly 40 years. He spoke rarely and was very choosy. 'Hello, Charlie,' he said softly.

'Yeah, Pop.' That's what I called him.

'Listen to me, son ... today the world will blow up, we will all die. Will you hold my hand when it happens?'

'Yeah, Pop, sure,' I said.

'Charlie,' he said, 'will you please pray with me?'

'Yeah, Pop, sure. We will go together.'

That's how madness gets to people. It's death – everything is death. The old boy knew he was dying, so he foresaw an end, but he was basically afraid. He wanted to be told it would be sweet ... he needed reassuring.

Another example is the Ape Man; he killed Catweasel, a notorious paedophile. Catweasel was a beast and he got what he deserved, but the Ape Man himself is insane. I call him the Ape Man, as his features resemble a caveman. He will not mind me saying this, but he is a lunatic and should never be in prison.

What about Chris Brand? He drowned a con in Norwich Jail some 20 years ago. Chris was only 20 years old, a young man on remand. But Chris has serious mental problems; in HMP Woodhill, CSC unit, he got depressed and set fire to his own hair. He swallows items like razor blades; he cuts himself. He's a bloody sad case who should not be in jail.

There is no end. There is no cure. It gets worse with time. Cure? How can you cure an institution? We are bricks crumbling in the walls of despair. Death is inevitable for us all. But the insanity is here to stay. 'Oy, cunt, who are you looking at?'

'Me?'

'Yeah, you!' SMACK! It turned out he had a dodgy eye. He wasn't looking. But he could have been.

I leave you, in this chapter, with the pain of the family of an Asian youth battered to death in his cell by a known violent racist. A skinhead, Robert Stewart, murdered Zahid Mubarek at Feltham Young Offenders Institute (YOI) in March 2000. The court of appeal overturned a ruling from a lower court ordering the Home Secretary to hold a public inquiry into the 'systemic failures' which led to the murder.

Mr Justice Hooper had found that the right to life guaranteed by the European Convention on Human Rights required the Home Office to carry out an independent investigation into the death of the 19-year-old first-time offender, who was serving three months for petty theft.

Lord Woolf, Lord Justice Laws and Lord Justice Dyson ruled

that a public inquiry was not necessary and that there had been no violation of the European Convention on Human Rights Article covering the right to life being protected by law. So what chance does anyone have when it comes to using the European Rights Act in his or her favour?

The Prison Service has already been found to be at fault. The Appeal judges established this; an inquiry into this had been held and the family were invited to be involved. The cause of death had been established by Stewart's conviction for murder and there was no basis for prosecuting any member of the prison service. They said there were no 'factual unknowns' which would impede the family from bringing a claim in the civil courts for damages.

After the judgment, Imtiaz Amin, Zahid's uncle, said, 'We're devastated. All this effort has just been thrown straight back at us. We've been told to shut up by the court. Why was Zahid sharing a cell with such a racist individual? How was such a premeditated murder allowed to happen?'

Imran Khan, the Mubarek's solicitor, said, 'To me, this is a travesty of justice.'

So there you have it, just another con killed in his cell ... so, fuck it, there are plenty more to take his place – see, this is the pressure placed on us cons serving time. Every day is survival of the fittest and if one of us does get slaughtered, what happens? Fuck all. Maybe you can see why I am the way I am!

Hey ... the prison system used to operate like a ship ... the *Titanic*! It went well and then suddenly it sank. Wanna know why? Drugs! You might think cannabis would have been unwelcome in prisons. Far from it! I myself don't go in for it, but those who did would chill out and behave themselves, and then the mandatory drug-testing of prisoners came into force. Cannabis stays in the system for 28 days or more, whilst crack and the like is pissed straight out of the system, making it harder to detect. Yet the likes of crack and heroin turns cons into killers. Never seen a con on cannabis want to kill anybody, but seen lots on the hard stuff want to run through walls, and could have done. Maybe cannabis should be prescribed for violent prisoners ... just a thought!

6

MONSTERS AND BEASTS

I've been hurting 'beasts' for years. I did one in Risley in the '70s with a lighted gag in the eye (I could smell it burning). Did he scream! Like a rat caught in a lawn mower. I stabbed one in the arse in Wandsworth in the '70s with a 6in nail embedded in a broom; I bet that cured his piles! I hit another in Parkhurst with a dumbbell in the teeth; he won't be kissing any more kids!

You've gotta treat these people like shit. I cut one in Hull; I used one as a punchbag in Long Lartin; I fucking love it! Why not? They deserve it all and more. Gas the fuckers in Belsen. I'd like to get Michael Samms's leg and bash Brady to death with it, then ram it up Sidney Cook's arsehole ... and why not?

Beverley Allitt – angel with a fork! What is she breathing for? Shoot the slag, put her in with me and I'll freely snap her fat neck! Now she's a lesbian on £35 a week in Rampton. Nice room, TV and I'm in a cage with nothing! She kills babies ... I rob banks.

Charlie Smith of Broadmoor was a right character; I met another Smith in Belmarsh, all 6ft 7in and 19st of him. He was a lorry driver who'd cut up a prostitute, evil fucker. I kicked him in the head, a nice shot, too. He got a 'not guilty', but he was soon back in on another one. I'll kick him again if I see him! I'll kick him all day long 'til all the shit is out of him! I fucking hate nonces, despise them all!

Robert Black — please, Mr Home Secretary, lock him up with me, I'll look after Black for you ... I need a new punchbag! A monster if ever there was one — he killed three little girls. What's he allowed to live for?

Gordon Robinson was a serious candidate for the rope if ever there was one. I met that slag on C-Wing, Parkhurst, in '76; he killed three boy scouts — or rather, shagged then killed — in the early 1960s. He had served more than 20 years when I saw him. Fuck knows why he never swung! But I gave him a fucking good headache one day when I smashed him with a sock! (Well, it did have a battery in it!) I hit that cunt so hard I thought I had taken the top of his head off. I was covered in blood ... it felt good, though.

I've seen a lot of blood in my life, sometimes running under a door when a man's cut his throat. I can smell it, I really can; it lingers in the air. Blood has a strange smell, nothing like it to compare with, but we've all got to bleed, some more than others! You'd be amazed at how many lunatics in Broadmoor, Rampton and Ashworth have drunk their victim's blood, sickos, evil bastards.

There are a lot of paedophiles in the asylums, child-killers, abusers of the weak, fucking bullies in lust! Men who can't have a proper sexual relationship, 'cos they're inadequate. These pieces of shit make my skin crawl, I despise them; they stay clear of me, as my hate for them shows in my face. They fear me. They can smell my disgust yards away, so they rarely cross my path. Some have, and they've learned not to do it again.

I don't see them as humans; I see them as lumps of shit that need flushing away. But in the asylums now, the doctors seem to love them. They get the best of everything – jobs, nice rooms, privileges, good food and they swap their porn magazines and shag each other's arses and have a bloody good time of it. So after ten or twenty years they get out and jump another kid. You can't cure these monsters. They're evil. And what do the courts do. Send them back to their nice cosy rooms with a view! Would you release a rabid dog in a school playground? That's all a paedophile is ... a sicko.

Dennis Nilsen killed 15 people, chopped them up, ate bits, even slept with the stiffs, shagged a few, too. One weird guy! Queer as a bent ten-bob note. It was in the seg block in Albany Jail where I first kenned him out of the window. He came down off the wing and got some punishment; all the lads were slagging him off. But he gave as good as he got; he loves a verbal argument.

I remember he knew some of the cons' names and said, 'Keep on and I'll get word to the *News of the World*, and give your names saying that you're my lovers.' I had to laugh. He's a funny fucker, but not my cuppa tea; a bit iffy for me. I rate him as a monster, but say what you will against him, he's not a grass. A con cut him down in the Scrubs, and he didn't make a statement. I've known 'faces' to get compensation, so he's not a grass. He's everything else though. Nilsen will die in jail. The madness of it all is ... why keep him alive? What's the point? He's never gonna walk under the stars again.

Josh was a fucking animal! Make no mistake about it, a filthy beast. I first met him in Parkhurst. He came across as one of the chaps, but underneath all his smiles he was a typical bully. Quite a big guy, bald head, always wore prison overalls, but he was a sick, evil, twisted rat whom I despised. Soon, the entire system would hate his guts.

I was in the seg at the time, must have been the mid '80s, when the prick turned up. Reg Kray sent a message down to me: 'Watch a con called Josh!' It turned out he was up on the wing only to be chased off, as he was not welcome. His true colours came out; he was a sicko, a fucking pervo. Even in the block, he would climb up at his window and offer cons on the yard a fag or some sweets to expose themselves, while he stood at the window and pulled himself off.

A con dying for a smoke or a weak con would do it; it used to wind me up! Once I was on the yard having my one-hour's exercise. I was stripped off to my shorts, training. I could feel, sense, his eyes on me. I turned fast and saw his evil eyes through the bars; I jumped up and spat at him. He gave me a load of abuse, but most Jocks you can't understand when they're screaming at you. I told him, 'Shut up, you fucking perv.' Later, he got moved to Albany Jail, which is next door to Parkhurst. He ended up stabbing a young Arab in the head with a pair of scissors. The Arab, called Alban, was serving life for a terrorist crime; he was a well-liked kid.

Josh was up to his games trying to get his pants off. The Arab was not into it so Josh stabbed him. I later bumped into Josh in Wandsworth but, sadly, I was still in solitary and so was he, so our paths had a brick wall in between. He was one slag I wanted so badly to have a straightener with.

Incidentally, Alban ended up in Broadmoor. He was never the same after Josh stabbed him; it sent him a bit funny, made him sick mentally, probably paranoid. That cunt Josh has a lot to answer for. He has terrorised inmates, raped them and stabbed them, all for sex! He's a sick rat who needs serving up big time. I know he got out, but I heard he's back in, so I may yet get my wish. The fact is, I've no choice but to attack him, as he will sure attack me. With a slag like that you can't afford to turn your back ... he will put a knife straight through you. So, Josh, wherever you are, I'm dying for some of you and I won't need a pair of scissors!

One particular sex killer is evil. I bumped into him in the '70s in Walton Jail. He raped and killed two old women in Cheshire. The screws slipped him on the wing, thinking that none of us knew who he was, but it was bang on! The rat! We all emptied our piss pots in his cell, while he was in there; there was shit all over him, all over the bed and the walls; he soon vanished.

Another slag is the devil on legs, one evil bastard and a nasty piece of work. The only good thing I can say about this sack of shit is he will die inside. I bumped into this turd in 1975. Nobody liked him. He was serving time for mugging a vicar. Big time, eh, mugging a vicar? Last of the big-timers but, apart from that, he's a sewer rat in jail. Our paths crossed and he got hurt. I entered his cell and cut the rat. Like all rats, he made a statement. He later got out and killed four old people. Strangely enough, one of them was a vicar – so he's got this thing about the clergy. He changed his name and was sent to Broadmoor. He's a complete fucking lunatic, but a madman who gives real madmen a bad name. I often think to myself, if I had killed him that day up in Hull, then four people would be alive today.

Bernie Erskine came into my face in Hull in '75; he's one evil slag. He gave it the large – put on a great act – but I saw right through him! I just sensed he was not all he made out to be, so I went out of my way to find out. He boasted about his robberies like he was some sort of John Dillinger, but he kept it quiet about the young girl he'd raped. I found out through a good source, and put it to him. His face went white ... as ever, denial.

I've never yet met a guilty sex case. 'She led me on, it wasn't like that ... she's out to frame me, blah, blah.' I hit him smack in the teeth before he could get out any more lies. The girl was just 16 years old! 'Cunt!' SMACK! 'Stay clear of me.'

Days later in the recess, while slopping out, I just had this strange sense something was about to happen and it did. He came at me from behind a toilet door ... with a jug! He slung it at me. I managed to duck, but some of the contents splashed my head. It was hot, very hot! Then he lunged at me with a 'tool' in his other hand. Like the cunt he was, he missed.

He panicked, lost control ... and he was mine! I stepped aside and allowed him to come through, then with a kick to his right knee, I put him down; the rest was easy ... he's only good with little girls!

The top of my head was a bit sore; it was cooking oil he had had in the jug. It was meant for my eyes and face, and then I would have been his for the stabbing. Erskine disappeared after that little lesson, but I'd say he never learned from it. Never did bump into him again, sadly; but he remains an evil bastard in my book. A cowardly evil bastard, who couldn't even stab me up properly, what a pathetic specimen of nature!

I'll tell you what insanity is! The system, it's crazy; it's also very evil, unpredictable and dangerous.

Donald Nielson, the 'Black Panther' — not to be mixed up with Dennis Nilsen — has the devil in his eyes, black holes of madness; he's now served 28 years, only another 25 to go ... he's dead.

A dead man screaming, they should have hanged this piece of shit for what he did to Lesley Whittle, stuffing her down the drain; they found her naked, hanging on a ledge. He said it was an accident! Yeah ... some fucking accident; he should have stuck to the post office raids. You need a brain for kidnap and ransoms; he hasn't got a brain, just a strong urge to kill. He's a killing machine, a pure psycho, a power freak and one lethal little madman!

I bet you're glad he's never going to get out, unless he escapes, but after 28 years he's still in max secure, still Cat 'A'. He walked around Full Sutton like a mouse in a cage looking for a hole, praying to escape.

Now this may upset a lot of people; if it upsets you, then I say do something about it — don't be a lemon. Act on it before it's too late. Strangely enough, it didn't affect me — but it will one day. Years ago, they had special visit rooms for 'monsters' so that decent people would not have to see or mingle with them.

Well, let's face it, would you sit feet away from the Ripper if you could help it, while you're chatting to your son/husband/brother? Well, nowadays there are no such 'Special Rooms' for the monsters, they've been done away with. (The Special Rooms, not the monsters, sadly.) They have visits in the same room as you when you visit your loved ones. I have my visits in my own Special Room, so you can't see the likes of me. As if I'm the monster.

At the time of writing, they prefer and insist that I'm kept locked behind a steel cell door, so on that basis I have refused to accept any of my visitors, except my legal visits that are conducted with me sitting behind my inner meshed and barred cell door. But they even tried to fuck my legal visits up by insisting that they should be closed visits, with me behind a bullet-proof glass barrier; they can go and fuck themselves.

Thanks to a threatened legal action, they bottled out of facing a judicial review ... weaklings! This is not the end of it either — Europe, here we come! But why should I have to speak to my wife through a steel door and not even get to see her or hug her? What about my mum, too? All that will change, you'll see.

So let me tell you how these paedophiles, rapists, beasts and granny abusers are eyeing your lot up. Your little kids are in danger. The Prison Service are taking the piss by allowing a possible incident. An offence doesn't have to have been committed by touch alone ... did you know that? By just looking in a certain way, they can cause alarm or distress and that's a criminal offence.

Now let's look at it in a sane way. A paedophile loves kids, and your kid has come up to see Daddy, and let's say, for instance, the kid gets grabbed! What does Daddy do? I'll tell you ... he destroys the monster, and Daddy ends up with a life sentence. Poor Daddy. So why was Daddy put into that position in the first place?

What if a child-killer grabs a kid and strangles it? Come on, what then? It's too fucking late complaining then. Your kid is history. What if a rapist fucks an old granny held hostage? It could happen. Get real. So I want you all to write to the Home Secretary or your Member of Parliament, and demand answers. Are you safe?

Well, I'll tell you, you're not safe. How can you be? Once you're held hostage, who's gonna save you, the screws or Daddy? No fucker can save you. It'll take half a second to twist and snap your spine or rip your eyes out, or bite a lump out of your tit.

These maximum-security jails are full of bad monsters and beasts – Duffy, Nilsen, Cannon, that's just three! There's a whole wing full of them – '120' – they're segregated from us, but they use the same visits room. So it's a mockery, an insult, a fucking disgrace. Add it up. They're segregated from us, but not from you. We see them on visits, but not on the wings or workshops, so what's it all about?

Well, there's a theory. 'Cos I'm not the sort of man to cause problems, in time I will also be allowed to have my visits in that room. What if I stood up, walked over to a monster's table and stabbed him in the eye with a pen or a spoon? Or even just my finger, which is worse than being stabbed with just a spoon. Then, say, I took his visitor hostage and shouted, 'OK, boys, it's a siege ...' Is that not duress? Are we not being put into a situation to do it ... well?

Take, for the sake of argument, Sidney Cook, the high-profile child-killer. I am not going to take the chance of him attacking a kid. 'Outside', I can grab the kid and take him to safety, but in that room I can't leave it, neither can the kid. So what can I do? I have to hope that Cook doesn't grab the kid. Fuck *hoping*! I'm a realist. I act on impulse; if I get one little itch, I'm off at 200mph.

Sidney 'Catweasel' Cook and Robert Oliver were part of the paedophile gang in the '80s who killed Jason Swift, why not hang them? These scum raped him and other kids, and then killed them! Catweasel died in Whitemoor, having been strangled; the rest got out. They fucking got released; can you believe it?

Now, how I see it, who visits a monster? Would you visit one? Could you? Well, if you do, you're a monster, too. A rat is a rat; it's not a mouse. We are all of us in some sort of category or other. I'm a madman, but I'm not gonna jump on your granny and rip her pants off or kill your kids. So have I made myself clear on this? You're put in danger. Don't allow it to continue. And the con you're visiting is also put in a terrible position, 'cos if he reacts, he will get more years added on — you'll lose him for longer. I predict in time an incident will occur that will shock the nation and everyone will say, 'Why, how did it happen?'

I love my mum, she's my angel, and I adore her. Outside, if I felt she was in a dangerous place I'd have her move out fast. I can't do that in prison, so I have to act fast and stop the danger. If it means I have to attack, then I will, 'cos no monster will grab my mum, ever. And these faceless, spineless prison chiefs must take all the blame for allowing it to happen. As I said, it doesn't affect me yet, as my visits are closed.

Your man will point the monsters out. 'Hey, look, love, over there. That's Black, the triple child-killer. They say he killed ten more ... Oh look, it's Straffen; he killed three little girls with his bare hands; I hope he don't grab our Sally ... Oh look, it's Brady. Hi, Ian, want a cup of tea? Blimey it's ...' Get the picture?

Fucking get real, 'cos that room is a fucking trap for your kids. Recently in Whitemoor Prison, Micky Bullock went on a visit to see his family who travel down from up North; his daughter is 13 years old. She would not take her jacket off, because of monsters in the room. Now Micky has made it clear, he will kill one if one so much as makes a move towards his kids.

These rooms are potential hell-holes, 'cos when it happens it could well end up a bloodbath. Have a good look around that room. I bet a monster is eyeing up your kid. If you take some deep breaths, through your nose, you'll smell the fear in that room. It's a nightmare. You'll pick up on the evil.

You've probably been raped 20 times in the minds of these sickos. So what is the answer? Either you lot petition, protest, get it changed or some poor sod will end up getting life. But the main question is, how can they change it? I know for a fact up in Durham Jail there is now no segregation wing; monsters mix in the wings. I blame the cons for this, and I'd say now, act on it; stop allowing the prison chiefs to put you in such hazardous situations.

I'd say, 'Hey, Chief, sling two monsters in with me for the night.' Would they? Would they fuck! It doesn't happen, I'd kill 'em! So get real, lads, act on it. You don't have to kill them. Just make it hard for them — shit in their beds, piss in their tea, don't let 'em sleep, use them as punchbags. Get a big rapist to burst their arses. Don't allow them to mix. The screws are taking the piss.

So why is it in the max-security jails the monsters are on 43 (prison Rule 43 – protection for the vulnerable prisoner) and protected, and we can't mix, but they can use our visits room to put our families at risk? Is it not insanity? I'd say it was evil, and totally unprofessional, if not wicked, dangerous and unacceptable.

And don't kid yourselves for one minute that it's safe, 'cos it ain't. Those paedophiles probably have their hand on their cocks as the kids come into that room. Get fucking real, a paedophile loves kids. A child-killer loves kids. A train-spotter loves trains. I love a bank. It's life, a fact, we are all into something, but we shouldn't be. All of us do something we shouldn't. You eat too much, you drink too much and you can't help it. These monsters can't help it either, 'cos they're sick in the head!

I'm a godparent. I've got a niece, too. I'm a lover of kids. I'm a lover of my mum. I love my family. I don't share them with monsters to drool over. So think about it now before it's too late. Digest it all, 'cos what you've read is truth.

The system is insane! Some jails now force cons to mix with the sex cases, people like Black, Nilsen and the Bradys of the world. These pieces of shit should all be in special wings, not mixing with us. Would any sane person want a mass rapist or sex-killer living next door when you can have me living there protecting the community? You wouldn't get paedophiles messing about in the neighbourhood I was in. I predict, soon, a disaster in jail – murders. It's got to come and it's only obvious. We can only take so much shit – we don't want monsters in our face. What do they expect us to do?

I mean, do you think this sort of conversation could take place between Ian Brady and me?

'Hi, Ian, fancy a game of chess?'

'Oh thanks, Charlie.'

'Err ... fancy one of my fresh-made apple pies, Ian?'

'Oh thanks, Chas, err ... you got any child porn?'

'Err ... no, Ian. I don't use it myself, but I'll ask the Beast of Basildon for you.'

'Who?'

'Oh, he's the new con. He raped 14 little girls.'

Now get my drift ... it's fucking sick. Let's get real. Let's stop fucking about. Robbers discuss robbery; burglars discuss burglary and ram-raiders discuss cars. Get fucking real, Mr Home Secretary, and stop mugging us cons off. A paedophile takes kids. We don't want the scum in our face! Your shit prison psychologists may love them, and your muggy screws may enjoy associating with them, but us cons don't want them on the landings. I say it's all madness throwing us all under the same roof, but the sad thing is, some poor sod will end up with life over it. It's what the headquarters want – to kill them off.

Free people do not want paedophiles living within their communities, so why should I have them living in my community here behind bars? I'm no second-class citizen, although some of you would like to think so.

My right to go out and make a wage to support my family has been stripped away from me; my right to enjoy my possessions peacefully has been stripped away from me; my right to have access to educational facilities has been stripped away from me; my right to a life without pain and suffering has been stripped away from me; my right to have open visits with my family has been stripped away from me; my right to freedom of expression has been stripped away from me; my right to continue family ties has been stripped away from me; my right to lead a dignified life has been stripped away from me; my right to father children has been stripped away from me; my right to vote has been stripped from me ...

During Strangeways Prison riot ten years ago, I was in the segregation block in Parkhurst Jail, Isle of Wight. I saw the *Sun* newspaper; it was my saddest day in prison, and how I longed to be in that riot. The greatest prison riots ever in the United Kingdom, and I was not in it. It hurt me to miss that.

I'd have got the biggest knife I could and tied it on a broom handle, and gone on a stabbing mission. There would have been that many paedophiles' mutilated bodies lying about that the place would have resembled an abattoir! Rivers of blood? I'd have cut off the dick of every paedophile! I'd have gone for the monsters and with over 300 of them in Strangeways to stab up ... what an achievement, what a victory! Strangeways' riot was the cat's bollocks, the riot of all riots, a complete insane hellhole gone up. I hope they do a film of it. If I'm out, I'd like to play a part in it, and if we can get some real monsters, I could then show the world how to exterminate them with a spear. So where's the next roof? Will I be in it? Will there ever be another Strangeways? Oh, yes please.

How I used to love catching a beast in the recess or shower or sitting in the TV room with the lights off. I hit one slag in Full Sutton 20 times with a large, square PP9 battery in a sock. Won't see him again. They slipped the pervo on the wing, but you soon find out in jail. There are ways to find out — bent screws, cons that remember, slip-ups and old newspaper cuttings.

Who remembers Chapman, the 'Barnsley Beast'? Ring a bell? Raped a good few girls up North. Got life in the 1970s. A big chap, ex-Army. I arrived at Long Lartin Jail in the late 1980s and they put me on A-Wing; the first smiling face I saw was Johnny Walker, who'd been fitted up with 20 life sentences. He was one of the Birmingham Six. He served 17

years and was then freed. 'Innocent' John was a lovely boy. Big Albert Baker was there, another lifer, and a slag I'll call Don. Don came into my cell. 'Hi, Chas,' and he marked my card, who's who and all that.

It was Don who said, 'The Barnsley Beast is on the wing.'

'OK, yeah, where?' He was opposite our cell. I waited and watched him come up the landing. Once he hit his cell, I slipped in like a tornado. 'Oy, cunt, what's your fucking game on the wing with all of us? Nice cunts like you give us criminals a bad name.' I pulled out a 7in tool. 'Want some of this, do ya?'

'Look, Chas,' he said. 'I've been on this wing ages. I don't bother anybody.'

I said, 'Well, don't fucking bother me, cunt, or you get it.'

Next day, I saw Don come out of his cell and go into the Barnsley Beast's cell. I shot in the beast's cell again. 'What's Don doing in here?' I asked.

'He comes in and puts a bet on. I'm the wing bookie, Chas.'

This blew me away! Remember, 99 per cent of my bird is in solitary, and here I am on a wing with the chaps, and the Beast of Barnsley is the fucking bookie! It doesn't add up.

I shot in Don cell and punched a hole in his two-faced head. Cunt! Telling me who and who not to speak to. It turned out he was £20 down on the books, so if I'd done the beast he'd had saved £20. What a slag! I later found out there were other beasts on the wing. I lasted a couple of weeks before I blew up, and used an iron bar on some of their heads.

Little Alfie Lodge was a Welsh armed robber, and I respected him; he helped me a lot 'cos I was sure to kill someone. That's 'cos prison is evil. This Beast from Barnsley had a serious row. Three cons went into him with tools. The four went to hospital, so it's no joke. Ronnie Owen could have got me killed; or, better still, he'd kill Chapman. Either way, Owen would be dead. I hope you read this, Owen. You're worse than the Beast. At least he's not afraid to have a row. You're just a gutless cunt!

Paedophile monsters — those pieces of shit are abusing and destroying your kids. A monster grabs a kid, destroys that kid physically, mentally and even the kid's soul is destroyed; in some ways it's a blessing if the kid dies, 'cos no kid should have to experience such inhumanity and brutality.

The Railway Killer John Duffy is a fucking monster. Murdering bastard, he raped a load of women. With his laser eyes, the cunt wouldn't have any eyes if I bumped into him!

John Steed picked up two prostitutes from King's Cross, and shot one dead in his motor. Turned out he was a serial rapist. Nasty bit of work! He put his mood swings down to steroids; eventually, he got lifed off. He spent a good ten years in the '43' wing. I landed in Full Sutton seg unit and he was there. He stayed in his cell so people couldn't see him, but I knew it was him as my memory is spot on. He was giving it the big one out of the window to the lads.

I lay on my bed and I thought I knew that geezer ... that name ... and he knew me. Soon the whole seg was at him. 'Beast, beast, beast!' He soon got his week in, but the strange thing is, even though we are all locked up in solitary, I felt like I could get to him. I was on a ten-guard unlock, but I felt maybe I could grab a screw and demand to get Steed's door open; I wanted to attack him so badly. But I was mysteriously moved back to my cage in Wakefield and it was there I heard ... John Steed had hanged himself in his cell at Full Sutton.

I was fucking made up; it had taken him ten years to realise that death was the best thing for him, and it saved some poor sod from getting extra bird for him.

But this really makes me think — look at all the number one beasts: Arthur Hutchinson, James Lang, Peter Pickering, Peter

Sutcliffe, Paul Corrigan and Ian Brady and so on. None of them are ugly. Look at Ted Bundy in the USA. All these guys are good-looking men who can pull a bird. I've always wondered about that. You would think a monster was ugly, a hump on his back, a person who can't chat up a bird, but it's the opposite. So it proves my point — they're born evil! Insanity drove them mad in the womb!

So the monster gets caught and once they're in court, they can't escape the evidence, so what does the court do? Send him to prison. How terrible for him! Life. He goes on a nonce wing with a bunch of other nonces. He has a colour remote-control TV (for his kids' programmes).

Oh yes, he'll watch all the kids' TV programmes. All those boy scouts ... lovely. He will have a nice warm cell, bed, carpet, curtains, even a kettle, electric shaver, radio cassette and clocks ... shall I go on? Cosy or what? He will have a job in prison so he can buy his smokes and tins of salmon. Videos are screened on a Saturday night. He will get nice visits and association (being allowed to mix with other prisoners).

He will be able to go into other cells and share stories with other paedophiles and swap police statements and photos. Photos? What sort of photos? Didn't you know? The police take photos of the dead, mutilated bodies and those monsters get them through their legal team to use in their defence — sick or what? Me, I tried to use footage of me being beaten up in prison by screws and Jack Straw banned it, yet Mr Home Secretary, whoever it is at the time, allows paedophiles to have explicit photos of kiddies, dead kiddies. Now that's what I call insanity!

They swap their victims' statements. Let's say a boy of ten years old gets raped. They swap it all and get their rocks off on it. Oh, they get to see plenty of counsellors, probation officers and psychologists. You know, all them stupid twats who say paedophiles are not sick bastards!

Now, let's get the facts out once and for all. These are not crimes of innocence. They're evil bastards and they can't be cured. They cannot be helped. They come into prisons as cowards. They are spineless people, so in prison they're model inmates. They're the screws' tit-bits – 'Yes, sir, no, sir, three bags full of shit, sir' – so all those cons are excellent. 'What a good boy.'

Year after year they lick arse, and then they get parole. Then they're back to your kids. All those years they've been dreaming of your kids, watching kids on TV, reading about kids in mags and mixing with a ring of paedophiles. It's like a community, they chat about how best to do it. Life training!

For example, an armed robber comes to prison, and associates with other robbers. They discuss the job, and where they went wrong. They learn from it, go out and try again. Some will win, others will lose; but they're robbers.

What the fuck do you think paedophiles think about – fishing? They're talking and dreaming of your kids, like I dream and think about banks. I'm a fucking robber. Get in my way and I'll shoot your legs off. I want your money; they want your kids ... OK?

So what's to be done? Look ... the courts and prisons are a joke, it's obviously not working. Research it; you'll see there are more kids being abused and killed than ever before. Why? Simple – there is no punishment. Paedophiles do not fear the consequences. But if you're hard on them ... sentence them to pain; rip their bollocks off and leave them to bleed or die.

Why bother sending them to jail? Why waste tax-payers' money? Torture them; destroy them once and for all. In fact, give me the job to exterminate them; let me give society a break from these monsters.

Patel got lifed off for sex crimes with boys. He was a nasty little bastard; if he's a true practising Muslim, why is he shagging little boys' bums? 'Cos he's an evil little slag! The system made a terrible mistake with him ... or did they? Maybe it was a planned mistake, as the system seems to enjoy making mistakes.

Patel was sent to Parkhurst! Now Parkhurst when it was a Category 'A' prison was full of good, decent cons, proper villains; all the good robbers with any credibility have done bird on the island. All the gangsters, all the hit-men and all the top faces — if you haven't done Parko, you haven't done bird.

All the chaps do not tolerate such filth on the wings; Patel had to have some and did. He was found in the recess with his throat cut and with a broom rammed up his arsehole. To all paedophiles, let it be a warning as to what can and will happen if you enter a real prison. The last I heard, Patel is now in Whitemoor '43' wing! He has to wear plastic pants, with lots of padding, as he's now totally incontinent. He walks like one of those puppets in *Thunderbirds*. Nice one, eh?

Brady and Hindley, the two sex cases, have been a big downfall in my journey through hell; I just start to itch when they're near me. I'm a bit of an analyser; most of them can't look a man in the eye, saving all their eye contact for their victims — little kids or women. Basically, they're fucking cowards, evil, perverted scum. When I started off my bird, I was on a mission to wipe out the cunts!

Ian Brady — force-feed him with scorpions or throw him in with a mass rapist, and let him get shagged to death. You've gotta be as evil as them; fight evil with evil, violence with violence ... an eye for an eye. Stop pussyfooting about! Destroy the monsters!

Myra Hindley — burn her, make a lampshade out of her skin and send it to Dennis Nilsen! Cut out her entrails and post them to the Ripper ... second Class, of course!

Give me a nonce and I'll teach them a lesson of life ... don't fuck with kids. Have you heard of something that paedophiles call 'life training'? Basically, it's where they seek an underage girl or boy and get their parents' consent to take away their innocence. I'll fucking show them life training ... chuck them in the cell with me for five minutes!

It's those paedophiles I love best. It's like trapping a rat in a corner ... fear! I like to watch them cower and beg, and some even shit their pants. All are maggots. Any bloke I know in or out despises them and any man who says different is a liar or a nonce himself! Why make excuses for them?

I'm sick of doctors making excuses, and those welfare workers, they're complete mugs ... nonce-lovers. 'His daddy never got him any sweets when he was a boy.' 'His mummy beat him!' It's all shit; a nonce is a fucking nonce!

Take Ian Brady and Hindley − the tax-payers have fed and clothed them for 36 years. What for? What good are they to society. They're no fucking good in jail. Brady and Hindley should have been executed 36 years ago. They're not human, so why keep them alive?

But let me leave you with a fact about Moors Murderer Ian Brady. He wants to die, and they won't let him, so they force-feed him. That's insanity! But I say Brady is a good actor, 'cos he's had over 36 years to kill himself. He's only good at killing kids! Even after he's been locked up for nearly 40 years, he's still spewing out his evil.

Very recently, the brother of Moors Murder victim Lesley Ann Downey died in a house fire in Manchester on New Year's Eve, along with his seven-year-old daughter. Tommy West, 45, of Fallowfield, Greater Manchester, was house-sitting for his stepfather, Alan West, who was in hospital for a hip operation.

The fire at the house on Princess Road, Moss Side, killed Mr West and his daughter Kimberley. A 40-year-old woman and nine-year-old boy, thought to be Mr West's wife Lesley and son Stuart, were also injured. If it wasn't for Brady, these people would still be alive. Why's that? Because the whole situation would have been different if Lesley Ann Downey was still alive; they'd probably all have been out partying on New Year's Eve, but what did they have to party for after all that Brady and Hindley had done? Two more murder victims to add to Brady's tally – off with his fucking head.

Beasley, the Guernsey Beast, got 30 years in the late 1960s for raping young boys. It was impossible to get hold of him; the Beast spent 20 years of it on protection under Rule 43. I met him in Albany in the '80s. Finally, I got to squirt shit and piss at him through a shampoo bottle. In Albany Jail, on the Isle of Wight, the fat cunt used to walk past my cell window in the segregation unit on his way to the workshops, so I caught him a blinder. It was a sunny day, and I was waiting for the nonce to walk by. Short and fat, he looked what he was; 'nonce' was written all over him and I was going to add to that with some piss and shit!

'Hi, Beasley,' I shouted. He stopped and looked. 'Hey, over here ... it's me.'

'Who's that?' he asked.

'It's me, your old buddy,' he came closer ... squirt, squirt! A spray of shit and piss hit him in the face and neck. 'Lick it up, you beast.' What a shot! Sorry it wasn't acid. Yeah, a lovely day that was. Beasley, the Beast I pissed on.

Peter Cook, the Cambridge Rapist, was another one I fucking hated. It was Parkhurst in the early '70s when I bumped into that evil bastard. I thought, Hell, it could have been my mum. He'd raped ten women, most of them young students; but the public don't really get to know the full details, unlike us cons!

The scumbag didn't just rape them; he destroyed them

mentally, and buggered them in a leather mask with 'RAPIST' written on it.

One day I just felt depressed; he was on the wing and I just had to give him some. I followed him to the recess and smashed his crust in with a mop bucket. I was gonna stab him up but a screw was coming so I left him on the floor. That was nearly 30 years ago, and he's still locked up. Let's hope the cunt dies inside, 'cos if he gets out, some poor sod's in for it. Those nonces can't be cured except by a hole in the crust. He must be nearly 70 years old by now, but a nonce is a nonce!

Fred West was in Winston Green Jail in 1994, and I was only two cells away from him! He was on remand, but I only saw him through his spy hole in the door as he was on a Cat 'A' nonce Rule 43 protection.

One day, I peeped through the spy hole and there he was sitting at a table looking at something. He looked like that idiot Benny out of the old *Crossroads* series. He ended up hanging himself in that cell. I used to shout to him through the window at night, 'Fred, you're gonna die in jail ... why not do it now, be a man ... die!' I'd like to think him hanging himself was down to me. I'm glad he did it; one less nonce to feed!

I thought Rose West would have done us the privilege and followed her husband.

She's about 200ft away from me on the 'She' wing here in Durham Prison. I don't think I'll be here much longer, so by time this book comes out, I'll probably have been moved again.

On a windy night, I'm sure I can smell Rose's whiff (especially when she's had a plate of Durham stew). I'm amazed that she hasn't been stabbed out yet! I hear from the screws she's in a lesbian affair now, slimmed down to 9st.

What's she living for? She put her own kids through hell, she's a paedophile ... strangle the witch. Personally, I'd lock her in a byre with a mad bull, that's all she's fit for. I pity the poor bull!

If the courts or prisons don't step in, then it's time society did. Demand the death penalty for paedophiles. OK, it might not stop overnight because these crazed animals can't resist a dabble, but it would slowly start to extinguish them from our lives.

Pop pervert Jonathan King has hired a minder to protect him from attacks behind bars. This supposed tough guy and paedophile lover is being paid by the King of the paedophiles in phone cards and tobacco to watch his back. King is doing a seven stretch for abusing underage youths. He was sent down in November 2001 and now he pays the price, but what gets me is why some straight-acting con in Maidstone Jail offers him protection.

Another con broke King's nose when he was in Belmarsh and, to give King credit, he didn't grass up his attacker. As I've already mentioned, I know faces who have made statements for the same thing happening to them. But I don't condone what King did to them kids.

This geezer who is protecting King, is doing a three stretch for unlawful imprisonment. What a hard case, eh? Probably trapped some innocent cunt in a room just for the fun of it ... just like me taking hostages! All I can say is that if he loves paedophiles so much, then he's a monster just like them and he's a target just like King. Glitter gets out and King replaces him — like attracts shite!

Well, I'll keep hating the system and the paedophiles. I'll never accept it. Would you? And when I get a chance to chin one, stab one, spit on one or stamp on his face, I'll do it. And if I'm an evil fucker for doing it, then so be it. All I'll say to that is, pray I never catch you bastards outside. Keep praying just that, 'cos I'm your worst ever nightmare. You paedophiles are filth.

Now here's a turn up for the book if ever there was one. The current Home Secretary, David Blunkett, has plans to introduce mandatory life sentences for serious first-time sex offenders. I'll believe it when I see it! This has only come about because of pressure from the press demanding action for 'Sarah's Law'. OK, that particular law only relates to paedophiles on the Sex Offenders Register, but the rate of new sex offenders coming out into the open is startling; Blunkett knows he has to act now. I mean, when we've got the likes of Jonathan King having his own fucking minder in prison then it really is taking the piss!

Blunkett stated, 'There must be no more cases like that of Roy Whiting [the killer of Sarah Payne], a man sentenced to four years for a terrible kidnap and sexual assault of a child, who went on to commit an even more horrendous crime. If someone has been convicted of a dangerous, violent or sexual crime they must be given a long prison sentence − including, in some cases, life − and made to serve it in full. If there is a recognised risk that they may offend again at the end of their prison term, we need to make sure they are kept under close supervision ... The police and probation service must have the powers to monitor such people for as long as necessary.'

He went on to criticise the media. Get real, Blunkett − I don't speak for myself, I speak for the likes of little Sarah Payne. If anyone recalls, I wrote in one of my earlier books that the man the police had in for questioning over the Sarah Payne murder did kill her and that was before it even went to court! You see, we get to find out these things even behind bars, if only you knew the half of it, but I doubt they'd let you get to read it 'cos they'd ban such a book.

Without the media, we'd get nowhere fast. I might not like some of what the media write about me, but when it comes to naming and shaming paedophiles, they've got my blessing. The *News of the World* and the *Sunday People* give 'em stick. Keep it up, boys.

Victor Miller – now there's a case for hanging. I had Victor Miller three cells away from me in the CSC unit, Woodhill Jail. He's a natural '43', a dirty, child-killing nonce! He killed a young boy after he had had his evil way with him. We didn't see him, we could only smell him – he refused exercise. These people need to be reminded that they're evil monsters. He didn't even leave his cell for a shower. I really do think capital punishment should be reintroduced for such evil filth, especially when people like me have to listen to them brag about noncing and killing a young newspaper delivery boy.

Ray Gilbert, Keith Pringle, Ferdie Lieveld, Schultz and me just couldn't take any more. It had to go off, and did! What did it for me was his boasting: 'I did the kid, so fucking what, who's gonna do anything about it?' When my door unlocked, I ran out, mad. The screws just froze. I leaped off the two landings and landed on the ground floor. Insanity had driven me mad again; the screws legged it and I had the run of the place. I smashed the cameras, the doors and the kitchen lights and I then got a bit of metal and started bashing on Miller's solid steel cell door. 'Come out, come out, wherever you are ... Miller!'

'No, Charlie, please, Charlie, I'm sorry, Charlie!' The beast shit his pants as I started coming through. I wanted him so badly, but as usual it was me who suffered most, as the riot mob rushed in. It was my turn. Shields crash into you; they're on you; they bend you up, bash you and then restrain you in a body belt and cart you off to another hell. More pain, more suffering, more isolation ... there is no end to it.

A van arrives and you're slung in, naked, wrapped up, your head is throbbing and they lovingly make sure your property is smashed to smithereens. Photos ripped and letters missing. Their evil ways always amaze me! Why destroy a photo? What's my mum done to them or my dead brother or my departed dad?

Brutalise me and punish me, but why fuck with my property, my memories? Why snap my radio aerial? 'Cos they're cunts, that's why! I've had this madness all my life. But the sad fact is you never see who does it; you think you know but you never really know. Some screws will say it's wrong, no need for that, but some love it; it's their buzz! So Miller gets clean pants and I get all this.

The way they keep sex cases happy behind bars is beyond me. If you've had the good fortune never to have been in prison, then it's kind of hard for you to grasp what I'm getting at.

How else can I put it? Let's say you live in a quiet village and then the local farmer hires his field out to a load of hippies for a rock concert. Would you care? Would it affect your karma? Something is bound to upset your peaceful life and that's what monsters and beasts do to us straight cons.

Screws go home, but we have to stay behind bars in the stench that these monsters give off. I smell death on them; they smell like a butcher's waste bin. Keep sending the fags to Hindley, 'cos she ain't never gonna see the inside of a shop to buy any. Play them at their own game.

I can't do any more. I've done enough, and when I do try to catch one, I only get smashed up by the screws. Screws love 'em, 'cos they're no trouble. Maybe some will say, 'God, Bronson doesn't half go on about it ...' Maybe I do, but so would you if you saw what I saw. If I had a TV set and a nice cell with nice visits then maybe I'd not hate them so much. But I'm a fucking animal; I'm in a cage; I've got fuck all and the paedophiles have everything. I've got it worse than a monster.

And in addition to these beats and monsters, there's a whole load of top-notch killers who'll never see the outside again: Victor Castigador (murdered two security guards and a cashier by setting them on fire); David Copeland (the Nazi nail-bomber); Kenneth Erskine (the 'Stockwell Strangler', killed seven pensioners in three months); Malcolm Green (killed a prostitute then a tourist, dismembering the body); Archibald Hall (the butler who killed his boss's family and several others); John Hilton (killed two men after serving a life sentence); Arthur Hutchinson ('the Fox', stabbed a bride's parents and brother to death at a wedding reception, then raped the bride's sister); Colin Ireland (tortured and killed five men); Arthur Jackson (shot one man and attempted to kill a woman); Fred Lowe (multiple con killer); Robert Maudsley (triple con killer, and ate the brains of one of his victims); Peter Moore (killed four men and tortured more than 50); Dr Harold Shipman (the most prolific serial killer in UK history); and Roy Whiting (child-killer).

And to think, I've shared the same roof with some of these guys! Now that's madness!

7

DEAD MEN BREATHING

The corridors in Broadmoor, when I was there in the '70s and '80s, were called galleries. They're dull, grey, echoey and gloomy with potent smells of bodies, sweat, fear and madness. Drugs can be inhaled from the corridor air.

Let me tell you about the medicine hatch. At breakfast time, lunch, tea and supper, the loons will queue up at the hatch for their medication. Some will swallow the pills or the syrupy liquid; others will be injected. All come away with dead eyes; most come away dribbling and have that mad look of hopelessness in their eyes.

The smell is one of depression; it drifts down the gallery with a cloud of despair. You will see many of the loons slowly shuffling up and down the gallery with blank expressions, drug-induced, dreaming of walking in a field or a break away. Few will do it for real; it's a dream!

They're basically lost in time, living on a memory. Then out of the blue, one will start to laugh, then another, and then more, until the cacophony becomes a signal for all to follow suit. They're all laughing hysterically, even crying! Nobody knows why. One will fall and have a fit; more laughter and more insanity. The laughter travels down the gallery; more come to join in, the nurses arrive ... it's a regular occurrence.

Laughter breaks the despair, but when it dies down it's back to the shuffling. Some will watch TV in the day rooms; they sit in easy chairs and just stare at the TV. If there's a power cut and the TV goes off, they still stare at the dead TV screen. Some who play games often erupt into violence. 'Bronson, you cheated.'

'I never, you did.' Slap! More laughter erupts; madmen laugh at violence ... they love it.

Some just sit alone looking into space; they're all hopeless, soulless ... dead men breathing.

All meals are eaten in a dining room, three loons to a table. This can be a crazy time, and some have gone berserk at mealtimes. Nobody knows when a madman will flip; if he doesn't, then how can anybody else?

Just going for a piss in the asylum can be a major event. You have to have eyes in the back of your head; the urinals are opposite the toilet door. Often, you will see two sets of feet in one cubicle and hear noises. You don't have to be Einstein to know what the noises are; a pumping, squelching or rubbery sound; a pant, a sigh, a moan, even a scream. They're not playing Scrabble! Even at the urinal you may get a loon hanging around for a peep; I've lost count how many I've given a slap to! 'Go on ... fuck off, how many times do I have to tell you, one man's meat is another man's poison!' It's bloody hard work to keep your cool!

There's a constant supply of dildos in the asylum; you just would not believe what some loons ram up their arse! Would you really want to have stuff like shampoo bottles, large carbolic soaps or a giant black sausage rammed up your arse.

Some have even been caught in the act. One crazy bastard rammed a lump of wood, wrapped in a plastic bag, up his arse! (No doubt with lots of Vaseline.) The wood got stuck; it's insanity! I bet the doctor had a laugh getting it out.

Now I don't know how true this is, but it was often spoken about. One lunatic used to put a mouse in a bag and pop it up his arse as he liked the feel of it moving inside him. I actually did ask him, but he never denied it or admitted it. He would, no doubt, take the truth to his grave. I told him to try a rat. With luck, it would rip his insides to shreds, so we could all have a real laugh!

There was one famous loony who was a 'yogi'; believe me, he could bend his body like elastic. He was seen once in the bathroom in a crazy position, all bent up, giving himself a blow-job. I think a few of the loons tried it themselves, as many of them had bad backs soon after!

Canteen day was always a crazy day. Unlike prison, asylum inmates come under the control of the NHS (the National Health Service in the UK), so they get more money. In the '70s and '80s, I used to get about £10 a week wages, plus I could spend my own money. Today, my wages in prison are between £2.50 and £4.50 per week, so you can see the big difference between what I was allowed in the asylums 20 or so years ago and what's allowed today. You're better off being mad!

It was awesome for me to spend so much! The canteen was like a proper shop — clothes, sweets, food, games, watches and all sorts. It was like Christmas every week for me! Now bear in mind 90 per cent of the loons had been there for 20 or 30 years, so it was all second nature to them. So you see why few had any teeth and so many were fat. The amount of sweets, ice cream and cakes they got was amazing, bags and bags of it. Now I don't mind a sweet myself, I love a bar of chocolate, but this lot were buying sacks of it; boxes of chocolates, eating it like it was going out of fashion. Like their lives depended on it, stuff it down or die. You'd have to see it to believe it!

Smokes? Benson & Hedges and cigars – they were on 60 a day. That's why at night you could hear so much coughing; it was like a fucking cancer ward.

And to cap it all, there was the once-a-month disco-crazy but true. The female loons would come over and we'd boogie, giving it some stick on the dance floor. You'd be amazed at how many John Travoltas there were! When the slow songs started, the smooches would start. You could see the girls loving it, grinding their pussies right into the loins of the madmen. Most went back to their wards with sticky underwear.

Me, I believe it's just more trouble, more tension, more frustration; if you can't do the biz properly, why bother? All the cameras on you; what if the girl has a wobbler and throws a fit or gets violent? Nah, it wasn't for me. I only went to two discos in five years and that was two too many, but it all happens there. One loony got his foreskin caught up in his zip; blood all over the dance floor (now I'll bet that bloody hurt). Often, the girls got caught wanking the loons off; male loons came back to the wards with the girls' knickers. The girls would go back to their wards with the guys' pants ... love bites, lipstick, it all goes on. There has been the odd pregnancy, and it's no good them denying it as it's a fact, and it's rumoured there is a lot of AIDS in Broadmoor. Well, that's probably fact, what with all the arses getting pumped!

There are some strange people in those places and I believe there are no stranger than the doctors, psychiatrists, psychologists and the nurses. Why? Imagine it's your job, forever discussing lunatics, reading their files and living amongst them. Surely it rubs off?

I've never forgotten one bloke who was sacked and prosecuted for being a paedophile. It was in all the papers in the early '80s. Fucking slag, locking me up and going home to watch kids performing! Nurses have been involved in many incidents over the years. Sex abuse and brutality! So I believe the madness does rub off; after years of working with loons, it must do!

Think about it. Sitting in an interview room discussing with a patient why he cut a woman's tits off and ate her uterus. Why the paedophile strangled the boy. Why the rapist shot 17 women. It rubs off! If you sat down with me and constantly heard about my armed robberies you may well want to hit a bank yourself. You learn and you become what you learn. The staff become a part of the insanity! The majority of madmen have committed sex crimes or are sex killers.

Why is it the Yorkshire Ripper is so loved by the asylum? Because all the doctors want a part of him. He is the cream — they love a notorious sex killer. 'Let's get into his brain.' 'Let's be the doctor to cure him!' It's a fact; the more they've raped and killed, the better treatment they get. Personally, I believe the only good Broadmoor ever did for the Ripper is when he got an eye stubbed out. You can't cure a monster. Why try?

Some of the staff were perverts. I've seen the way they watched us in the showers, all eyes on our meat and two veg! The casual touching of a naked madman; I've seen it! The lustful eyes ... not all, but many are that way inclined.

So what sort of man chooses to become a psychiatric nurse? Let's not beat about the bush, it's not an easy job; would you want to do a job in which at any moment you could be attacked or even killed? It's a job that's not normal, locking up madmen, so all credit to them, and many do a good job, but the others are basically strange! They look strange, they've got that mad look: the madness has rubbed off on them. Watch how they walk; big boots, chewing gum, shouting, swearing and basically acting like 'louts'. And a lot of brutality did and still does go on, like Rampton in the early '80s, in which lots were sacked and some were convicted and sent to prison.

Look at Ashworth paedophile ring, which was a big investigation recently. Too much goes on in them, some very suspicious deaths as well. So what's being done? Does it still go on? Let me tell you — it always will, simply 'cos the insane are vulnerable people; many have no families. Whether they live or die is irrelevant to anybody.

Are there any benefits in group therapy? Do me a favour! What a lot of bollocks! Face facts — could you do it? What's the point of a group of loonies talking about madness, their evil crimes, murder, rape, buggery and so on? And you've gotta sit there and listen to it. I'd jump up and smack them in the teeth!

I don't like to know or wish to know how someone buggered a three-year-old kid or how they strangled an 87-year-old woman. What's the point in it? Isn't it personal between you and a doctor? Why talk it over in a group? Asylums don't work like that; how can they, you have to live with each other. It's bad enough thinking of the crimes, but having to listen to them is beyond belief. I'd say it's evil, unnecessary, and it can't be right.

When it's my turn, do I have to tell 'em all where I buried my money? Why I rob a bank? Why I shot a grass? It's fucking obvious why I do what I do, but I don't talk about it to a bunch of loons, or to anybody.

I'm not that mad, am I? Or am I missing the plot? Could it be me who's bonkers? Put me in a group therapy situation and take the consequences, 'cos I'll not be able to control myself if they go on about such evil. I don't want to know why or how they jumped on a kid. Why should anybody have to listen to them? I'll just stab the cunt in the eye with a pen! Now fuck off!

Group therapy! It doesn't work, it can't work, and whoever set it up is a dickhead.

INTERVIEW WITH CHARLES BRONSON

Now then, Charlie, is it true you were in all three max-secure asylums?

Yes. Broadmoor, Rampton and Ashworth.

How long were you in each of them?

Broadmoor for five years, Rampton 11½ years and Ashworth for one year.

Why?

Why what?

Why were you there?

Well ... I suppose 'cos I was mad! That's why people are sent there.

Were you really mad or was it all an act?

Blimey, what a question! I'd say I was more dangerous than mad or more unpredictable than mad, maybe a little strange. Yeah, I was what you would call 'strange'.

Dangerous?

Well ... violent, yes. I'd sort of caused havoc in the prisons, and they wrapped me up and sent me to the asylum for some serious treatment.

Serious treatment?

Well, you know, lots of kickings and drug abuse and solitary and dehumanising and depressing me, that sort of treatment.

Did that really happen?

I never lie, I've no need to make it up!

Is it true you were up on Broadmoor roof?

Yep, three times, my hat-trick of rooftop protests ... I'm king of the roofs!

Three times?

That's what I just said. Oh, I do love a roof.

How many roofs have you been on in the system?

Now then, let me see; Hull '75, Liverpool '85, Leicester '88,

Parkhurst '89, Wandsworth '90. Almost made Winchester and Broadmoor '81, '83 and '84. Yeah, the '80s was a good decade for roofs! I do love a roof.

Why?

Why?

Why specifically a roof?

Let me tell you, there's a lot of maggots in the penal system; 'yes, sir, no, sir' men grassing each other up for promotion, evil, slimy rats, with snake eyes – smelly vermin.

Charlie, you're getting a bit carried away, let's stick to the roofs of the asylum.

Where was I?

Hat-trick at Broadmoor.

Yeah, '81, '83 and '84.

Let's have '81, and why ... how?

Right, '81 it is! It was pissing it down, a right bad day. I was one of a dozen lunatics going over to the canteen ... we was Norfolk Ward, intensive care madmen. Norfolk was the danger ward; we was all pretty much the same, unpredictable! Broadmoor had good wards, but Norfolk was the pits – brutality, drug control, seclusion and utter pain. I'd had enough, I'd seen it all and had it all, it was time to kick some ass, and so I decided to fuck 'em up big time. A nice roof does just that. It caused havoc, it caused disruption and it gets maximum publicity. I wanted the world to know about Broadmoor. It was time people understood about the hell behind this wall.

Were you alone?

Oh yes, I always work alone, I even rob banks alone.

Can we stick to the roof?

I was only gonna tell you about some of my robberies.

Another time, Charlie!

Err ... where was I?

You were about to kick some ass.

Yeah, you've got to hit those jerks where it hurts; in the pocket, damage and destruction, rip the place apart, so the best way is to demolish the place, then let them pick the pieces up later. So I broke free. Some fat guard tried to stop me, so he got it in the crust. BOSH! He went down like a sack of shit; I went up like a monkey, up the pipe on to a window, swinging across and up on top of the world. Top of the world, Ma!

What did you do?

I shouted over, 'Oy, get me some French fries and a nice fillet steak, mushrooms, tomatoes, a pot of coffee and pineapple and cream, and a slice of apple pie.' I started work − crash, bang, rip. It's amazing what damage one man can do in half-an-hour. In six hours there truly is not a lot left to rip off. Loved it! Sweat, blood, rain, pain, aches, bruises, wind and sky, it's awesome but it's beautiful.

Beautiful?

Yes, beautiful, better than sex, better than a lottery win, better than anything ...

Better than freedom?

Hell, it is freedom, up there is heaven! I'm free, as free as you! Free as a butterfly. Plus, I'm the governor. Sure it sounds insane, sure it's crazy, but it's true. I'm free, it's a sense of happiness and nobody or nothing can stop me ...

A bullet?

Yeah, maybe, but these maggots ain't got the spine to pull the trigger, they're only good at attacking me ten at a time and injecting me. Slags!

Did you hurt yourself up there?

Me? Hurt! Nah, pain's the game. What's pain anyway?

It's a form of pleasure, a stimulant to life, like a sting from a bee, it livens you up. It gives you that kick up the ass you need to survive adversity; it's lovely, like a bowl of prunes.

Prunes?

I do love a prune, good for the bowel movement.

Yes, Charlie! Let's continue!

Yes, I'm a born climber, see! I love heights; I once climbed a 24-floor block of flats from balcony to balcony, just to get to a geezer I wanted. Broadmoor roof was my next; the 'Birdman' needed a nest, a perch, a platform. A man can only take so much shit and I had taken enough! Up on that roof I destroyed the myth of Broadmoor. Broadmoor is not invincible, and I'm the proof of it. I beat the crap out of it, not once but three times. I cost them a million bucks, so kiss my ass.

I was the king. I practically brought them to their knees; if every madman there would have done what I done we could have ruled the planet! How do you stop such a flow of madness? I slung the slates off and I ripped out pipes and wires. I demolished the fucking hellhole! At night, in the rafters, I'd lay there looking up at the stars ... it was peaceful. I thought about it all, who I am, what I am, where I'm going, all I've lost and all I've gained. Respect is priceless, I've earned it, I've bled for it and I've died a thousand deaths for it. These roofs, to me, represented power and strength within. My hat-trick crippled them financially, spiritually and mentally. The madman drove them mad with sleepless nights.

Charlie, did you ever think you would die up there?

Die! Me, die? I'm too young to die; I'd only die if they were to shoot me or climb up and throw me off.

Would they have done that?

Nah! I told them, 'Come up and I'll grab any one of you and dive off.

Did they come?

Would you have done? Nah, I was alone with the bats and the lovely countryside of Berkshire; lovely country, can see for miles on the roof.

Was it true you were called a killer by the media whilst you were up there?

Yeah! They love to sensationalise. They sell papers with lies, they get rich off my back, like blood-sucking leeches, like maggots in a corpse, chewing, sucking, stealing life.

Did you kill?

Let's say I've never stood trial for murder.

Any regrets, Charlie?

Well, I've just one — it's the Strangeways riot. I missed it! The biggest riot of the system, and I missed it! I was in the block in Parkhurst and when it blew up I was gutted. I felt bad; I should have been there with the boys, kicking ass. It's my biggest sadness. I'd have got a big meat cleaver out of the kitchen and gone on a mission. In fact, I'd have gone home and took 1,000 cons with me. I'm gutted ... I'll never get over it.

Blimey, you are sad!

Sad is not the word ... I'm devastated.

Well, thanks for your honesty. Is there anything else you would like to say?

Yeah! I want to say to all the lunatics in the asylum — keep the faith, don't give up 'cos you're better than them who cage you! And if you feel strong you'll be strong ... stay alive, boys; kick some ass!

Also, a big thanks to my mum, 'cos without her love and support I'd not be alive today.

Anybody else, Charlie?

Well, yes, just one last word. A special thanks to all the Bronsonmania fans, all the great people who stand by me and support me; my club is now awesome and it's spreading, it's like an incurable disease. But it don't kill, it cures. Cheers! And good luck to you all.

8

BROADMOOR —
DEAD MEN DREAMING

Broadmoor Hospital was originally named Broadmoor Criminal Lunatic Asylum. The first patients to arrive there were 95 women in 1863; male patients arrived the following year. The asylum had been built following the Criminal Lunatics Act of 1860; it's uncertain why Crowthorne was chosen as the site. The Mental Health Act of 1959, which came into operation in 1960, changed the name to Broadmoor Hospital making it into a Special Hospital for psychiatric patients of dangerous, violent or criminal propensities. Its role was to treat these patients.

The patients include persons sent by the courts either because they are too ill to defend themselves in court or are deemed by the magical Mental Health Act not to be held responsible for their actions. Others are sent there because it is thought that, for their own sake and that of others, they should be treated in a secure hospital where they are unable to leave the treatment situation. These people need not necessarily have broken the law or have appeared in court; the decision in these cases is made by the doctors.

Following the escape of a homicidal patient, Straffen, who allegedly killed a little girl in Arborfield, there were calls in the village for some sort of alarm system to give some warning of an escape. As a result of this, a siren was set up including six satellite sirens, which are tested each Monday morning.

Should there be an escape, then the people in the village suffer from this siren blaring away for approximately 20 minutes. Then the 'all-clear' siren sounds for at least another 20 minutes when the patient is eventually recaptured, regardless of the time of day or night! If there is an escape from Broadmoor, Crowthorne comes to a standstill for the duration because roadblocks encircle the village and cars are checked for the missing patient.

Since 1992, there have only been a handful of security breaches at Broadmoor, including an escape in 1993 and a rooftop protest in '96.

When I arrived at Broadmoor in '78, my old mate, Ron Kray, was there; he warned me to be careful. Ron had it all sewn up ... good visits, nice food, nice cell, TV, the lot. But even Ron had to be on his toes.

Rooms? They're really cells with high ceilings, cold stone floors and cold walls with dull colours. The cell ... sorry, the *room* door is solid oak with just a spy hole in it

The daily routine in Norfolk Ward, the 'intensive care' section at Broadmoor, starts at 7.30am: wake, wash, shave, empty pot, shit and piss.

The recess, where all this piss-pot emptying and washing takes place, stinks like a farmyard, but most are so drugged they don't smell it. Some fall over with their pots of shit; you may be lucky to get a five-minute shower! Some loons walk about naked with erections while in a daze; all laugh and point, 'Look at that!' 'Size of that!' 'Let's pull it!' 'Let's suck it!'

'Come on, boys, behave!'

This mixture of stink, laughs, cries and screams makes the morning a hell. Things happen ... madness, insanity beyond reality, then breakfast and more madness.

Pills – first medication time – pills, syrup and injections. Alcoholics, quickly up for a fix, all into the day room – soft chairs, carpet, curtains, windows, grey walls and a bookshelf with old books, which are all out of date.

Games – Monopoly, chess but most just sleep, dream, talk to themselves. TV on or off, they stare at it with dead eyes. Nurses watch, a fight breaks out ... restraint ... injection ... gone! Won't see them for days or weeks.

Lunch – 12.00pm, five tables, three to a table, serving hatch, steel shutter, not allowed behind it. Nurses serve up more medicine, more sleep, more TV, more thoughts, maybe a fit in between, hysterics or a fight, always something. One loon may rush a nurse, attack and hurt, because he'd been done short on the chips. Lunatics never forget. Barry Quigley would go strange, stand up and run at a nurse, punch and run off laughing.

Michael Smithers bit a nurse's ear off! Why did Mick do it? I'll tell you why – they drove him mad. Mick's solid stuff, a real blinder. Me, I became a zombie, the forced drugs turned me mad, soon I was insane, shaking and, like the rest of the loons, waiting to take my pot of juice.

Sleeping whilst shitting; I once squatted on my pot and fell asleep on it! I woke up with the pot stuck on my arse! I've had so much serious mental pain I've banged my head on the door to give myself a physical pain to take away the mental torture. I've jumped on nurses so they would jump on me. Beat me; give it to me! Why? Why not? Pain is a pleasure to escape the madness.

A beating can and does help, 'cos mental agony is the killer – it destroys. You have to escape it, so what's it like to queue up for the drugs? Shuffles, stares, shakers, dribbles, stony silence, it's a fucking hell on earth. Swallow! They then say, 'Open your mouth, stick out your tongue,' to see if you've swallowed. Shuffle back to your chair, vision blurry, dry mouth, out of breath, sit down, watch the rest! Fucking die, you poor fuckers, kill us!

Bed time – 7.30pm! Time for bed, walk to your room, strip off outside the door, put your clothes in a box, get checked. Lift up bare feet, lift up bollocks, pull your cheeks open, pull tongue up! If you don't do it, you'll be jumped on and they'll do it for you. They pass you pyjamas, you end up tired, depressed. I used to bury my head under the blanket hoping I'd never wake up. There was fuck all to wake up for, only more hell, more drugs and more inhumanity!

I remember one night, I was asleep on the floor and my mouth was up against the crack of the door. I felt a bang and a shout. 'What you doing down there? You OK?'

In a daze I said, 'Yeah.' I was sucking the draft, getting the air on my face; I was going through a claustrophobic state in my sleep. My window had a locked shutter on it so the draft under the door was my way of survival. How low can a man get? How low can they push a man? I was a rat in a sealed cage with no hope!

It was the 1980s, not the 1890s ... how could it be? I'll tell you how; it's an asylum and in these places it can happen. We are the insane; who listens to us? Why should you listen? If you did then you'd be classed as mad!

It was not 'til I crashed into Broadmoor that I realised just how many paedophile scum existed! God ... you just don't know how many, all crammed into the asylums like pilchards. Prison's bad, but the asylums are 100 times worse! And it's in your face.

I walked into a cell in Broadmoor only to witness one of the sickest sights I've ever seen. It was in Gloucester Ward back in 1979 ... I went into a lunatic's cell to collect some tapes I had loaned him. I should have tapped on the door ... I was shocked to see three loons prancing about naked. One was bent over a chair chewing on another's dick; the other was up the second one's arse; they were in their element. 'You dirty fuckers, where's my fucking Abba tapes? You sick, twisted, fucking ...' It put me on my toes. It turned out two of them were nonces! And the slag who had my tapes, he had raped and killed a 79-year-old woman.

I had to watch myself in that place, 'cos I was in the minority. I'd say 75 per cent of the inmates were 'nonces', if not 85 per cent, so it's a battlefield ... if you want it to be! Fortunately for me, most of my five years there were spent in solitary, otherwise I would have lost it and become a killer. I'd have had no choice. Would you accept living next door to the Ripper or the Stockton Strangler? I had some close scrapes in that place; well, it is a madhouse!

Ian Ball was a nice chap; I liked Ian. Who's Ian Ball? Remember in the '70s some loony grabbed Princess Anne, almost kidnapped her? Well, that was our Ian.

Ian was very unlucky; that day, he shot a cop's finger off in the struggle. It's common knowledge he's a dead loon walking, and three decades later he still walks the asylum grounds.

I met Barry Williams there. He shot dead five innocent people. I asked him why. He shrugged. 'Don't know!' Strange answer. He was a weird case ... devil eyes, mad eyes, black pits of insanity. I could smell evil on him. Five innocent people – bang, bang, bang, bang, bang – and he didn't know why. Pity he never shot that Norman Parker, 'cos then there would be no *Parkhurst Tales*.

In the 1950s I met Donald Hume there; what a nice chap he

was. I admired him, a lovely old boy. He chopped up a geezer and slung him out of a plane over the Channel, and then he robbed some banks in Switzerland. He spent 15 years over there in jail. Then they brought him home and put him in the asylum. He's now done more than 40 years! Time flies by for us all!

I'm coming up to 30 years ... 30 fucking years! I told you it's mad. Like the time Bob Maudsley and John Cheesman kidnapped Alan Francis in the Boot Room on Somerset Ward in Broadmoor. Sadly, Alan died a most horrific death.

At their trial at Winchester Crown Court, both Maudsley and Cheesman said, 'Send us back and we will kill again!' They had killed to escape hell! (A great shame it wasn't one of the doctors they had killed. I'd have respected them for that.) They both got life. Then Bob, as I've previously mentioned, killed twice again in jail. That's madness for you. They kill in Broadmoor and all of a sudden they are both sane and sent to a jail. Is there any sense in that?

Bob kills two more and suddenly he's sane! The whole system is nuts! You can't be insane one day and then sane the next! You're either one or the other. Or are you only insane when the system wants you to be? Or shall I rephrase it ... you're only insane when they drive you insane! Insanity drives me mad. Now do you get my drift?

Asylums like Broadmoor are Victorian. They are designed to break men, but they still live in the shadows of fear. The Broadmoor walls touch the sky. Few ever escape. Most don't wish to, as institutionalisation creeps in. Sadly, most in Broadmoor are dead men dreaming. They masturbate their years away, forever dreaming, until one day they can't get it up and then they die. Some fight it, but all lose!

The drugs will beat you. They inject you with hell. Psychotropic straight to the nervous system, you can't even scream or move. You're a bag of shit and it's all over: you're history. So you learn to ride it, until the opportunity arrives to kick some ass! Then you give them hell, but then you lose again, but you ride it, and that's how it goes. Insanity!

I've mentioned events that happened in Broadmoor in previous books, but I'd need 100 books to cover the Broadmoor years! So I'll give you a taste of some of the events that I left out. I can't go into them all, as there are people I have to protect, good people. Some things have to go with a man to his grave! I'm not Norman Parker or John McVicar! Yeah, McVicar.

And since McVicar's been out, he's now like a fucking welfare officer, putting his nose in where it's not wanted. I personally don't like him, as he is another one who acts the large ... gives it the big 'un. He actually believes he's a top journalist using his big words, but it's fuck all. He's just who he is ... an ex-con. OK, I might be laying it on a bit thick here, but when I hear certain things, I say it how it is. Hey, good luck to him, I'm pleased he's out there, 'free'. I don't wish jail on nobody. I'd even let out Rose West ... someone's bound to shoot the fat slag!

Don't it all make me laugh! Parker with his tales – where's the facts? You want facts ... I'll give you facts.

Some lunatic used to pay lunatics a tenner a time if he could watch them have a shit. Ten fucking quid! He would go with them into the cubicle and just watch! The nurses all knew ... male pervo nurses.

I had to put a stop to it, as it made me feel just a little bit sick. I pulled him into the recess one day and give it him big time, mostly body shots. No sooner had he fallen, I picked him back up and gave him more. I used his body as a human punchbag. I just ripped into him; I felt a desire to destroy this bag of filth. What sort of man pays a tenner to watch another man shit? It's beyond me!

Outside, I'd just have put him in a hole! I couldn't swallow that! Could you? Imagine outside, being approached by that sort of thing! Try to imagine it! This is insanity at its very best, and if you allow it to, it will eat you up, rub off on you and destroy you. You become sick, one of them! I advise you to fight it 'til you drop dead. Don't become a part of it or you're lost. Dehumanised. This is asylum life ... a different kind of survival.

One loony sat in a secluded room. She was mad, but she could not accept it; so she was neither sane nor insane. She could not be either until she knew herself, so in limbo she had to die. She kept stuffing toilet roll into her mouth. They found her choked to death.

Someone got a lovely pair of trainers from his mum for Christmas, the best pair he had ever had, but it was the nylon laces that he couldn't take his eyes off. They found him hanging in his cell.

Another one was a silent type, very nervous of people; shy, introverted, nobody would believe he could scream so loud ... well, he did drink a bottle of bleach.

One lunatic never got any letters. He would talk to himself, get old envelopes and pretend they were sent to him. 'Look, look, I got ten letters today, twelve yesterday and eight on Monday. I've had 50 letters this week.'

One wally, dressed in black, would march up and down the corridor, with his little Hitler moustache, mumbling about Jews and gypsies. Funny to see, but deadly dangerous and, at times, he would break into hysteria and scream abuse. He would have to be restrained and injected.

Oh! Dennis Nash was at Broadmoor for 30 years. He used to have an aviary in Gloucester Ward. Loved his birds, did Dennis. He also used to have sex in there with his boyfriends. He even had a mattress in there for it. Fucking mad or what?

One old loony used to walk up to people sitting in the day room, fart in their face and back off. I know it's not nice to hit old boys, but he should not have done that to me. I picked up an ashtray and slung it at him. I never meant to smash his skull open. I felt a bit bad about that, but he never farted again. I cured him. I cured him in days ... Broadmoor hadn't been able to, not in 40 years of trying!

I remember the day a big black guy stabbed a white guy in the eye. It was over, would you believe, a spoon of sugar. The poor lad lost his eye, simple as that. I saw it, it's not nice ... the scream never goes away, I still hear it, and I still smell the fear of that lad. He knew he'd lost that eye. I can still see the big black guy's smiling face. A sick smirk, he enjoyed it; he was a psycho. The psycho had hit. Such is life, a day in the asylum. I saw things that never leave me; each incident is a scar!

A lunatic has a fit, he loses it, he smacks his head ten times against a wall, blood, lots of blood, tears and snot; he falls to the floor crying, a heap of disaster born to suffer! I saw a lunatic headbutt a door and knock himself out. Another trapped his finger in a door, more blood and more screams. Fights, biting, scratching, stabbing, a kidney ripped out, a testicle, more screams, shit ... lots of shit! They love it, write on the walls, draw faces ... the stench never leaves you!

Suicides — you read about them ... but you don't know the truth. If you were to see it, you would go insane! Cut throats, cut wrists, hangings, suffocating, eyes bulging and tongues protruding, more shit. Suicides always shit themselves ... did you know that? Life's final shit, the final act of madness; smell that, you rats! Clean me up, you pigs, zip me up in the bag, you scum, and get me out of here ... Get me the fuck out of here!

The asylum years taught me a lot about myself. Bear in mind I'm the only lunatic in the United Kingdom who has spent time in all three max-secure asylums. Don't ask me which is the best, as how do you compare insanity with insanity?

Mark Rowntree had to be one of the most puzzling madmen

I ever met. He looked like any normal 20-year-old lad to me, good-looking, a sense of humour, smart and pleasant. Then I'm told he stabbed to death a whole family of five including two kids. What can you say? I asked him why. He said, 'I felt a bit depressed.' That was it! I can accept a guy snuffing out a load of Old Bill, judges, drug-pushers, 'nonces' or even traffic wardens, but what can you say? Fuck all!

But, believe me, not all were insane. Guys like Ron Greedy, Chris Reed, Lenny Doyle, Steve Sloane, Mickey May, big Phil Baxter, big Steve Roughton, little George Heath and Micky Smitken. Micky bit off a screw's ear, but the screw was a pig anyway, so who cares? Ear today, gone tomorrow, such is life.

A lot of the asylum staff were mad ... you can't work in madness and not be affected by it. Some had mental breakdowns, some turned to booze and several got caught shagging arses! Insanity drove them mad ... or did I drive the whole of Broadmoor mad?

As you now know, I hit their evil roof three times, great moments of victory. But you can't win; you rot away in a hole. My asylum years taught me how corrupt it all is. It's a wonder Norman Parker wasn't a part of it, he would have loved it there.

I was honoured to have met Diana Dors, Terry Downes and Acker Bilk when they visited Broadmoor. Jimmy Saville as well, but Diana to me was amazing; I've never met anybody quite like her. That was all down to Ronnie Kray. Ron's pal there was Charlie Smith, who'd got life for killing a tramp, and then he killed a cellmate in the Scrubs. He's been in Broadmoor since 1980. I thought he was OK. Obviously, he was Ron's bit of meat; Ron spoiled him with gifts. Charlie was his 'plaything', but when Charlie absconded I knew what he did outside, and he knew I knew.

Kate Kray's sister was close to Charlie then, but she isn't now and neither is Kate. Charlie, I'll say now, that you're no better than a maggot; I'll not bother saying what! But live with it, cunt. Insanity did drive Smith mad.

I see that Denis Nilsen is always in the press; he might as well have his own press officer, suing the headquarters because he can't have his hardcore gay mags. Well, I want a box of apple pies! If that cunt can have his filth, why can't I have some pies? It makes me puke up to hear all this nonsense. He shagged and killed 15 fellas!

I met Ned the Neck in Broadmoor in 1979. He had been sent to Broadmoor in the 1940s during the war. He was caught on a bombsite up a stiff's arse! He had been getting his rocks off with all the corpses! What a fucking sicko! If being bombed up isn't bad enough then having Ned the Neck stab your ring piece is the pits. When anybody died in Broadmoor, we all used to shout, 'Ned, Ned, it's your birthday.'

There really are some sick bastards about; how many more are out there? They can't all be locked up, can they? How many more Fred Wests are out there? Hundreds, if not thousands! I just can't understand how anybody can shag a stiff; it's beyond my comprehension. But then again, I am mad! So I'm told.

Glen Wright was, and probably still is, mad. He's from Northampton, the birthplace of my old dad. Glen came in serving a three stretch and got lifed off for two alleged murders inside and he's still fighting it. Well, this guy has got to be the number one shitter in the system. He's forever protesting – dirty protests – but we all like Glen 'cos he does at least fight for his rights in his own way.

Glen, like me, hates monsters, so I respect him for that. He got that nail-bomber Copeland who blew up part of Soho in London, near a gay bar ... Glen bashed him over the head with a teapot. Glen also gave it to Michael Stone! Stone, you might recall, was convicted of the murder of Lin Russell and her daughter, Megan, in 1998, and he lost his appeal in 2001. As well as being a murderer, Stone also likes cock. I've got it on good authority from contacts at Wakefield (Monster Mansion) that Stone was found hob-nobbing (literally) with another inmate when both were caught naked behind a barricaded cell door. A screw broke down the barricade and Stone turned lemon like the perverted killer that he is and threatened him. And, fuck me, that's the prison they want to send me to from Durham, where I am at the moment. Can you imagine me with Stone? I'd be barricading him and me in a cell for a few rounds and it wouldn't be for hob-nobbing ... it would be for knob-chopping!

Never mind how tough you are, hardness doesn't come into it when they rush you and stick you with a hypodermic needle! You're out of the game. The tranquillisers can knock out rhinos. It's fear, don't kid yourself. I fucking despise drugs, but these slags pumped me up with it, as they do with most. Restraint pants down and slap, in it goes! I've had needles snap off in my butt 'cos my buttock muscle was so tense and rock hard with fear! Will they inject me with petrol or an air bubble? Are they going to kill me? I won't be the first or the last. When will this nightmare end?

You wake up in a pool of piss, sweat and even blood. Drowsy, aching, restless, zombified, senseless, dry eyes, blurred vision, shaking. You're a fucking wreck, a dead man dreaming, dehumanised. The door unlocks, ten white coats ... 'Take this tot, take it or another injection!' You take it and ... back to Disneyland, back to death, weeks, months and even years of it. End result — a wreck, a lazy, fat, tired-out bag of shit. That's insanity, that's torture, that's the truth.

'No more, no fucking more,' on your knees screaming, 'No more ... come in and bash me! Beat me senseless, but no more of this shit. Stop killing me slowly, shoot me, hang me, stop destroying me, no more!' It's a nightmare, a hell and I've lived it and breathed it!

Broadmoor creeps into your blood; the walls touch the sky and the grounds suck you in; it's even got its own burial ground. We called it the 'Madman's Hole'; it smelled of fear: a stillness and even the birds seemed to have stone faces like their eyes were made of marble. So many monsters, men of hell, I don't know how a sane man can keep sane in there. No living thing is safe ...

Did you know that the Ripper is so evil that even the plants in his room at Broadmoor refuse to live! Yeah, that's true! Now we all know Prince Charles likes to talk to the plants, well, let's just say they are able to sense the difference between good and evil; they're sure as hell trying to say something about the Ripper's soul – it's lost!

Not too many have had it away from Broadmoor! Well, not since it became max secure. Bear in mind it's over 100 years old; up 'til the 1960s, it was just a wall. Any lunatic could hop away. In the early 1900s the loons were allowed out in working parties, and plenty ran off. All that stopped in the 1950s when monster John Straffen had it away.

Straffen was born in 1930. In his younger days he would play truant and by the age of ten he was attending a school for the mentally retarded. By the time he was 17 he had assaulted a child and was committed. Released in February 1951, he went on to strangle two girls to annoy the police! Pronounced unfit to plead he was sent to Broadmoor.

In April 1952, Straffen escaped from Broadmoor only to be captured a few hours later. During Straffen's few hours of freedom, a little girl, Linda Bowyer, went missing. She was found the following day in a nearby field, strangled to death. When Straffen was interviewed by the police, he said, 'I did not kill the little girl on the bicycle.' This was before they had asked him about the murder.

Straffen appeared in court in July 1952, and entered a 'not

guilty' plea. His ability to plead was accepted on the basis that three doctors had asserted that he was now fit to plead, partly because he understood four of the Ten Commandments.

The trial was abandoned after a juror was heard to say that he thought Straffen was innocent and that the crime had been committed by one of the witnesses. Amid great publicity, the judge, Mr Justice Cassels, stopped the trial, empanelled a fresh jury and the proceedings began again and this time Straffen was found guilty and sentenced to death. A reprieve was, however, forthcoming and he was indoctrinated into the prison system and not to the asylums, as some would have expected, spending all 50 years in maximum-security prisons throughout Britain.

Straffen insisted he hadn't killed Linda Bowyer. Amazingly, it has come to light that three independent witnesses all heard what might have been the child's final scream at 7.00pm – 20 minutes after Straffen had been recaptured! In my heart, I feel that Straffen did kill the little girl. Even if he hadn't done it, he was still a monster and deserved to die for the other child murders.

During the 1960s, there were some dramatic escapes from prisons and asylums. Our very own Frank 'Mad Axe-Man' Mitchell, his legacy lives on; a great guy. A couple of other celebrated escapees are Ronnie Biggs from Wandsworth Jail and Blake, the spy, from Wormwood Scrubs.

Lord Mountbatten eventually turned the whole fucking prison system upside down in his report, creating maximum-security jails such as Albany on the Isle of Wight. The very first all-electric prison followed and then Long Lartin. So jail escapes became less frequent, but nothing is impossible.

Alan Reeves proved that in 1981, and so did Len James Lang. Alan's escape was a classic, a beauty. I'll always remember it. Why? 'Cos I was there. Alan had been in Broadmoor since he was 15 years old; he had killed a fellow lunatic while he was there. It was doubtful he would ever have been released, so he went anyway. After 15 years of being locked up in hell, he flew out like the eagle he is. Alan flew out on a summer's day using a TV antenna as a hook! Up and over! Whooooosh! The waiting car sped off, Southampton Docks, a nice ferry ride. Some madman, eh? Fucking genius!

J Lang, now he was a different sort, the killer of a 16-year-old girl. He fortunately only made it out for a few hours, 'cos when he jumped down off the wall, he broke his ankle. Shame it wasn't his neck.

But escapes from Broadmoor are so rare. Now it seems the wall reaches the sky, with its cameras and fences – it's all super max. The lunatics are pretty much secured. But one day some genius will fly. It's like a rat in a cage ... it keeps on gnawing, it's wanting out. Nobody wants to live in a cage ... not unless they're mad!

I had a pop at escaping in '82 but it fell in. Caved in on top of me; quite upsetting to think about it. I hate defeat, so I prefer not to go into that; it hurts. I recall one loon who was trying to escape with a spark of an idea; he climbed up on the wall, flapped his arms and dived off to fly. Poor sod was in the infirmary for six months, legs and arms in plaster, but he tried. I felt a bit sorry for him. Well, I did tell him he could fly!

Another nutcase thought about cutting himself so he could get to an outside hospital; the plan was to run off while he was there. He cut his throat and almost bled to death.

So many loons come up with mad plans, but that's all they are, mad plans that can't possibly work. There was one nutcase who starved himself for weeks. His plan was simple. Starve! Get skinny, smear his naked body in butter and slip through the bars. 'Look,' I told him, 'your fucking skull won't alter, no matter how much you starve!' But he wouldn't have it. He went down to six stone, tried it and gave up. But you gotta hand it to them.

Another climbed into a cardboard box when a washing machine came in and got two lunatics to carry it out with the rubbish. All you could see was them struggling with it! So that soon ended, and all three were put into seclusion.

One got a job down the gardens, but he only lasted a day. He dug a 12ft hole to plant spuds. He told me later he was going to go down 20ft, then start to tunnel under the wall. 'Why 20ft?' I asked. He had no answer. The guy was crazy. You've gotta laugh.

While prison still has its spectacular and dramatic escapes — the helicopter at Gartree, or the ones at Whitemoor and Parkhurst — sadly, they're now so rare and are mainly things of the past. But let's be honest, nothing can beat a good asylum escape.

And while I'm at it, Frank Mitchell got his name 'Mad Axe-Man' for the Broadmoor escape. He broke into an old couple's house with an axe, but he didn't harm them. Quite the opposite, they loved him. Frank was a big, strong man, a gentle giant. He only ever got violent with the guards 'cos he could have a right fight.

Anyway, his feet were all busted and bleeding after running for 20 miles with Broadmoor boots on; evil fucking boots they were. I know 'cos I also wore them. The old lady bathed and washed his feet. He had a nice meal with them and they all got on well with each other. It was the Old Bill, as usual, who sensationalised it all. Frank had his problems like us all, but he had morals. He would never have hurt old people, but a label sticks like shit to a blanket, and it went with him to his grave. A great guy and a true warrior – RIP. Enough of escapes, as it always gets me excited.

Now a bit on dormitories! Yes, yours truly was once in a dorm in Broadmoor. Me in a room with other madmen; not a nice experience. Now let's be sensible about it, lunatics and murderers sleeping in the same room? Don't get me wrong,

I'm not saying I was scared, but let's just say I slept with one eye open.

I just could not believe I was ever in a dorm. I had almost strangled to death a paedophile in Rampton; I was described as the most violent man in penal history; I was not happy; and would you want to sleep in a room with me? Or, better still, with ten fucking madmen?

It still makes me smile, even 20 years on, me in a dorm! I only lasted a week. But it was a week I'll never forget. Insanity at its best! Snoring, farting, wanking, stinking smelly feet, shouting in their sleep and sleepwalking. And, of course, the 'gay flings'! I was like an eagle, watching every noise and every movement, I was alert. No fucker was gonna waste me in the night.

Some of those loons were mad killers. One had killed five people; six would mean a bag of chips to him. I did most of my thinking in that dorm; I had to, my sanity was at risk. What if they all got together to plot on me? What if one fancied me or maybe planned to kill me? Kill Bronson and be the one everyone will know. Killing me would put him in the history books.

To say I never liked the dorm is an understatement. I hated it; it was making me ill, sick in the crust. I began to imagine myself going berserk and wasting them all, but what choice did I have? This was madness with a capital 'M'.

I studied them carefully — eyes, facial expressions, movement. One fucking strange move and I'll kill the whole lot. I'm too young to die, I thought. Hey, they could be plotting on gang-banging me; it would be all over the papers: LOONS GANG-BANG BRONSON. No way … I'll kill them all. On the first night, I smacked one in the chops.

That week will remain with me for ever. I was smack in the centre of a nightmare and it made me psychotic.

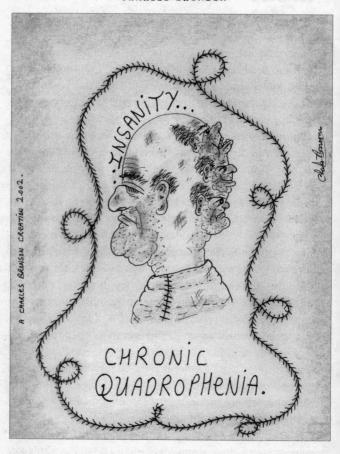

On the second night, I found two of them in the recess having it off! I felt sick, two old faggots in their heaven. I kicked them both up the arse. 'Go on, fuck off, you pervo sickos.' The fucking state of the sad bastards, baggy skin, dead eyes, smirks for smiles, panting and playing with each other's skinny, smelly dicks. Get me out of this nightmare! They all knew who I was, but who were they? Who had they killed or raped? They never looked like blaggers to me.

'Oy, cunt,' I shouted to one, 'what are you in for?'

'Me?'

'Yeah, you!'

'Err, I killed my wife!'

'Oh yeah, what for?'

'I was ill,' he said.

'Ill! What had she done to get wasted?'

'Nothing!'

'How did you kill her?'

'I strangled her with her tights.'

'Yeah, I bet you stuffed her panties in her mouth as well and done her up the back door, you filthy maggot!' Looking at another loon, I said, 'What about you ... you over there with the evil eyes?'

'I'm a rapist,' he said.

Oh yeah! Big tough guy, eh? So who did you rape?'

'I'd rather not say,' he replied.

'Oh, he'd rather not say ... oh, so sorry for being personal, forgive me. I walked over to the bed and bent down and whispered, 'Cunt ... who did you rape!'

'Err, my daughter,' he said.

'How old?'

'Ten years old,' he replied.

'You cunt, you sick cunt.'

I then said in a loud voice, 'All of you, listen to me. Listen, I don't like you, I don't like this place, you're all sick ...' It went quiet, too quiet, unnervingly silent. 'Err, sorry, lads, I got a bit upset there! I'm just having a go at the filth. If you're not filth, my apologies, if you are, you're filth!' That's how that dorm affected me, big-time crazy!

A week of it drove me nuts. I'd never fit in; I was not one of them. I had nothing in common; I'm a robber, a villain, not a fucking nutcase. Was I as mad as them, but to a higher degree, maybe more dangerous – psychotic? Was the problem me or were they actually thinking like me? Could they have wiped us all out? I believe they could and would if they had a gun or knife or a tin of petrol. The difficulty is, with me I can do it with my hands. To snap six of their necks before the others woke up would be a massacre without the weapons. How close it was, a nightmare come to reality! Screams beyond humanity!

The rest of my years in the asylums were spent in a solitary room. But even then in the early hours in my own mind I used to picture them, the whole asylum, asleep next door, in all the rooms and all the dorms. What were they dreaming and thinking and what horrors hid behind their faces. What depravity played in their brain? It's no secret; there are a lot of sick bastards in them places!

I met them all in the asylums. Anyone who was anybody I've met! Hell, you just don't realise who they are half the time, 'cos half of their cases never reached court; there was no trial, no media, it was all swept under the mat owing to insanity. Like the loon who cut up a prostitute and sent her tits to a national paper. Like the many mass killers who wiped out their own families. I bet loads will have butchered their kids and wives and in-laws. You'd be amazed at how many murders they've committed – four, five or even six killings and, to look at them, butter wouldn't melt in their mouths – insanity at its best ... or worst.

The religious freaks are the worst killers, as they do it for God, and they're saved, blessed. They kill evil, you see! Then the sex killers, they're the lustful killers; they dribble as they mutilate the bodies of their victims; some will chew the body and leave their DNA behind.

Then there's the jealous killer; now they're a sad lot, all they do is cry and feel sorry for themselves. Then there are the psychopathic killers; they're cold as ice, pure wicked and you can see the hate in their eyes. It's hate that motivates them; they often laugh as they destroy. Some even ejaculate as they plunge in the knife. Some will tell you it's better than sex.

Most killers become pitiful. There is no higher crime than taking a life, but believe me, most live in a very sad world – I would say 90 per cent of them would turn the clock back, 'cos as the years fly by and they become old and more alone and isolated, they all regret it. Even the insane have regrets — believe it.

Asylums are crazy places, with crazy rules. If you're not mad when you arrive, you are when (or if) you leave. I was lucky, I got slung out; they couldn't afford to keep me any longer. I was Britain's most expensive lunatic to keep caged. I cost Broadmoor £1^1/$_2$m in damage – three roofs prove it.

So there I was at the table, just about to pick up the teapot and pour a cuppa! And I caught the evil look on one of the lunatics' faces on my table. This big black guy had stabbed a fellow lunatic in the eye before. I shouted, 'Oy, what's up with you?' He was sweating, shaking, staring at me. If looks could kill I'd be ten times dead. His breathing was heavy, a sure sign of an attack; do I hit him now? Do I walk off or do I wait for the attack?

I reached over and grabbed his neck tightly, ready to punch in his insane face if need be! Squeeze – 'Slow down, chap, pack it in ... I don't need it,' I said, through gritted teeth. 'But you're gonna fucking get it if you don't stop.' He eased up. The madness disappeared. My eye was safe, 'til the next time. That's how it comes on. He'd have shot me if he had had a gun. A knife, and I'd have had a hole in me. Any other place or time I'd have just hit the slag. But you have to make allowances for the insane. Why keep bruising your knuckles on their skulls?

Asylum life is lethal! You can die as easy as a cup of tea; at any time you can be killed, and for nothing.

I went through a period during which I couldn't keep off the establishment's roofs, it was a serious urge I had. To look at a drainpipe and start shaking with excitement ... nobody knows the feeling of hitting a prison roof, not unless you've done it. Let me tell you, it's like a lottery win — it's power. You're the governor; it's a kick in the teeth to the system.

When you're on a roof, you're free, under the stars, fresh air, alone. I used to get a hard-on when hitting a roof. They'd shout up, 'You wait 'til we get you down; we'll smash your legs, beat your arms and twist and snap your toes.' What nasty fuckers they are; they're insane, beyond help.

But Broadmoor's roof was so special to me. It was heavenly. It was my way of fucking them up, and causing maximum damage and confusion; make them pay for it, cause them problems. Make them think, Best not fuck with Bronson.

I was Britain's most expensive lunatic to keep locked up. That roofing contractor loved me, but the others hated me, despised me. I was their embarrassment. They would have killed me if they could have got away with it. You could see it in their eyes. They would shout up, 'We've got a wild big syringe waiting for you, full of psychopathic drugs. You'll fucking get it when you come down.'

I'd shout back, 'You gutless fuckers, don't threaten me with your drugs. I'll fucking rip your faces off, evil screws. Nurses — don't make me laugh. You're rats in white coats. You're evil beyond belief, beyond humanity. All you know is causing pain and misery.'

The female loons would all watch me rip the roof off Norfolk and Essex Wards. They would shout to me, 'Yoo-hoo, yoo-hoo.' I'd watch them hang their tits out the bars — beautiful tits. How long does a man have to go without sucking a tit? They would moon me, lovely juicy arses up against the bars. With a breeze I could almost smell their sex, so near, but so far, it fucking hurt. I'm only human — all that pussy looking at me. 'Show us yours, Charlie.'

I flipped it out. 'Yarhooo, look at this. YARHOOO.' They screamed with laughter. I'd flop it about a bit. 'Have that girls.'

'Boootiful ... looovelly,' they all screamed.

But it's depressing. I soon got fed up, so I'd go back to ripping the roof off. I'd have another shit through a hole in the ceiling and it plops into an office.

'Dirty bastard,' someone shouts.

'Fuck you, screw, that's all you're worth, shithead.' It's a hate factory, a war zone and a mental fight.

Every morning, the weeds would be blowing about, the cold sets into the bones, your teeth rattle, your knees hurt and your fingers go numb. How much more pain can you endure? Your eyes are full of grit; your body is full of splinters. You ache, you curl up in the foetal position, you fall asleep and you dream of your loved ones. You shake with cold and pain.

A new day. Sun, warmth, but the hunger has you — pain in your guts — so you eat slime, moss out of the gutter. You eat some pigeon eggs; you drink water out of the tank on the roof. You survive! Again, they abuse you.

Sunday — emotions. You consider death. Then you believe you're dead — you died the day the court sent you to Broadmoor. You're insane. Insanity is death.

Have a wank, swallow the sperm, it's protein, it keeps you alive. It really will keep you going. Bet that's blown you away! I bet the SAS do it and worse besides! You learn to survive when you're alone. A pigeon, eat it raw. I'd eat a lunatic or a screw or a doctor — 'Come up, I'll eat you, raw.' Fuck the SAS, SBS or even the SS ... I'd eat them! Man has got to go on. Eat worms, spiders, cockroaches ... anything, but survive.

The slags below start to fry mushrooms and omelettes so I can smell it. They're cooking so it smells. They know I'm hungry and it's torture. They're using psychological warfare. It drives me mad, but how do you drive a madman mad?

There was this room in Norfolk House Intensive Care at Broadmoor. We called it the 'plastic room'; it had a plastic window, plastic jug, plastic mug and even the bed was plastic. You ate from plastic plates; you used a plastic spoon. You became plasticated, and through your hazy, drugged vision even the nurses' faces looked plastic. But this room was also used to apply mental and psychological pressure to you. It had bloodstains on the rails, walls and ceiling. Speckles of blood were splattered so as to intimidate the lunatic – behave or get it big time. Drugging us senseless was not enough; they wanted to destroy us in every way.

It was evil beyond anything you can imagine, and you stayed in that room 'til they said you could come out. They didn't need to lift a finger in order to apply certain types of punishment. You had to shit in the potty. They wouldn't empty it. You slept in there, ate in there. You got your fresh air for one hour a day, but only if they said so. People just don't realise that a madman has no rights. They say, 'You're too dangerous to come out,' so you stay in and you get no exercise. You get fuck all.

They will antagonise you, kick your door, whisper outside so you can hear it. One used to smoke outside my door and blow it through the crack. They would mess with your food – spit in it, put drugs in it and even steal half of it. They would give you a change of clothes, which would be dirty, or wouldn't fit you. You would say, 'Hey, it don't fit,' but it would have to do until the following week. Often I'd rip them up, then they would say, 'Well, now you can't come out.' It would be seen as if it was me who was mad. But they drove me mad.

They would have a TV set in their tea room and turn it up

loud. I knew all the soaps and the films, but I never got to see any of them. It was a living hell in which they drove us over the edge. The plastic room began to smother me, like I was wrapped in cling film. I went through bouts of claustrophobia in which I'd scream and bang the door for hours, 'til my feet and hands bled and I was exhausted. I'd lie on the floor, breathing the draught under my door, as I felt I had no air. The window was sealed with a plastic sheet and a shutter. I'd lie there in a state of severe depression. I'd hear footsteps. It would stop outside my door, and — bang! — the door would reverberate in my face. I wished the door were open so it could be my head. 'Kick me to death, just put me out of this misery.' I used to hear the screams in the night of the madmen's nightmares — in time, it was me doing the screaming.

More drugs, more loneliness. You become a zombie and part of you dies. Your dreams are no more. A black hole sucks you in deep; you're in the plastic room. This room had an oblong hatch, which locked on the outside. They would open it up to pass things in, such as tots of medicine. It had an inch-thick, see-through plastic covering. Some days, I'd just stand there looking through at the insanity of life in Broadmoor and, believe me, it was mad. What I saw through that hatch was my worst fucking nightmare come true. Soon, the plastic room was to be my home — my saviour.

I never fitted in; I could not accept this insanity. I'd watch the lunatics walk by in their pyjamas and dressing gowns to slop out. To watch them carrying pots of shit, full to the brim, spilling as they walked; shit and piss, smells coming through my door, polluting my space. A screw in a white coat would be pressing the nozzle on a can of air freshener; I'd get a whiff of scented air to kill the stench, but that stench never really goes away. The plastic room was a living sewer; my pot only got emptied when they chose for me to do it.

There were no bell buttons in the cells at that time. To get attention you had to kick the door, and then they would say, 'You're too aggressive,' or 'You're too bad tempered.'

I'd say, 'How the fuck else can I get your attention?'

'Don't get cheeky,' they would say, 'or you get fuck all.'

The cunts were turning me into a beast. A zoo would be better than this. I'd watch the nurses stuffing their faces with fruit and sandwiches (ours), and I'd watch them smoking. 'Die of cancer,' I'd shout through the door. 'Cough your guts up, you German SS scum.'

I'd watch the loonies; some would come up to my hatch and look through. Their eyes were spaced out, mouths open. Some would have a sick look, a look of doom, dribbling. I'd tap the hatch and shout, 'You OK, you OK?' Some would nod and some would just look, 'til the nurses shouted, 'GET THE FUCK AWAY FROM THERE!'

I've seen other loons being wheeled into the men's room for electro-convulsive treatment, and when they were wheeled back there would be blood on the pillow, shit on the sheet; the trolley looked as though a wild animal had been on it. He had just had some shots of electricity into his brain.

After spells in the plastic room, I would live amongst the mad; I became one of them, so much so that I now enjoy being with the insane. They're better than the sane. These guys are full of mystery and you never know when they'll flip, or what they'll do next. That's why I love them.

Madness becomes a comfort. Let me explain. We all get times of stress, anxiety and boredom, so what do you do? Outside, you have options – hit the booze, drugs, go for a run, a gym or a good fuck. We all have to find our release, or we die of a stressed heart. Broadmoor in the 1970s had no gym, so what could we do to release our stress? At times you couldn't even pull your cock, as the drugs took away any feelings. You're impotent so you only have one way out and that's madness. My way was to rip roofs off or attack. I'd get smashed down, beaten and taken back to the plastic room. But I'd be free of stress, until it built up again.

Others had their own ways. They, too, would fall and be trodden over, but madmen have a strong survival instinct. We only fear ourselves and that's our true fear. Just what will we do next? Will we go on a mission we can't control or will we go to bits, never to be put back together again – the Humpty Dumpty syndrome? The fear of jumping off a skyscraper – it's not the diving, it's the thought of the landing, but we're all capable of such madness.

Michael Ryan – why did he shoot up Hungerford? Dennis Nilsen – why did he kill all those innocent young men? Why did the Ripper rip his name into the history books? I'll tell you why – madness beyond their control. Call them monsters, but their mums love them. Just thank your lucky stars it's not you or your son or your father, because it could be.

Ted Bundy – look at him, a nice chap, good-looking, women loved him, but inside his heart was madness. The electric chair burned it out. He fried like a sausage for his madness. Ted could easily be your uncle or your cousin or your twin brother. Ted Bundy lies in every man if you allow the evil to eat into your heart.

Sane today, madness tomorrow, you can't stop it, it's like a growth of cancer and it spreads; it sucks away your senses. My advice is simple – don't fuck with the insane, as, like an elephant, they never forget, never! That little thing you did 20 years ago may end up your worst ever nightmare, as you may forget it, but a madman never does. You may owe him 50p, but he owes you a knife in the back. Don't fuck with madness.

There are killers out there amongst you, watching, waiting; it's time you woke up to smell the coffee. You could be next. A noise, a shadow and it's your turn to die; some are born to kill, others born to be killed. Which are you?

Predators hunt; prey is for picking off. Madness is for ever! We even smell different; our hearts don't beat, they tick. Our eyes are different; we don't just see, we also pick up vibes. We are probably dehumanised and way past our 'sell-by' date, totally unusable, bitter as lemons.

We have the beauty that the sane don't have; it's like a warm glow that protects us. I challenge any sane man to spend a single day in the plastic room, and not come out insane! For me, I could easily go back in, and accept it like a tortoise wears a shell; maybe I never left it or it never left me.

Away from the madness, there's also a lot of sadness. Please believe it when I say great sadness. Asylums are full of sad, lost people, and it fucking hurts to witness it. I'm not a soft touch or a weak man, but I've felt compassion for my fellow madmen and women! Sure, they can seriously piss you off. But when you get to Hawthorn and understand them and see their sadness ... I've walked into a room and seen a guy bashing his own head on the wall. Lumps, bumps, blood. Why? Crying, hurt, pain! I've hugged them, told them not to, talked to them, tried to help them, bathed their heads and faces.

Do you know why they do it? 'Cos they hate themselves. They're ugly and they're unloved – they're just fucked up, lonely people. Bang! Crash! It's their way of expressing their inner pain. I've seen it so often. Some I've helped and others have been beyond help.

One old boy I used to love to chat with in Broadmoor when I got the chance was Alan Depreze, a caged man for more than 40 years. He went to Broadmoor in the 1930s. I fucking loved this white-haired, white-moustached old boy. I'd get a bag of soft sweets and him and me would sit together and eat them and I'd listen to all the old mad stories. Then there was

Unlikely but firm friends.

Top: Lord Longford (now deceased) championed my cause.

Bottom: Jim Dawkins, the 'hard-boiled screw', worked at Belmarsh and became a good friend to me.

Top: My 'doppleganger' Micky Peterson giving a bit of lip. Micky Peterson was my name before I changed it.

Bottom: Micky Peterson with Screaming Lord Sutch shortly before he committed suicide.

My other namesake. A picture of the actor whose name I adopted –
signed by the man himself.

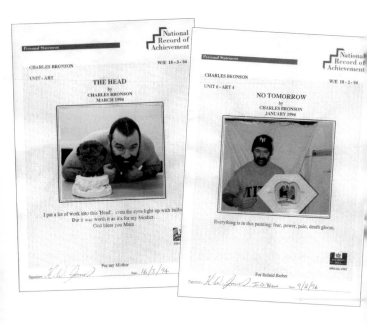

My art has played a huge part in getting me through the insanity of solitary.

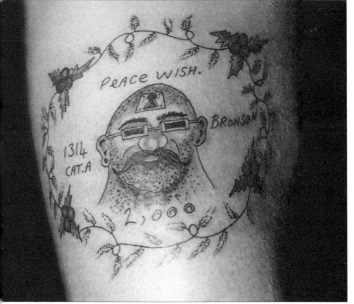

Top: Punk rock band the Swellbellys giving me a noisy salute.

Bottom: Charlie Bronson tattoos for all discerning fans.

Top: Me and the infamous Fred Lowe.

Inset: With another faithful companion – Bertha the medicine ball.

Above: Paul Flint, me and Tony McCulluch.

Right: A tribute from Tony Simpson (*left*) and Dave Courtney (*right*).

Top: My brother Mark, with my dad.

Bottom left: With my late brother John, in HMP Whitemoor 2000.

Bottom right: Harry Marsden, always putting on boxing shows to raise money for worthy causes. A real diamond.

Top: My close friend Dee Morris and my Mum, Eira, holding the belt I was given by Mike Tyson.

Bottom: Dee with my pal, the boxer Matt Legg at a protest about my release.

In Leicester square with their banner with, *top*, Matt Legg and, *bottom*, Ifty.

Top: Dee and my brother, Mark, at a charity event.

Bottom: The crowd assembling outside Downing Street.

Top: My pal Dave Taylor and other supporters join the fight to free me

Bottom: Dee and Red Menzies show off their t-shirts as they wait outside Downing Street.

Walter Prince, 50 years in Broadmoor, and Eric Davies, a 45-year man. All three died while I was there. They were all buried in Block Eight – Broadmoor Cemetery. They were in hell before they died and the only love they got was from their fellow madmen. Hell! I respect the insane. They're the cat's bollocks to me.

Rumours flew around the asylum. 'Don't you dare get a blow-job off anyone you don't know, 'cos you might get it bit off.' I'm told years ago a Broadmoor female did just that. As sexes mix, it's possible it did happen.

Night-time in the asylum is a time to reflect. You need that time to come to terms with each day. The madness you've seen, you need to analyse it all, study it and try to find the answer. But for some there is no answer.

When the door opens in the morning, it's back to madness. A naked body walks past. Shouts of, 'Get some clothes on,' or 'Empty that shit,' or 'Clean your teeth.' There's always a smell of shit in the asylum, body odour and sweat, a smell of despair. Some are so badly drugged up they forget if they've wiped their arse. Some fall asleep on the bog. They've got drugs to make you sleep, wake you up, make you shit and to make you eat – all sorts. Drugs, drugs and more drugs.

Insanity, I believe, truly can get you through it all; if you can laugh, you'll survive it. If you cry, they make you cry more. If you scream, they love it. To see a man cry and scream is their way of saying, 'Shut it, or no sweeties.' Say that to me and I'll smash your fucking skull in the first opportunity I get. It takes ten of them screws to bash one lunatic up; it takes just one of me to do it to them.

That's the reality with me. Don't take liberties. When the Ripper arrived in Broadmoor he was on Ron Kray's ward. Ron went up to him and told him the score. 'Don't fucking look at me and, when I walk in a room, that's when you walk out, got it?' For ten years that's how it was. Ask yourself, what if the Ripper had looked? Monsters have to be put in their place otherwise they take over. You have to lay down the law from the word go.

I met Dickie Langrell in Broadmoor in '79. He was over 50, small, 5ft 4in and 9st, harmless looking, but he was a complete psychotic. He'd hear voices and then attack. One day the voice told him to attack me. He flew at me and jumped on my back trying to bite out my neck. Fuck me, what a dangerous fucker! I smashed him up into a wall. I managed to prise him off, and then the nurses took over, injected him and segregated him. Days later, he carried on as if fuck all had happened.

One geezer got a glass jar and rammed it into a nurse's face. Why? 'Cos he didn't like the colour of the nurse's socks! Another lunatic went into the recess and kept nutting the toilet door ... 'til his head went through it. A loon was having a shit at the time. Imagine that!

Let me leave you with this thought! Some will say, 'Don't listen to Bronson! He's mad! It's all lies.' I say this:

1. Yes I was certified insane, but to leave the asylum one must be certified sane!
2. Have you got a certificate to say you're sane?
3. I have!

I also say, in some countries it's an offence to deny the existence of the Holocaust. It's called 'Holocaust Denial'. I believe I have gone through as much if not more than any Holocaust survivor and for anyone to deny this is, in my opinion, 'Brutality Denial', and they should be brought before the courts and slung in an asylum!

How anyone can go to the extreme of visiting the scene of such atrocities as carried out in Hitler's death camps is beyond me ... just visit your local asylum. Have a look at the padded room or the plastic room! Remember one sure thing — I tore Broadmoor roof off; I cost you plenty. You never beat me! You never could beat me! I was just too sane for you insane fuckers.

9

ARSEWORTH AND RAMPANT

Ashworth High Security Hospital is situated in Maghull, ten miles north of Liverpool city centre. On this site there has been a hospital for over 100 years. A prominent local merchant, Thomas Harrison, originally owned the estate.

In 1878, it was sold to the overseers of the Liverpool Workhouse – Liverpool Select Vestry – who used the large house as a convalescent home for children from Liverpool workhouses. Eventually, in 1911, construction began on a new hospital to be used as an epileptic colony.

In 1914, the 'Lunacy Board of Control' bought the whole estate, including a large unfinished hospital. Before it could be pressed into use as a State Institution, however, the hospital was taken over for the treatment of shell-shocked soldiers from the Great War.

In 1920, the Ministry of Pensions took the hospital over and it was not until 1933 that it became a State Institution. In 1948, the hospital became part of the new National Health Service and, in 1959, the Ministry of Health took over responsibility for running the Special Hospitals.

In the 1970s, further enlargement came when the decision was taken to build a fourth Special Hospital to relieve overcrowding at Broadmoor. There was still land available from the original estate in Maghull, 50 acres of which was made available for the new Park Lane Hospital.

From 1974 to 1984, Park Lane opened in stages. Unlike Moss Side Hospital, a high-security wall, completely separating it from the rest of the site, surrounded it. Moss Side and Park Lane shared some facilities but operated as independent hospitals.

In 1990, one of the first acts of the new Special Hospitals Service Authority (SHSA) was to merge the two hospitals. On 19 February 1990, the new hospital, Ashworth, was born. The old Moss Side Hospital became known as Ashworth South and East, and Park Lane was renamed Ashworth North. Ashworth South, the original Moss Side Hospital, closed in 1995. I have also spent time in Moss Side, making me unique in that I've been in all the best lunatic hospitals.

In March 1991, the hospital was severely criticised in a *Cutting Edge* television programme alleging the widespread abuse of mentally ill patients by staff at Ashworth.

A public inquiry was chaired by Sir Louis Blom-Cooper QC, which put forward 90 recommendations. There was a call for wholesale culture change at Ashworth. This led to a further reorganisation of the hospital and much work to try to change the culture of the institution.

In April 1996, the hospital became a 'Special Hospital Authority' when the High Security Psychiatric Services Commissioning Board (HSPSCB) succeeded the SHSA.

The capacity of 520 beds was gradually reduced. As one of the three Special High Security Hospitals (Ashworth, Park Lane and Broadmoor), Ashworth receives patients from the North of

England, Wales, the West Midlands and North-West London. Approximately 80 per cent of patients have been convicted of a criminal offence, most of whom are subject to restriction orders. The average length of stay is eight years – a small number of patients will never be ready to leave and will spend the rest of their lives at Ashworth.

Ashworth Hospital today consists of two sites – Ashworth East and Ashworth North. Ashworth East has six refurbished wards, two newly built wards and the Wordsworth Ward, a new 16-bed ward. Ashworth's female patients are located on the East Site, as well as a large number of mentally ill men. A high wire wall provides physical security.

Ashworth North has 17 wards with a total capacity of approximately 370 patients. The Personality Disorder Unit (PDU) and most of the male mental illness wards are located on the North Site, which also contains extensive recreational, rehabilitative and educational facilities. A high concrete wall providing very considerable physical security surrounds it. Ashworth is now Europe's number one maximum-security asylum. Home sweet home!

There was one little pervo in Ashworth I had some fun with. I couldn't believe his cheek, he just blew me away, but he was only little, so I couldn't hurt him. He was just simple. 'Chas,' he said to me in a low voice, 'can you sort me out a pair of bird's soiled knickers?'

'Eh? Where the fuck am I going to get a pair of soiled panties?'

'Well, Chas, you do get lots of visits, can't you smuggle me a pair in?'

I just couldn't believe the little fucker. 'Go on, fuck off!' But I had an idea. I had a word with my pal, big Phil Baxter. Phil was a Brighton lad. He'd gone beserk with an axe, but he never killed anybody. He got sent to Ashworth. Phil's just Phil, a great guy; he'd help anybody, and is a good man to have on your side – powerful, like a horse!

He got hold of a tiny pair of pants and he sewed on a bit of frilly stuff. When he finished they looked real, he then rubbed the crotch area around his arse. I then rubbed it around an old tin of pilchards and we sprinkled talc on it and tied it in a cellophane bag. It was ready.

I pulled the little pervo. 'Oy ... seeing I like you ... I'm on a visit tomorrow, my pal's bird is up, no promises ... but I'll ask her for her panties.'

'Will you, Chas? Please ... please ...'

'Yeah, don't go on, I'll ask.'

'Chas, please ask her to sort of damp them a bit.'

I looked at this fucking poor sod and I felt a strong urge to put his nose into the back of his skull. 'Yeah, yeah, I'll ask her.'

'Chas ... thanks.'

So it was all planned. On my way back from my visit, big Phil would pass me the bag from his window so when I walked on the ward the pervo would see me, so he'd have no doubt where I got it from! We were on Hazlett Ward, Dr Hunter's ward; he was a decent old psychiatrist, 'mad', but a nice bloke.

It was my old pal Ray Williams who came up to see me that day; he was in fits of laughter. I told him, 'Ray ... it is a nuthouse!'

As I got back to Hazlet Ward, I grabbed the bag off Phil and put it in my shirt. The pervo was waiting at the entrance, eyes bulging.

'Chas, Chas, Chas, did you ... Chas?'

I winked; thumbs up.

'Chas, Chas, really, Chas?'

I walked to his cell. Phil came over. 'Nice visit, Chas?'

'Yeah, Phil.'

We both went in the pervo's cell. I pulled it out.

'What's that, Chas?' Phil said.

'Oh, it's a present for my little pal here.' His eyes were bulging ... he was fucking drooling.

'Fucking panties, isn't it?' Phil said.

'Yeah,' I said. 'Red hot, straight off my bird.'

'Chas, Chas, let's have it, please, Chas.'

Phil and me left him with it. We looked through his spy hole; in ten seconds he was pulling himself off as he smelled them. What a sick bastard, what a sad fucking world it is! Those panties kept him alive!

There were a lot of loons in these places, but some were not as mad as you might think — some were crafty fuckers. At night-times, they would ring the night call bell when they knew a female staff member was on night duty. For ten minutes they would be talking to them through the spy hole in the door. 'Please, miss, I can't sleep, talk to me,' and the woman would talk about any old shit; he would be pulling his dick!

'Ooh, that's better, miss, when you talk to me, you've got nice hair, miss.'

'Do you think so?'

'Yes, miss, ooh, miss, you are nice.' I suppose they must have known and others used to expose themselves coming out of the shower and deliberately dropping their towel to show a female staff a hard-on. It was their buzz!

There were rumours that some loons were shagging the staff, but that wasn't for me. I stayed clear of all that. It's just not me, not interested; more trouble than it's worth! But the faggots in there were beyond belief. One nutcase stuck a toilet brush up his arse. He made it into a thick dick shape and covered it in Vaseline — whoosh, right up — but it got stuck! He never lived that down! They had to take him to an outside hospital for an operation. Well, it is an asylum! What did you expect him to do with a toilet brush? Clean the toilet?

And talking of toilet brushes, big Dave Taylor got stabbed with one up in Frankland Jail, right through his chest. The guy who did it snapped the head off, sharpened the handle and plugged

Dave up. He was lucky, very lucky! What saved him was the attacker left it in him; if he had pulled it out, Dave was brown bread! Fancy dying with a toilet brush sticking out of you. Dave later got out after serving ten years and ended up blowing a guy's canister off; he got lifed off. It's a crazy old world, eh?

Stevie Booth — now there's a guy I admire! Thirty years he's been caged up and is still a handful. He changed his surname to 'Peterson' out of respect to me.

The Kray twins loved Stevie, we all do. We once had a fight in Rampton over a pork pie hat. You couldn't make it up, could you? And fuck me, can he hit! We got dragged away, kicked to bits, injected and isolated, all over a fucking hat!

Later, Steve went to the dentist and demanded that he have two teeth taken out so he could have a gap like mine, so we would look the same. That's loyalty beyond belief!

I remember the day big Sam Ellis got a bit lemon with me. Sam's a big black guy, he had been in Broadmoor for 20 years and then I met him again in Ashworth. It was on the yard he turned funny, fuck knows why. It may have been the sun on his head; he was on a lot of medication. But he insulted me; he walked on my towel while I was sitting sunbathing! All I had on was a pair of shorts. I jumped up and nutted him so hard that he flew up in the air, all 18st of him. We never did speak after that.

Mark Rowntree — now there's a strange guy; he killed five, knifed them, two were kids. Met him in Rampton and then later in Ashworth. He had a pretty face; sad there's no acid in the asylum.

And a Broadmoor queen had problems, big time. I'm not sure if he's a bloke or a woman. He falls in love with people, wants to own them, gets very jealous, possessive. Out comes a tool. BASH! An old boy, ugly, big nose. He moved to Ashworth about the same time as me.

One day I was out in the garden getting some sun on Hazlett

Ward, which is next to Gibbon Ward where this guy was. As I walked past the cell windows, I heard a moaning noise. Curiosity got the better of me. Fuck me, if it wasn't him getting his arse shagged ... and he saw me. 'Hi, Chas!' It was as if he was just casually greeting me in the street.

I've seen the loons sitting on the grass talking to a ladybird; I mean really having a conversation. I've sat next to them just to listen to what they're saying. My fucking brain hurts looking back at all this shit. Talking to a ladybird! A loony in Rampton made a hole in his mattress and shagged it every night, until another loony put a razor blade in it. Ouch!

One loon in Ashworth used to pay other loons $\frac{1}{2}$oz of tobacco for their soiled pants. I pulled him one day, 'Oy, how much for a bird's soiled panties?'

'Fuck me, Chas, I'll give you the world!'

So back I went to the fake panties scam. I found a very small pair of pants and got another loon to sew some flowers on it, as I'd done before, then I rubbed a bit of fish in the gusset, and some aftershave, I then put them in a plastic bag.

After a visit, I called him into my cell. 'Fresh off my bird!'

'Chas, Chas, let me smell. How much? ... Say the price, anything.' I gave him a whiff. 'Chas, Chas, how much?'

'Get me two giant bars of Galaxy a week for six months.'

Sadly, I moved soon after, but that tells you the madness I was surrounded by.

A loon in Ashworth came at me one day with a sackful of snooker balls, and missed my head by a whisker, I grabbed him and took him into my cell. 'Right, cunt, what's your game?'

'You kept looking at me,' he said.

Was I hearing this properly. 'What?'

'You kept looking at me.'

I never did. What would you do? I put him on my bed and sat on him. I began to squeeze his neck 'til his eyes bulged, then

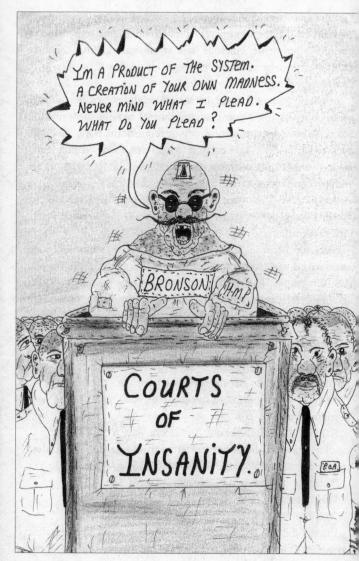

let go. Once he got his breath, I squeezed again. I could have wasted him; I got him up. 'Now listen, mad or not mad, you're dead if you ever so much as look at me again.' I eyed him like a hawk. Really, I should have killed him. Why allow a loon to take you out?

One day, I'd just come back to the ward from the gym, had a great work-out, and went to my room to get my shower stuff. Once I'd showered, I saw two pairs of feet sticking out from under the curtains, lots of 'ooohs' and 'aaahs' and sighs and pumping. Got a bucket of cold water, ripped off the curtain and let them have it! What I saw will live with me for all time! There were three of them, not two; one was, somehow, lifted up on the other's back. It blew me away, dicks everywhere! Oh well, whatever turns you on, I guess.

Now see why I had to get out of them asylums? It was causing me great problems, but it was one hell of an experience.

In 1910, Rampton Hospital, in Nottinghamshire, opened as England's first State Institution for mentally defective people considered to be dangerous. Broadmoor now specialised in the insane and Rampton in the mentally deficient.

I was recently asked by the prison padre, 'Hey, Chas, what's the maddest thing you ever did, ever?'

I gave it a lot of thought and replied, 'You won't believe it if I tell you.'

'Go on, Chas, tell me!'

'Well, it was back in the 1960s, I walked into a church and hit the father with an axe and set fire to the organ.' The padre fucked off. Obviously, I'd made it up. It will stay with him for years. That's how I handle madness, by using psychology!

Once, I was in a class, and there were about 12 of us, all long-termers. I think six of us were Cat 'A'. We had this woman teacher; now I don't want to be nasty, but she was coyote ugly. She had a smile that made her look like a bulldog sucking on a lemon! I asked her in a whisper, 'Hey, miss, have you ever thought of being a model?' I got her all sweet, then I said, 'You could model them horse bags.' Would you believe she ran out of the class and I got banned! They banned me for telling the truth. I can't fucking help it if she's ugly, can I?

I told you, prison can be insane. I personally don't give a fuck if she was Marilyn Monroe, I just spoke the truth. I've nothing against ugly people, they're sweet by me. They can't help but liven our days up. I actually love a freak. The uglier the better, same as midgets, I love them, giants too! Look at my mate. 'Duchy No Legs'. He was born with no legs, but I love him to bits 'cos he's a survivor; he puts people to shame with his achievements and he's done a bit of porridge, so he's a brother of mine.

But that teacher was nothing compared to one ugly fucker I met in Rampton in the 1970s; they called him the 'Head'. He was about 5ft 3in tall, skinny and he had a fucking head like a donkey; it was awesome! Full of bumps, lumps and scars. I've never seen a fucking head like it, but what made it worse was the plastic helmet he wore, as he was epileptic, and the epileptics in Rampton wear these helmets to protect their heads when they have a seizure.

Let's try to describe it – this lunatic's body was like the body of a small boy with a man's head. I used to crack my boiled eggs on his plastic hat and wink at him as I did it! Hell, I wish I had a photo of that, what a fucking laugh that was; it used to brighten up my day. I'm not a cruel bastard, I just love a laugh – the Head was just a legend to me.

One old boy in Rampton I met back in the 1970s was Jip Carter. He had a little faded leather case that he treasured. Once a week he would go and sit in a corner of the Day Room and open up his case to look through his worldly possessions. I was privileged one day to be invited by Jip to join him. I sat in the corner with him, and I was one of very few to see what he had. Poor old Jip had been in Rampton since the Second World War. All his family were dead, and all he had in the world was the case. He showed me photos, old letters, certificates, books, a watch. By the time I had seen it all, I truly had a lump in my throat. And I'll always remember Jip Carter's words. 'Don't be mad, son, get out and stay out.' Jip died in Rampton, although he'd really died the day he arrived. Sad but true.

Mark Rowntree was a classic example! I first met the guy in Rampton asylum, then later in Ashworth. Mark was a young guy, a normal-looking lad, handsome, a good personality, fit and healthy and then — BANG! He lost the plot, killed five innocent people. Went berserk with a knife. I asked him why. And as I've already said about other loons, he just couldn't give an answer, as he had not known himself. Was it sexual? Was it jealousy? Was it for money? None of those, he just woke up and went on a mission. That's madness.

And there's nothing madder than the case of Nurse Beverley Allitt. They now make up illnesses; she's nothing but a child-killer, an evil bitch. She's in Rampton having discos and sex with lesbians. Lock her up in a dungeon; give the slag bread and water, for Christ's sake, she's a baby-killer. She isn't mad, she's evil.

What really gets me, someone like Allitt is diagnosed as suffering from a supposed rare psychological illness and the shrinks are over her like a rash! They can make fortunes off someone like that, writing umpteen books and going on tours of universities.

Allitt was convicted at Nottingham Crown Court in 1993 on 13 charges of murder and causing grievous bodily harm to children and babies! The shrinks have sympathetic views for people like her ... they are seen as tragic figures! But what about the grief-stricken relatives of her victims? Eight-week-old Liam

Taylor – murdered; fifteen-month-old Claire Peck – murdered, as well as the other unnamed victims.

The National Health Service should have been held directly responsible for the series of blunders that resulted on Ward Four, the children's ward, at the Grantham and Kesteven Hospital.

Munchausen Syndrome by Proxy. Basically, this is just an attention-seeking personality disorder dressed up in a fancy name! This disorder manifests itself in the uncontrollable urge to draw attention to the sufferer, often by the person causing self-injury or injuring those in their care.

On the Friday evening, the hospital postponed any investigations. By the Monday, Claire Peck was dead. On 26 July 1991, Allitt was charged with murder. In November 1991, she was formally charged. By the time her trial had started on 15 February 1993, Allitt had lost 5st in weight, supposedly as the result of a form of anorexia. She had been held in Rampton where she reverted to a childhood habit of self-harm by scalding herself with water and eating broken glass. Pity she didn't chew on some arsenic!

Allitt was even too scared to attend court; the jury returned their verdicts on 11 May 1993. On 25 May, Mr Justice Latham sentenced Allitt to 13 life sentences, four on charges of murder and nine for grievous bodily harm. What do they do? They pack her off to some nice, cosy asylum, 'cos she's so dangerous! Save the taxpayers a fortune and have her topped. Look at how the government have added 1p on National Insurance so they can spend extra on the likes of Allitt!

Allitt is a serial killer. And would you believe it, after the trial, Allitt's physical condition miraculously improved! She made a recovery in world record time!

Since then, Allitt still plays her little games. She was rushed to hospital in Worksop, where she was treated for self-inflicted wounds caused by opening out steel paper clips and forcing them into her body. I'd have driven her to hospital to the tune of 'The Funeral March' and just as slow as it's played! Allitt eventually confessed that she had committed three of the murders and six other attacks. She is currently detained in Rampton.

10

THE MADNESS
OF LIFE

For every action there is an equal and opposite reaction. I believe my life is an impossible fight – no winning and no losing. The journey is that of madness, out of control, total destruction from here to the crematorium. You couldn't imagine at times how hard I think – so hard it fucking hurts! It rips me up, my soul's on fire and my heart is heavy and painful. I sleep with one eye open and my fists clenched; at times I awake feeling the stiffness of my jaw and the grinding of my teeth. I exist ... but I fail to live.

I am a creation of the establishment – I realise I'm not as strong as life itself, but I also realise death will suck me in. The eyes and fingers are pointing in my direction. For me, there is only one way, one road, one signpost – it reads 'Hell'. It's a one-way ticket; there are no brakes on my vehicle, there is no way out, only one way in. You can't hold on to time. You can't hold on to a missile.

Sometimes I stare into a pool of piss, I see my reflection, I picture a hole in my face, there's nothing there, it's vanished. I watch the maggots turn to flies, and they fly off with bits of flesh from my body. I attempt to wipe it clear from my mind, but the nice thoughts get swallowed up. I can't think nice for too long ... it would destroy me. Weariness would overcome me; I would crawl and drown in the piss. Like a stiff in the gutter of a ghetto with a poisoned liver, a filthy drunk who sucks his way from the madness of life, a journey of hopelessness. But somebody must have once loved him. Every lost soul once had a mother, an angel. No one is born a monster ... or are we?

The truth is basically screaming in your face. You can be with a partner for 30 years and still be strangers. He could be the local Peeping Tom and she could be the slag of the town — but will you ever know? The only sure thing you will know — you're going to die alone in the same way as you were born ... naked and helpless.

I held a newborn baby some time back; it's probably some low-life punk now, going around bashing old women up. Next time you see a ladybird it could be me! Never doubt nothing — anything is possible!

When you get a new car or bike, you've this urge to see how fast she can go. Well, a gun or a knife is the same! You need to test it. See what it can do. I remember my first shotgun, when I sawed off the barrel I was excited to see the power of it. So I went in a wood and shot at the tree trunks. Awesome power. Ripped them to bits.

Now I'm gonna confess something. It may amaze many, even shock, but I'm not really a tool man. Let me explain — villains love a tool, some just to get a buzz or high out of using them. I never have. Sounds insane? It's true, I don't get a buzz out of using tools. I'm more of a physical guy. I buzz from punching up bodies. I love using my fists and strength. Oh yes, I've used tools — plenty — but only 'cos I had little choice.

Sometimes you've got to get in and cut fast, and at times do maximum damage in little time. I remember once, I smashed in a door, rushed in and done a geezer badly – I used an iron bar on his legs. It was all over in 30 seconds. Strangely enough, I can remember the *Coronation Street* music on the TV as I bashed the fuck out of him. Dirty fucking grass. Still, he may have learned by it, 'cos he never grassed and I never even had a mask on. I wanted him to know; that's how I work. Look at me. See who I am. Sure, I'll go down for ten years, but I'm back out twice as ugly, twice as cruel and twice as vicious. So don't grass ... ever.

Unlike most, I don't fear prison – never have, never will. Obviously, I don't want it, I hate it, but it's the hate that drives me on to survive. Another time I took up a contract – three grand. It was early '70s. Three grand was big bucks, so I had to do it. The only problem was it was a pal's cousin. He had gone bad and was becoming dangerous to a forthcoming trial; his statement looked naughty to two guys on remand.

Look, I'm not heartless; a pal's a pal. I did what I had to do. Then I went to see my pal. He accepted it; he had no choice, because his cousin deserved it ... a copper's nark. That scumbag would not look the same again. His whole life ended up a nightmare, and I'm proud to say, it was down to me. The two guys got acquitted. I got my three grand, and the scumbag probably got a job in the circus as the ugly freak. That's how it is ... insanity.

There is no escape from madness! But what you can do is control it; if you're in control of it, you can use it to your own benefit.

I remember some years back, when I was about 17 years old, I was in a pub buzzing from the sound of the jukebox, the heat, the noise and the madness. Eyes fascinate me! Faces unknown; strangers. Somewhere in that crowded room, there's a madman. How lucky they were ... it was me. If only they knew, read my mind or picked my thoughts up. I looked just like any other 17-year-old lad — smart, healthy, not bad looking ... not ugly. But I always had this strangeness, like a barrier around me. Step inside and violence erupts.

I smashed one bloke straight in the face. His teeth embedded into my fist. Blood spurted out. I nutted his pal. Crunch! I felt his nose snap. I kicked out and punched. I kept moving, but you can't fight the planet. Something hit the back of my neck; blows rained into my body. Screams, 'GET THE BASTARD!' I kept punching into darkness. I felt my entire body floating up. Air hit my face, lungs. Pain erupted. 'DO THE BASTARD!' That's all I remember, then I awoke in hospital. Fuck me, who wants to be a madman? Believe me, it's a painful journey. For every punch you throw, you take 50 back. Incidents like that are a part of a madman's life.

So the question is, why did I attack? I'll tell you, or I'll try to. It's a challenge of life. 'They' were all a part of my existence. They had to beat me or crawl away, so they beat me. They beat me good, but not good enough, 'cos 30 or so years later, I'm still laughing. You have to waste a mad dog. You can't afford to play games, and that's what it is, a fucking game, a gamble, win or lose.

She was in her late 50s, plumpish with a nice face, a beauty in her day without a doubt. I was maybe 16 years old, hot-blooded and dangerous. I got up off my seat. 'Hey, lady, take my seat.'

'Thank you,' she said.

'You're welcome, lady,' I replied.

I bent over to the geezer in the next seat. He had one of those faces, what I call 'maggot features'. He looked what he was, a fucking rat. Probably married, two kids, mortgage, H/P, debt — a typical fucking maggot. 'Yeah, you ... you fucking maggot.' He went red. 'Why didn't you give the lady your seat then? You filthy fucking maggot. Not good enough for your seat, is she? Not your type.'

The woman spoke. 'Please don't cause a scene.'

'Sorry, lady,' I replied.

I got off at the next stop, or I'd have punched the maggot's face in. Is it madness or just me? Would you put your tongue in my mouth and feel 100 per cent safe? Could I or would I bite it off?

To love somebody, I believe, you become that somebody. You think alike. You start to look alike. It's more madness. A human's love can wrap you up in a new seat of madness. She wants the meat, the muscle and the power. Man wants the challenge; after all, we are the predators — women are the bait, the food, the catch.

I read an article in a magazine: 70 per cent of women love it up the arse. What's all that about? Are they insane or just perverted? Crazy bitches! What sane person wants ramming up the arse? OK, it takes all sorts. Me, I'd prefer a plate of chips, with lots of Daddie's Sauce and a nice mug of tea, sweet tea.

She was red hot, so hot that she melted on my dick. I was 37; she was 18. I'd just spent 14 years in the can. I mean, imagine it, 14 years without a woman and then ... bang! I've got an 18-year-old blonde bombshell sitting on my dick, bouncing up and down. 'Jelly Baby' I called her. Why not? She was lovely, beautiful! Her body was a dream.

As she bounced up and down, I closed my eyes and thought about going to war with the planet. I wanted to get so into her ... disappear inside her, and shine out of her face. Fuck with Jelly Baby and it would be me there to fuck with them.

We got in a lift. I held on to her tight, so fucking tight. Three guys got in, two black and one white. Young punks, probably tooled up, out to mug some old granny or two. I looked at them, stared, my eyes penetrate. I squeezed Jelly Baby close; she felt my pulse, the tension, heart, soul, pain. Something strange happened in that lift. A madness I've never had before. I got a hard-on! A fucking big hard-on! I started to smile at the three punks. Fuck me, this was insanity.

They froze ... they prayed that lift would soon stop. 'What's up, Chas?' she asked.

'Nothing, I'm just in love. I can't stop getting a hard-on. I can't stop wanting to kill the planet ... I'm fucking sick.'

'You're dangerous, Charlie ... fucking way over the top.'

I had this gun, nice little piece, but I'm really a 12-bore man. I like the feel; I love the noise. But I had this little piece, felt nice, cosy, safe. I used to fire it out of the car window at the street lights. Why? Why not? Why do you always have to have a reason?

We were in this pub together, just sitting there, like any normal couple. I'm not a big drinker; I can't afford to be, as I like to be in control. 'Gotta have a piss, back in two minutes.' I stood in the toilet, had my piss, washed my hands and then it started − my face, eyes, the reflection of me at the mirror. I felt this strangeness creep all over me. Like I wasn't there, like I was back in a concrete coffin − like my Jelly Baby didn't exist.

I'd experienced this before when my mum and dad picked me up from prison. We stopped by a garage, I went for a piss and ended up pulling the hand drier off the wall 'cos I felt the same way as I did back in the hell cell!

A guy walked in ... I clocked him. He would have run out screaming if he only knew! If only. I walked out breathing hot air, a rush of madness, screams in my head. Gotta get to the Jelly Baby. I sat down in silence. I held on to her. Jelly Baby asked, 'What's up?'

I held on. I whispered, 'You OK?'

'Yeah ... what's up, Chas?' She looked into my face, she knew. 'You OK?'

Fucking hell, I was ill; prison had destroyed me. I wanted to crawl inside Jelly Baby's snatch. Crawl right inside her and be safe. Nobody would ever find me, warm, no problems. But her snatch wasn't big enough.

Nothing ever lasts. I used to lick her body, like a toffee apple. I used to blow into her hair, watch it fluff up. I used to love waking up and smelling her next to me. The sweet smell of body — fresh, only an 18-year-old has that smell. Pure sex. 'Christ, Charlie, you've got another hard-on.'

'I can't help it, Jelly Baby; I can't fucking help it, babe.'

About the same time, Kelly Anne Cook was on the scene, one crazy bitch, a piss-head, but she had this way about her. She took me to this pub. I ended up taking a guy outside and smashing his face in. I left him lying in a flowerbed. 'Come on, Kelly Anne, time to go.' I was blowing guts away, just for looking at me.

One night, in Kelly's flat, it happened ... I had a breakdown! I don't really know how or why, but I lost it. Totally. She was her usual self ... pissed. I don't like to see drunks in my face; their breath stinks and they talk shit. 'Fuck off to bed, get out of my face.' I hear her being sick. It reminds me of the asylum.

I turned on a record ... loud! She came staggering in. 'Fuck off, Kelly Anne, go to bed.' She fell on the sofa like a bag of shit, so I left the room, ran the bath, lay in it, soaking, thinking. Time for madness!

A guy called Steven Oaks was in the next block of flats. He lived 12 floors up. A fucking rat. I'd been watching him for days. I'd done a bit of homework on him. He was taking liberties on the estate. Time I paid him a visit! So I dried off, got dressed and off I went. I started to climb the outside, from balcony to balcony. I do love a climb. I took the carving knife with me for company. I got up to the ninth balcony when some silly tart clocked me and started to scream. Silly bitch, so dramatic, who needs it?

I had a choice – carry on or go back. The Old Bill would be on the scene in 15 minutes. Do I need it? Nah. So I made it back to Kelly Anne's. I sat there watching her snore off her booze binge. Crazy ... days later the 'pigs' burst in on me. The whole police force knew it was me, but it never mattered, as they had me on a jewellery raid. I was back in, back where I belonged. I was dangerous at this time – unreal and full of madness.

I knew the pigs wanted me badly. They fear me. Fear is paramount. They're shit fucking scared of me. They came tooled up, a dozen, with chains and coshes. 'Bruise the beast!' 'Get too close and you'll lose your throat; watch his teeth.' 'Don't step into darkness alone! Take him out.' I'm immune to madness, but I want to love before I'm killed. I need to melt into a body of tenderness.

Those weeks I was free, I knew the door would crash in on me. I knew the madness would return. It never left me. I left prison, but prison never left me. I stank of it; everyone could smell the fear. The pain never goes. Crash – they're back in to wrap me up. They carry me away to the padded room. Would you believe it, I've still got a hard-on. Madness has no cure ... it's for ever.

I had gone into my local pub. Fred was the local villain, he was double my age, and had done bird for armed robbery; he was feared and respected in the town. He had his own table and chair in this pub. All the local criminals zoomed around him, like he was some sort of king.

He called me over. I felt 10ft tall. 'Mickey,' he said, 'sit down.' He called over for a drink for me. 'I've been hearing things about you. Good things. But it's time you went up the ladder a bit. How do you fancy a bit of serious work?' He had so much gold in his mouth that when he smiled he looked like a brass doorknob. I jumped at the chance of making a few extra quid, so it was all set up for me.

I was to grab a bag on its way to the night safe outside a bank. The driver takes off, drops me off at a safe house and bingo. A description of the guy I was to grab the bag off was given; the time and the place was all set; it would be as simple as eating an apple pie. This was my first ever bit of serious work, and from this I knew I could only get better and richer. It was a Saturday, about 6.20pm; we were waiting. I spotted him. The car started up. I got out. CRASH! I almost hit him through a shop window. I grabbed the bag and away ... simple!

By the time I landed at the safe house, I was close to shooting my load. Excitement and happiness washed over me; I was like a dog with two tails. I was so high. A buzz I've never experienced. I was to celebrate that night with the boss. I'd bring him the cut, and the driver and I'd be well sorted. He told me the amount we'd get paid should be about three to five grand. The takings in the bag would be about 50 grand. So it was big bucks. Awesome! I was 18 years old and about to be rich!

I opened the bag and emptied it on the bed — roast beef sandwiches, a cake and a flask of coffee! I'd swiped some guy's lunch bag! To say I was gutted is an understatement. I fucking cried! But I will say, the roast beef had mustard on it and I enjoyed it. The biggest thing was walking in the pub to tell the boss. He took it well. He laughed and I learned from it. That's how crime is. Up and down. Win some, lose some. I actually gained from it, as I became a better criminal, more alert and more serious.

But looking back, it's all insanity. Maybe that incident was really an omen. Was I really being told, 'Give it up, Micky, 'cos you can't ever win. You'll lose, one day you'll lose big time ...' I don't know the answer, but I'd know every roast beef sandwich since has made me smile. Oh, and the geezer I hit, I often wonder how he must have felt. I bet he thought, Christ! I'm living in a right tough area. I got mugged for my lunch bag! There's a lot of humour in madness. You can't help but smile.

The second bit of work I did for the boss went like clockwork. A nice few bob. Shame I had to crack the guy on the skull ... silly man wouldn't let go of the bag. Oh, well, that's life. The only real heroes are dead or seriously injured.

In the system, I was on one drug that gave me a constant hard-on, throbbing all day and night, pointing out of my pyjamas – kinda hurts. The drugs fuck your system up. Constipation, vision, shakes, dries your sperm up, muscular spasms, restlessness, senility, rots your organs ...

Fuck me, why can't somebody just love me? Why do I have to do this shit? I'm a victim, I'm a beast and I'm no longer a human. Now see why I destroy it all, now see why I'm what I am? I've fought these slags for nigh on 30 years.

Imagine what my brains are like. It was in the 1970s the prison wanted to give me a scan, but it was the POA (Prison Officers Association) who stopped it, saying I was too unpredictable to take out to hospital. In those days, only specialised hospitals had the machines to carry out brain scans. I was refused, even when the doctor wanted me to have one. At Parkhurst, they gave me an EEG (Electroencephalogram) which records electrical activity in the brain to pinpoint areas of sensory projection, the localisation of tumours or of epileptic foci, and so on. The doctor told me that I really needed a CT (Computed Tomography Imaging) and CAT (Computed Axial Tomography) scan. Again, the POA said, 'No way. He's too violent and unpredictable to take out to any hospital for a scan.' The scan machine cost a fortune, and they

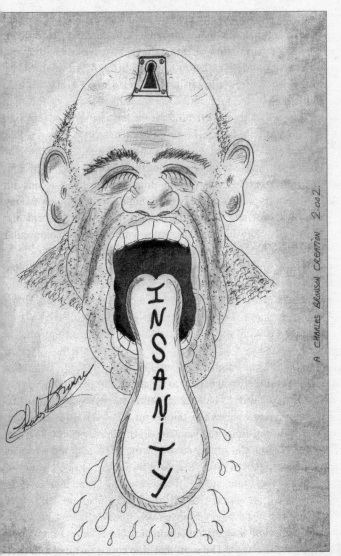

actually made the authorities afraid in case I'd smashed it up. So I've never had one.

To date, a number of medical experts believe I suffer from a form of epilepsy. What do I feel about it? Well, I believe I've some form of low-grade brain damage and I always have done. I can't be normal to have lived like I have, can I? What makes me explode? Why do I lose it? Simple – it's a brain dysfunction – damage. Maybe a growth, a tumour or a scar. A scan could show this up and prove if I did have damage. Now what would the authorities say to that? Then where would that put the system? I'd say a few million pounds out of pocket, and my release from prison because they refused me the scan in the '70s at Parkhurst.

Epilepsy affects 1–3 per cent of the world's population. It is a medical brain disorder causing a tendency to develop fits or seizures. It affects men more than women.

I should add, I'm not as bad now, but I still get serious pains in my head. I won't take medication, neither do I talk to doctors, as I don't respect them or trust them. Why should I? How can I? Those hypocrites! Most are afraid to go against the system.

When I was at Whitemoor Prison on my hunger strike, because they'd taken my art materials off me, the doctor allowed the block screw to torture me. I was on a 40-day hunger strike and, by law, a man on a hunger strike should be in the hospital under observation. I mean, if it's good enough for that monster Brady, what's wrong with second-class me being hospitalised? But I was kept in the block! The doctor was frightened of going against the system, and losing his lovely big fucking fat pension!

After ten days on hunger strike, you are automatically moved into the hospital. He couldn't do it, as he feared the POA. So again the system law and the medical board lost. But how?

With me it happens time and time again; it will always happen as they put security before health. If I fall sick, I die, it's as simple as that; it will be too late to treat me, as security will always come first.

If I do have brain damage and I later die, I'd like it to be known at my cremation that the system killed me by refusing a brain scan. Whilst I'm alive, they will always get away with atrocities. It will only be after my death the full truth will appear. I'm living a death as it is.

Take outside — freedom. What is it? What does it mean to a madman? We go years through a lifetime with no love, no sex, no nice food and no nice clothes. So when it comes, we choke on it! The kindness strangles us; we can't cope, so we make pigs of ourselves.

I remember sex. Without blowing my own trumpet, I was a nympho! I could not get enough. I was so happy; I was like a kid in a sweet factory. A ten-hour session is just the start. I'd lay there looking at her body, smelling it, licking it, like a lion with a piece of meat, wondering about the organs inside, how it worked, why it worked. I used to enjoy the beat of her heart. I could put her heart in my mouth and let it pump away. I'd love to go into her body, and just swim around her veins. I'd just look into her eyes and drown myself.

I was totally obsessed with another body so close to me. I wanted to watch her pee. Why? Why not? So I could study her, check her cunt and see if her pee was clear or misty. Now I know somebody is gonna say, 'Hey, this Bronson geezer is a right kinky cunt,' but I would argue it to be more a fascination. I don't want to be pissed on like those dirty bastards!

I feared she may die and I had to protect her. I'd dress her and slip her panties on her like it was my body. I'd feed her. When we walked out, I'd hold on to her, hug her, breathe on her and look at her. I'd become her and I began to smell like her and even my dick smelled of her. We once had a bath together, she got horny; we did the biz in the bath. I thought, fuck me, what a way to die. Let's drown on the job!

I believe a sexual relationship is based on fear. She wonders, is he as mad as he appears and what's he thinking? Why does he look at me that way? Why did he do that? He's a pervo. Can I spend the rest of my life with him? Where does he go when he leaves? Is he a bisexual? Why does he lick my face? Why does he scream in his sleep? Will he ever kill me?

He thinks, has she ever had it up the arse? Why does she get so wet? Is she a tart? Will she cross me? Is it my money? Does she love me? Is my dick too small for her? Was she looking at that guy?

A relationship is basically insanity. A closeness like sex is awesome; the very thought of having seven inches of human muscle pumping away inside another body is frightening ... breathing, panting, sweating, scratching, biting and screaming – is it not madness?

Have you seen a woman orgasm? Is it not insane? Eyes bulge, mouth drips, teeth, spit, sweating; it's terrifying, but it's wonderful, it's a bit scary. Then you sleep, cuddle, hug. It's crazy. Madness at its best! So I say, enjoy life, get your dick sucked plenty. Get your pussy stroked plenty, live in madness, enjoy madness. Fuck away the blues. Keep on fucking 'til the angels come. 'Cos the angels will come, sure as there's a hole in your arse. Madness is beautiful.

I believe man is madder than woman. Why? We are more complicated! Think about a man – have you women ever thought what it's like with three pound of meat and flesh hanging from your body. I believe women are jealous of men, as we can stand erect. We are stronger and faster, but alas we have the weaker minds. I believe women are mentally strong. Too smart.

I can talk nicely and comfortably one to one, but in a crowd I sweat. I get urges to attack. I get bouts of madness. Maybe in time I'll get myself a little cottage or an old lighthouse, and live alone with some pets. I said I would never remarry or live with another human, but along came the beautiful Saira ... hit me like a whirlwind. Thanks to an e-mail sent to my fan club, she found out where I was and now she's my wife.

Life is insanity, treachery, evil and falseness beyond belief. Take my ex-girlfriend, Joyce Connor. She got released from a six-year sentence, having served four years. It was tough for her, I mean double tough, 'cos she's from Canada. I wrote to her for four years; we helped each other through, we laughed and cried together; our pain and misery were as one. We rose above adversity. Her big day came – freedom. My pal, Dave Courtney, picked her up from the station in a limo. She had a big party bash, organised by my great pal Joe Pyle, waiting for her at the Million Hairs club in London – champagne, grub, legless! James 'Le Prince' Nicholson organised photos in the press and in the media for her. That was on the Friday. Months in advance we had planned a phone call for 2.00pm on the following Sunday.

I was excited. I rang ... she wasn't in. I put the phone down, all choked up. I felt the madness creep into my head. I looked at my reflection. Shall I rip the phone off the wall? Shall I rip a hole in this hell? I controlled it. The madness passed. Ten fucking days later I got a letter off her. I sent it back. It's over!

Shit! Who needs it? Why? How? For four years we were one! We'd never met, but her letters were magic. Then she does that. That's madness. But I won't slag her, as she's let herself down, not me.

So the insanity goes on winning. Romance was in the air. She was a sweet girl who got six years over madness. She had Class 'A' drugs on her when she was caught flying into the UK. Good luck, Joyce. I mean it. I loved you to bits for four years;

it could have been 40 years if you were at the phone when you were supposed to be. I can't accept your excuses; that call to me was precious. It depressed me, hurt me. Thanks. I really mean that because otherwise I wouldn't have met my beautiful Saira. I mean, who wants an ex-druggie for a wife when you can have an angel?

I'll give you a fact. To all those people scared of cockroaches, do you want to know how to stop them coming in?

Every creature is afraid of something. Cockroaches fear slugs and snails; don't know why, but they do. This is what you do. Get a nice big fat slug or snail and rub it up and down the floor at the bottom of the door on the area where you think the cockroaches come in. It's the slime that keeps them away! A cockroach won't pass over that slime; you'll be cockroach free!

Now what relevance has that to insanity? Just imagine you could do that with sane people. You spot the madness and, before it gets in, you block it out. One day that will happen with gene therapy. People will be able to say, 'Hey, I don't want my kid suffering like Bronson did, cut the bad genes out.'

A doctor in Parkhurst, Dr Cooper, once told me that, when I lose the plot, I am demonic. Now I'm gonna tell you a story about Dr Cooper. It was, as I've already explained, back in 1978, when Dr Cooper, along with two other doctors, certified me mad. This incident I'm about to tell you occurred on C-Unit in Parkhurst, 1976.

I walked out of my cell and I felt like some action. It was one of those days that needed livening up. I stood outside my cell door and leaned on the rail and watched the cons come out of their cells.

There were never more than ten on C-Unit; we all had our problems or we wouldn't have been in there. Some had massive problems. I was one of the lucky ones, 'cos I was the only one serving a fixed sentence — the rest were lifers. I used to drift into bouts of dreamlike states, wondering what it's like not to have a relevant date for release. The very thought used to send a cold shiver through my body.

I'd watch them slip out; I'd watch them walk up to the hot water boiler to make tea. I'm a born analyser, see. I love to watch life in action. Ron Kray was walking out of the shower, and Ron loved a bit of action himself.

'Hey, Ron,' I shouted, 'look at this.' He looked as I somersaulted over the rail and landed feet away from a screw. 'Could have been your head that, screw.' He was white with fear, as I'd just jumped 12ft from a metal walkway. When I landed it took him by surprise.

'Fuck me,' he said, holding his ticker, 'Don't do that.'

I tapped him on the head. 'No problem.' Ron loved stuff like that; it used to make his day.

That incident got me a call up by Dr Cooper. Dr Cooper asked, 'Why did you do that?'

'What?'

'Jump from the landing and frighten the officer.'

'Hey, what if I broke my legs or neck? Would you then be worried about a fat lazy screw?'

'It would have been your own fault. Now why do you do such strange things?'

'Look, Doc,' I said, 'I'm a man of many moods, but I'm like a bird in a cage; I hate it. I get fed up, long to be free, to fly. All this jail is no good to me. I do those things solely for my own sanity.'

'But you can't continue to do them.'

'Why?'

'It's not normal.'

'What is fucking normal in jail?'

'Behaviour.'

'Then I'm abnormal,' I replied.

OK, I wouldn't do such stunts now, but back then it was just a mad laugh.

Now let me tell you my opinion. I believe Dr Cooper actually likes me, and he's a little bit jealous of me. He probably dreams of doing some of my stunts. If he had attempted that jump, he would have smashed his ankles or even misjudged it and landed on the screw's head. I wasn't on that unit long, but the short spell I had, I loved it with the Kray twins. It taught me a lot.

I had a few work-outs with Reg in the gym. He was one hell of a skipper, and to see him on the bag was a treat – lovely mover with tremendous punching power. But the immortal words of Ronnie just blew me away: 'You're bloody mad, you are.' That, coming from Ron Kray, was a compliment.

Ron Kray was moved to Broadmoor in 1979 from Parkhurst, having been diagnosed a paranoid schizoid. He was prescribed drugs such as Dipitec, Medicate, Stelative and so on. It seemed to keep him stable and calm. For me, it had the opposite effect, making me depressed and clumsy and unhealthy. But Ron made the best out of a bad set-up and he lived in Broadmoor like the king of the castle. He made it work for him and around him. He had a nice room with a TV, carpets, curtains and a bedspread. Ron was Ron; he used the place to his advantage. Nice visits, good food, nice clothes; he even married twice, first to Elaine Miller and then to Kate Kray.

Kate brought a lot of sunshine to Ron; she made him laugh. I'd say she helped Ron over some bad times. There's a lot of good in Kate; a good heart, a good soul and, no, she never married Ron for money. Kate had her own money. Kate married Ron because she idolised him; she felt for him, so Ron plodded on, and did his time peacefully 'til he died.

Ron used to watch me throw the roof slates off; he loved it. Ron loved a rebel; he thrived on it. His mum, Violet, used to leave me meat pies in a box when she visited Ron. Charlie, Ron's brother, used to pop in some magazines for me. The Krays were a special breed — salt of the earth! Ron was mad, yes, I won't deny it, but he lived by morals. Ron drew a line; if you stepped over it you'd get fucking hurt. That was Ron, a madman who had lots of self-respect and greatness! I loved him like a father. Ron once said to me, 'Charlie, madness is a gift of life.'

11

VENGEANCE IS MINE, SAYETH BRONSON

A lot of stuff has been written about me, but I'd like to put the record straight. A geezer sent me the Paul Ferris book recently, *The Ferris Conspiracy*. Now I've never met Ferris; I've heard of him, in fact some of my pals speak highly of him, but after reading the bit in which I'm mentioned, the guy's been misinformed.

I won't bother with the details, but remember this: get your facts right, Ferris, before you slag people off. It's men like me who have fought for all your prison comforts, your curtains, your rugs, your bedspreads, your nice visits and your flask. *Me*, Ferris!

I've spent my whole adult life fighting for cons' human rights, but I've never had any benefits myself. I've stopped the pigs bashing cons; what have you fucking done? You have never been next to me in a cage; I never saw you up on any of the roofs protesting for better treatment and conditions. That was me, Ferris, doing it for you. It's me who's had to take the full force of my actions, and all I get is people like you slipping me into your muggy book as if I'm some sort of animal!

If you had met me, maybe you would have a different opinion, then I could have accepted your judgement. You mention some great guys in your book, men I admire, but to judge me without meeting me ... who the fuck do you think you are? That's insanity to me!

Talking of insanity, Riff Memhet, a serious armed robber who copped a 21-year sentence, exchanged words with me one day through the closed doors. I'll always remember what he shouted. 'Bronson! You're a liberty-taker ... you wrapped that poor governor up in Hull Jail for nothing.'

I was lost for a reply, I was in shock! I felt lost, like I no longer belonged in jail. How can I have taken a liberty by kidnapping a governor? He is the system ... he runs our life; I'm a prisoner ... it's my duty to wrap up who I want! I said to Memhet, 'As long as I don't wrap you up, what's your fucking problem?'

It was the same in Parkhurst when I came out of my cell in the late hours and smashed the jail up. Cons were slagging me over it! It's a poxy prison I'm wrecking, not their homes! Or are they all insane?

Once, in Wandsworth, I was slopping out, dozens of us, scores of us, queuing up to slop our pots away. The stench alone depresses you. Some guy, somehow, spilled some of his piss on my boot ... accident or on purpose, who knows? But it was no accident as I smashed his head into the wall. I just lost it. I kept smashing his crust into the wall. My mate, Mickey Stevens, grabbed me. I was killing him! That's how you can snap. You don't get out of bed and say, 'Oh, I'll cave someone's crust in today,' it doesn't happen like that, it's just an explosion of madness!

Tony Martin, the farmer, got life for shooting two burglars;

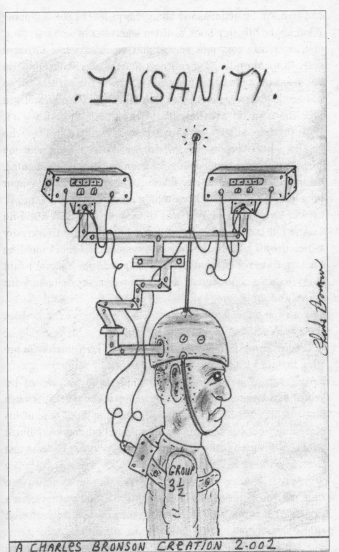

one died. An Englishman's home is his castle. The law is insane! What a joke British justice is ... two little pricks climb into your house to steal your property, and they could have had a gun or knife. Tony Martin, a farmer, lived alone; what else could he do but shoot the scumbags? Now he's got life! That's insanity!

I see mad Frank Cook's back in jail again. In his book *Hard Cell*, he wrote, 'Bronson will kill me on sight.' What a silly thing to put in a book! But you have to ask yourself why.

All his little chats on TV and radio and all his work with the 'pigs', and what do they do? Nick him and put him back in. Still, he always wanted to be the hard man of the United Kingdom. Why not stay in, Frank? Do society a favour, 'cos I think they're tired of your crap.

And I'm not gonna kill you, Frank, so why say it? I'm now at peace with myself. I've put all the madness behind me! But even so, I'd never crawl away from my past; I am who and what I am! No act and no regrets! I've not even got any sympathy for my victims, only some I should have hit harder. No doubt you'll be crawling again for some parole. No wonder you're a short arse; you've lost 6in by crawling around.

I remember in Full Sutton in the late '80s when Frank did me a big favour. I hit this big black guy in the TV room. He had to have some, as he was getting very silly. It was Frank who helped him up and took him away to clean him up. Frank later told me, 'It's sorted, no comebacks.' But the next day, I was moved up to Durham cage. I'm not saying Frank was involved, but if I had sorted it myself, I'd have made certain I was in the clear. See you in hell, Frank!

Albert Donaghue had the cheek to write a book on his life with the Krays ... what a fucking insult! He turned Queen's Evidence (QE) on the Krays. Some people just have no morals at all! He should crawl into a hole with that other 'slag' John Barry who went QE on the twins as well. Don't confuse him with Ian

Barrie, though, who is a gentleman! A loyal man, he served 20 years for the Krays, like the man he is!

I've got this thing about grasses ... I just get the urge to rip their tongues out and pop their eyes with a needle! I wonder if you could put your lips over an eye and suck it out! I'll have to try that if I ever bump into Berti Smails.

12

MAVERICKS

Lee Duffy once helped me trap a nonce in Armley Jail. That Leeds jail is one filthy shit tip. I collared this nonce in the showers; Lee Duffy was with me. Lee was a Middlesbrough lad, a hard fucker. He got out and was stabbed to death. Lee held this maggot while I opened up on him. I hit him a good 20 times, then I held him and Lee hit fuck out of him. Later that day, I found a tooth in my right knuckle. I felt quite sick to think I had a nonce's tooth in my body. Lee Duffy was a good lad and he hated nonces too! RIP.

Schaefer the Pen — I can't forget this con's name, up on D-Wing at Wandsworth in the 1970s. His father died and some slag screw upset him and it sparked him off. I was in the seg unit and when they dragged him down, I shouted, 'Leave him alone, you bullies.' Lovely fellow he was. Later, that same screw got done. That's how prison is, see. Even the screws can't always get away with it, we all have to pay a price, same as me. One day, I'll get it in the neck and maybe the screws will kill me. Nobody can escape in jail. Take the Strangeways Prison riot – who was safe there? I'll tell you – no fucker was!

Princess Fergie visited Wormwood Scrubs the day I was in the block. I saw her out of my window with all the faceless people. She got some verbal that day off the lads: 'Show us your tits, Fergie.' 'Give us a butchers at your bush, Fergie.' 'Give us a wank, Fergie.' It was funny ... I got fed up shouting after a while.

Leon Brittan visited Parkhurst when I was there. I'd have loved to have wrapped him up; what a hostage a Home Secretary would make! He was a nasty piece of work as far as Home Secretaries go. Jack Straw was a pussy compared to old Leon. Michael Howard was a little ferret! He caused some trouble! They just don't realise the trouble they cause when they get silly with new rules – why can't they leave the jails as they are? A jail is a jail; why pretend it's anything else?

They go on about how they are there to help offenders return to a non-offending life and what a cushy time we have in here – bollocks! Stop kidding yourselves ... accept it, we come in and go out later to catch up on where we left off. Behind every door there is a dream! In my case, it's a fucking nightmare!

Tommy Tedstone is a top legend from the 'Port' (Ellsmere Port), which was only a small place at one time, but it was a place to be proud of; its fighters are hard men, particularly Tommy Tedstone, also known as House Brick.

Look, we've all got skeletons in the cupboard that we hope to run from! I'm gonna come clean now. This is my confession to clean up a crazy incident. Fuck me, it's so long ago, but I've gotta clear a guy who all the Old Bill believes it was. So here goes!

Ellsmere Port, late '60s. I was living with my grandparents for a spell in Great Sutton, Belington Road. I was a hod carrier earning good cash, but I was also half a villain; nothing big, the odd smash and grab, the odd nicking a motor and the regular punch-up or two. The Ellsmere Port lads were a tough breed, guys like Ray Williams, Ray Hitchen, Scully and Eric Bell, brother of Bobby Bell, the wrestler.

So I got nicked and ended up in the 'old cop shop'. The new cop shop is opposite the Viscount pub, but the old one was down by the magistrates' court, in the town centre. The 'pigs' were kind of rough with me. Fuck me, I was only a lad, so I swore to myself, 'Round two, I'll have 'em!'

They charged me with criminal damage, but never nicked me for hitting out with a chair or jumping on them. Why? 'Cos they then gave me some of what I gave them — fair play. I've no problem, but I still want round two; that's how I am, see!

So I thought hard about it and decided they deserved a lesson. It was a Friday night; I'd been paid that day so I was buzzing. I shot down the alley of the 'pig shop'; all was peaceful and, in those days, only a handful were on nights.

I squatted and had a crap! I shit on a rag I found. Hell, I was laughing as I did it – well, I was half-pissed – then went to work. I put shit on the car door handles, gates, doors and bicycles, everywhere, even on the dog kennel doors. Took me ages, but I did it and scarpered.

Some time later, I bumped into Tommy Tedstone and he told me the story about when the pigs pulled him in and laid into him for shitting their place up.

'No!' I said.

'Yeah,' he said, 'and I never did it, Chas, but I'm only fucking saying, I never.'

'Bastards,' I said. 'Hey, I wonder who did it?'

'Fuck knows,' he said, 'but if I find out, I'll kill him!'

Confession time — Tommy, it was me, mate, sorry, pal ... but what could I say or do? That's how life is, brother. At least you're a man who can take what they can give and at the end of it all, you came out on top.

Andy Dougall was a big 19st Scotsman. I first met him in the 1980s in Ashworth. They were terrified of him; one day he just lost the plot and wrecked the ward; it looked like a fucking bomb site. They injected him and slung him in a van and moved him back to Parkhurst. The asylums just could not handle Andy! So that proves what a load of crap it all is. They want people off who are violent in prison, and then when we get out of hand in the asylum they can't handle us, so they re-write us off as sane and send us back to jail; it's mad, all mad.

But what do they send us back to? Treatment in torture? Andy originally got lifed off over castrating a poof. This guy actually found Andy half-pissed and sleeping rough as a homeless victim living in London sleeping in boxes and doorways. The geezer took pity on Andy and took him home. What a fucking brainless prat he must have been by taking Andy home!

Andy was one of Glasgow's most dangerous men. And when he awoke in the poof's bed, he found a hairy pair of bollocks in his face! That did it; the blade came out and off they came; his dick was cut off along with them. Amazingly the poof survived, but Andy got life. It's always the same, the good get the worst, as I don't know any man who wouldn't have done the same as Andy. Well, what would you have done? Think about it. You're waking from a lovely hazy dream and a pair of bollocks are dangling in your face, so what do you do?

Prison turned Andy mad. Up in Wakefield Jail, they got Andy on a lot of psychotic drugs but they just sent him more violent. He jumped a screw and almost bit his nose off, so they built a cage for him in the hospital. After a spell, he moved to Ashworth, then Parkhurst. It was at Parkhurst I next met him; it was on C-Unit, which was for violent men. Andy, now 21st, was sad to see. One day, big Chris Moody chinned him and Andy was so drugged he could not even hit back. I grabbed Moody and smashed his head into the wall; Moody was a big, fat, brainless prat from Hull. Andy later went to Bristol Jail, to their lifers' wing, and that's where he mysteriously died.

It was breakfast time at the hot plate; he threw a wobbler and smashed it up; the screws jumped him and he later died — they said it was a heart-attack. So many end up like Andy Dougall. I call them the walking dead — drugged up, fucked up and waiting to die. But we always say that a violent life ends violent. We have to accept it; we are what we are, so it's no good crying about it. Screws fear us, so when they come in to get you it's not with kid gloves and kindness. It's violence. 'Get the bastard, lads, kick his fucking head in; strangle the fucker; break his legs.'

Rosemary Kingsland and Terri Stevens got passed to see me when I was in the Wakefield cage. I had never met them before; Rosemary is a famous writer, having been responsible for the PJ Proby biography and many bestsellers. My favourite was the one she did on the natives of South America. She actually lived amongst them for two years to research their way of life; one brave lady. Terri is a brilliant singer; she's been compared to Shirley Bassey. Two lovely ladies I admire.

Rosemary was going to be writing my life story — or I should say we were discussing it — but it all fell flat. As usual, that's how life is ... up and then down, but no problem. There was a queue to do my story, at least ten good writers; in the end, Ackroyd did one and Richards did two others and a good job they did, too.

But that visit was one of the most amazing visits I ever had, if not the most amazing visit in the history of penal visiting. I was in the cage, a gruesome hole, in the belly of the beast; Rose and Terri sat outside.

We got chatting and I said, 'Terri, can you sing a Timi Yuro (Rosemarie Timothy Aurro Yuro) number for me, it's called "Hurt"! Timi Yuro is known primarily as a one-shot artist for her fantastic version of 'Hurt' in 1961. It was a record Ron Kray let me hear and it's a favourite of mine.

Terri said, 'I sing that number in my act.'

Well, to say I was bowled over ... I was blown away.

She sang it loudly:

> *I'm so hurt*
> *To think that you, you lied to me*
> *I'm hurt way down deep inside of me*
> *You said your love was true*
> *And we'd never, never ever part*
> *Now you want someone new*
> *And it breaks my heart*

> *Whoa, I'm so hurt,*
> *Much more, oh, than you'll ever know*
> *Yes, darling, I'm so hurt*
> *Because I still love you so*

> *But even though you hurt me*
> *Like nobody else could ever do*
> *I would never, never hurt,*
> *Hurt you.*

The whole fucking jail could hear it. When she finished, the screws were clapping and cons were cheering; it was brilliant. Reg Wilson was in the next cage; he said later it was brilliant. Reg was serving natural life, and he got more time for trying to strangle a governor. Hell, that was one visit I'll never forget.

Stories like this you couldn't make up; it's just fate, meant to be, it stays in your head, a lovely memory. And do you know what? She cried as she sang it, just like Shirley Bassey does, right outside my cage door. What a memory! What a singer! What a visit! Terri and Rosemary were both sad and disgusted over the conditions I was kept in, but that song just done it for us all. It was a part of history in the making.

Screws said later they had never heard a voice like it, and with it being in the dungeon it echoed so it was three times as loud; noise travels in a dungeon, that's why you hear the screams of the tortured souls having nightmares ... or getting a kicking. I've not heard from Terri or Rosemary for years, so thanks for that day. Fucking awesome!

Curtis Warren was in Armley Jail when I met him in the '80s, on remand for a big drugs trial. He was acquitted, then he later got nicked again and copped a 12 stretch out in Holland. Whilst serving the sentence, he allegedly killed a fellow con — such is life! He's said to be worth £100m, so they say.

If I owned that much I'd buy my own prison and have Dave Courtney as the governor and I'd have a special furnished cage built just for me. It would have all the mod cons, TV, bar, jacuzzi and I'd have my wife, Saira, in for Saturday nights. I'd make it a lovely jail and there'd be no trouble in the Cat 'A' section. Any trouble and then all the troublesome cons would be shot, simple as that. I'd have no fucking about in the Bronco jail, neither would Dave Courtney, but you'd be treated decently.

Tony Balderesso got out and blew his own brains out! He got trapped after a robbery; he could either give himself up and come back to jail for 20 years, shoot himself or let the pigs do it. He did it himself — bang! One good man he was — he chose heaven instead of coming back to hell.

Mick Ahmed is an old mate of mine. I first met Mick in the early '70s up in Hull Jail. Fuck me, he could have a serious fight, and that's probably why I took to him — I love a fighter. Whilst Mick was serving his sentence, his missus was playing about ... so he got out and blew her away. He sadly got life, but what a smashing man.

Big Patsy Flanagan carved Mick Ahmed up in Gartree, and almost took him out! Mick, to this day, has a big hole in his chest, but he was strong and survived. Patsy, I must say, took him a bit slippery, as Mick was just getting out of bed and was half-asleep. They were pals, too!

I was in Gartree in the 1980s when Mick's dad died; a sad day for Mick, I felt for him. His father was a proud Asian man, a very well-respected man; it blew a big hole in Mick's life. He's now out and doing well.

Ron Gibson got seriously served up in Parkhurst by a mob of Londoners, but Ronnie deserved it. He did get silly at times but he survived it and kept silent. That's how you suss a guy out. Many grass, go for compensation, play on the sympathy side and it may get them parole, but they're just rats and reptiles.

Sonny Carroll was a funny fucker, a typical Scouser. He got up on the bathhouse roof in Walton Jail for a spot of sunbathing. An all right game fucker, but done too much bird.

Les Joyce had a nice escape when he had it away from Maidstone Jail; he later died on the run. At least he died free!

Micky Fenton had a nice escape, too, off the van! We all knew he was gonna make a break; he was on his way for accumulated visits to his local jail from Parkhurst. He pulls out a tool and hijacks the van. Sadly, he only lasted a short spell and we were all gutted when he came back to Parkhurst, but it was a legendary escape.

That's always been my dream, to escape, but I'm under such heavy security. I'm forever cuffed up to two burly screws, plus I'm cuffed to myself! If I'm not like that, I'm in a body belt! How can I escape? It's just not fair, they don't give me a fucking chance! But now I'm older and wiser, I see no point in making an escape, 'cos I've got my family to think about. I do want to spend my autumn years with them in freedom ... legally!

Did you know Patsy Kensit's old dad was once nicked with Ron and Charlie Kray (nothing big), but it's probably his claim to fame to be nicked with the Krays! Jimmy Kensit was his name. Ron told me years ago, 'Strange how a lot of the big stars like to hang around with the "faces"'. Well, stay clear of me – you'll get a bad name with me. You'll end up in the asylum, I tell you!

Patricia Jude Francis Kensit, born 1968, in Hounslow, London, says that, early in her career, she was advised to pretend her father was an antiques dealer. Patsy's childhood memories are of criminals coming to her house. 'When I was little, I remember opening a door and seeing all these men doing what they called a "count up" in our living room. I'd never seen so much money. It was difficult for me as a child because I was never allowed to have friends over to my house like other children.'

Frank Conteh, John Conteh's brother, was a flash fucker. I think Frank was serving a six stretch – may have been seven. He thought he was his brother, John, and lived off John's image. What a fighter John was ... awesome! I'd say he was one of the finest fighters we've ever produced in his weight division; a natural born fighter he was.

Harry Roberts, Freddie Sewell, John Duddy, Charlie McGhee and so many other cop killers ... I've done bird with them all and all of them, believe it or not, are nice guys. Freddie used to make clocks; Harry used to make jewellery boxes and Charlie used to rebel against authority! He later died up in Frankland very mysteriously. Duddy died in Parkhurst from a heart-attack. You'd be amazed at how many die in jail, especially under mysterious circumstances.

Winston Silcott has had a tough old time of it. In 1984, Winston was the victim of a knife attack by three men at a party. Winston was handed a knife and ended up stabbing Anthony Smith. Winston reported the attack to the police, and was arrested. Two weeks later, Anthony Smith died from the knife injuries. His face and abdomen had been slashed, he had a lacerated lung, and had been stabbed in the heart.

Winston gets bail. But the following year, 1985, a police officer, Keith Blakelock, was murdered during the Broadwater Farm disturbances in North London. Three men were arrested – Engin Raghip, Mark Braithwaite and Winston Silcott.

All three men protested their innocence. Police photographs of Winston were released to the press forever condemning him a murderer. He was guaranteed an unfair trial for the death of Anthony Smith in the atmosphere of retribution.

So Winston was banged up for life with no future, but in 1991 the 'Broadwater Farm Three' were pardoned and freed. Mark Braithwaite and Engin Raghip were released, but Winston remained in prison, serving a life sentence for the death of Anthony Smith. Now that's what I call insanity! You win some and you lose some!

Big H McKinney killed five ... but did he? Some say he was a London hit-man, all 6ft 7in of him, but I say he got a raw deal. John Childs, the supergrass, went QE on Big H, putting him away for life, but 'H' is still fighting his case after more than 20 years. That's a long time to fight – endless time! He's still in max secure, an old man dying. I believe he's innocent, I really do!

Eddie Browning got life over the Marie Wilkes murder. It was a horrific case. She broke down on the motorway; she was pregnant and she got stabbed to death. Browning claimed he was innocent; I believe him and it turned out he was when he won his appeal, but not without serious mental scars. Browning has since cracked up and ended up in a 'nuthouse'. I hope he can fight it, I really do, but I doubt he ever can.

The compensation can't ever make it right! The system destroys people, turns them mad. Go ask the Birmingham Six how they feel or the Guilford Four, or all the other poor sods who have spent years in jail under this insane system. Go and ask the families how they feel, or see the graves (many died from the stress). Compensation can't bring them back. That's what it does, first insanity and then death! You die mad ... no one wants to know, people forget.

Ruth Ellis – do you remember her? You should do, 'cos this country killed her, hanged her 'til she was dead. She killed her lover, a crime of passion, and we killed her. Did you know women who hang have to wear big plastic pants to stop their insides falling out? It can be messy! You probably don't want to know, as you may not like to know the gruesome details.

Did you know most hangings never even snapped the neck of the alleged criminal, they choked to death? It's fucking madness; we hung Ruth Ellis in the mid '60s; she was the last woman to be topped in the UK. Not so long back, is it? A true tragedy of British justice. Ruth Ellis was the fifteenth and last woman to be hanged in England in the twentieth century. Fifty thousand signatures on a petition for mercy were sent to the Home Office. Typical of them, they took no notice of it. Just like the Home Office of today ... out of touch with society.

Albert Pierrepoint, the notorious hangman, had dropped more than 400 in his 25-year reign as king of the hangmen. At Holloway Prison, Ruth Ellis was led into the execution chamber at 9.00am on 13 July 1955 and, without fuss, Pierrepoint was to have Ruth swinging within ten seconds of her entering that room.

Her wrists were strapped behind her back and her ankles were shackled. She was then placed over the gallows trapdoor. Pierrepoint then placed a white hood over her head, securing it with the noose. He tightened the rope around her neck, adjusting the rope's suspension point about one inch in front of her lower left jaw. The lever was pulled; the doors opened with a bang – CRACK! Ruth Ellis's neck snapped and she was dead.

I met a screw in Wandsworth who had worked in Holloway,

and he swore he saw the ghost of Ruth Ellis. I believe him, 'cos if I was Ruth I'd have come back to scare the shit out of the system. What a wicked nation we are! I've met cons in the death cell waiting to be hanged; obviously, by the time I met them, they were reprieved and left with a life sentence.

Big George Wilkinson was maybe the most violent man in the system that I can recall. In the '70s he was a feared man, a big strapping six-footer with a 56in chest; no gym, just natural build. He was a Geordie, and he fucking loved a hostage or two. The cages were built for the likes of George, as he had awesome power; in Durham Jail he took the doors off!

Big Lenny McLean never did much bird; he was too smart for it. He knew how to stay out, but the bit he did, he did his way; if Lenny had ever got big bird, I think he would have found it hard to get out. Sure as day turns to night, he would have ended up in a cage for the incurable if not the insane, as it was Lenny's nature to lash out at idiots! Fuck with people like Lenny and you got a slap, so he would have been slapping screws all day long.

Billy Williams, or Bill the Bomb, is a classic example; anyone who knows the 'Bomb' will say, 'He's a diamond, a top guy, a true Eastender!' But in jail, Bill gets into lots of aggro, as it's his nature to lash out at mugs! If you fuck with Bill, you get a right hook, simple as that! And you could never count how many copped hold of that 'Bomb' ... you're out cold. But he's not a bully: he's just a man who lives by a code of conduct; he will warn you, tell you to behave, ask you to behave and then, if it don't work – BANG! Lights out!

Proper men are never gonna accept the life of a budgie; it's frustrating and soul destroying being told when to eat, when to get up, what to do and what not to do by a bunch of fucking idiots who come under the label of 'officer'. Well, they're screws, not officers; they'll never be anything in my eyes. They're jailers, faceless people; in fact, I'll go as far as describing them as misfits, 'cos I just could not see half of them getting a job anywhere else! Fortunately, there are always a few who shine through, decent men doing a fair job. Without the small minority, the whole system would fall and crumble at the seams!

The Ape Man strangled Catweasel in Whitemoor with a fellow inmate called Caine. They both got life for it. Catweasel was a right nonce; they should have got a gold watch each. But the Ape Man is no angel himself; he got put away for life for killing an old woman, and before that he did time in Ashworth asylum for 'noncing' a kid. I actually met the Ape Man in Ashworth in the early '80s; he was only a lad of 18 or 19 at the time. He looked like one of those *Planet of the Apes* stars; same face, eyes and nose. I always laugh when I see him, as he makes me feel good … well, compared to him I'm like Brad Pitt. But when he snuffed out Catweasel, it sort of told me he's not a bad chap; he did society a favour there.

I think I'll write a book, *Evil Bastards*, 'cos I've met so many of them. Do you know most evil bastards are basically cowards? Take that Hamilton scumbag who did the Dunblane Massacre. Why did he kill all those kids? Evil! Why did Robert Black kill those three kids? Evil! Evil is evil! There is no reason. Why did Ronnie Biggs nick £2m? To live to enjoy, but look where he ended up … back in old Blighty and in the clink!

Harry Johnson (Hate 'Em All Harry) I met in Walton Jail, Liverpool, in 1974. It was my first meet with him. Now all you so-called psychos out there, you're just fairies compared to Harry! Harry was the original psycho, fearless, hateful and violent. He could offer you a sweet with one hand and stuff a blade in your gut with the other … and then take his sweet back!

There was this dickhead on our wing, who put his nose where it didn't belong. I gave him a gypsy's warning, 'Oy, be careful,' but like all dickheads he didn't listen. Harry wanted to weigh him in for real. Bear in mind, Harry was now serving 20 years and he'd only started off with seven! I told him, 'Nah, leave it to me!' Dickhead was lucky it was me. I bumped into him in the recess at 30mph and knocked him out stone cold! Suddenly, Hate 'Em All rushed in with a table leg and gave it to him! CRACK! WHACK! I had to hold on to him. 'Blimey, Harry, slow down, you'll fucking kill him!' It was only then that I realised the true meaning of the word 'psycho'! It was all over Harry's face, eyes bulging, saliva and that sick grin; it sort of made my skin go tight.

I've fought from becoming a psycho; I don't want to be one. There's a time in a man's life when he needs some peace. Sure, we all need to turn it on at times of pressure, but Harry was stuck in the psycho league, and he later died in prison.

But I loved Harry and always did; I believe prison turned him into the madman he was. A true legend, he cut George Ince; and he fought his way through and attacked his fair share of screws. That's why I loved him ... he did the screws. And when he cut Ince, that was good for me. Yeah, Hate 'Em All Harry was the original psycho!

Charlie Kray may as well have been given the death sentence when he got his 12 years for drug-dealing. They locked him up in Parkhurst. He was unwell, a bad ticker! What the fuck were they doing putting him in Parkhurst? Why not a low-category jail, a cushy jail where there's proper treatment. Some humanity.

So he takes a turn for the worse; they rush him to St Mary's Hospital. They bring Reg over from the mainland to see his dying brother. Reg had been inside for 33 years; he, too, was an old man, and he was cuffed up like a dog. Then Charlie died. Before Charlie, it was his other brother, Ronnie, and eventually Reg – three brothers. The Krays are no more – RIP.

Charles Bronson, me, I'm a serial hostage-taker, the only one Britain's ever had, and all my hostages have been taken inside. I've taken 11 hostages over the years, although the total is not strictly true because the Dr Wilson incident at HMP Winston Green was a half-hearted effort. I just had him in a head lock for a short time before having the shit kicked and punched out of me — all caught on prison CCTV video, and seen by Jack Straw.

On the video, you see double-fisted blows pummelling into my torso; you see the boots flying in and you see upwards of 50 screws attending to my urgent need for a good kicking. The video footage was banned by the High Court, so you good people wouldn't see what really goes on inside prison. If this is a lie, then let the Home Office sue me and sue the publisher of this book. My legal team has the evidence; maybe Mr Blunkett might be interested in seeing it.

Each hostage siege is different; let's take the last one where I did the teacher Phil Danielson at Hull. I lost the plot, I was afraid, in fear of my life. Sure, I did it, but what made me snap? The system made it happen, like it makes me lose my mind, it drives me mad! They tell me lies and I swallow them and then I choke. Then I have to hurt people.

They want to see me in a hole. Pour more shit on me. Torture the mad dog. I never wanted it; I never deserved it, and so I grabbed the teacher. I tied him up like a Christmas turkey. He was all mine!

I got depressed, I mean big time — dangerous! I ripped out the washing machine; there were three inches of water on the floor. The room went black. My heart blew up. A death chamber; death row; sizzle! The live electric cable had dropped into the water I was standing in! That's how it is with insanity, but I survived it!

Two-and-a-half days later, I let him go free. I went back into the hole of shit, pain and agony, screaming all the fucking way. In that time, Phil Danielson, while in my custody, accused the Prison Service of abusing his human rights. It can be clearly heard on tape, which was recorded by the Prison Service. Now doesn't that tell you something?

Tony Crabb is a good pal of mine; he got life for a murder he never committed. His case will never go away. His solicitor, Vicky King, will not let it go away either. Vicky is one of those solicitors who fights all the way. She takes on cases others run from. Tony is in his middle 40s. Recently, he's been collapsing, with blackouts and serious head pains. It's fucking obvious to us all that he needs proper treatment, tests. His blackouts are regular! Screws have had to go into his cell, pick him up and put him on his bed. What the fuck do screws know? So you can see the madness in prison life. I'm a lunatic, but even I know he needs proper treatment; but the poor guy can't fucking get it in here.

Joe Varadis (Joe the Greek) got 18 years for armed robbery, all 5ft 3in of him. I rate Joe as one of the most violent men I've met. Screws and cons were terrified of Joe. Fuck with Joe and you get seriously hurt. It was at Bristol he put 48 stitches in a screw's face. The screw thought he could take liberties with Joe. Joe slapped him, or so the screw thought. He saw his shirt turn red and he soon realised he had been cut. Another time at Parkhurst, somebody said to Joe, 'Get to an outside hospital, it's easy to escape.' So he cut his stomach so badly his guts popped out! Joe was just violent, no fear.

He later got deported back to Greece but was shot dead on an attempted escape. That's Joe — pure madness at its very best. Born violent, lived violent and died violent. I met Joe in the Scrubs block in the '80s. At that time, I myself was very violent; it was around that time I dived on the new governor, and strangled him. Oh well, that's life. Unfortunately, the screws saved him.

Frank Birley was a tough fucker — fearless and awesome! One day, up in Full Sutton, two guys stabbed him, cut him up big time. But could they put him down? Could they fuck! Frank survived it. He got 15 years at the age of 20 for big-time robbery. He served his sentence like the man he was.

Once, up in Frankland, he hit a screw so hard he broke his jaw and cheekbone. Frank got out months later and was shot dead in an accident. His mate was carrying a gun, he slipped on a grassy bank and the gun went off! A sad end to a great man we all liked.

Frank had this aura of fear around him; when he walked into a room, you knew it. All knew it. Frank spent his time in max secure, all of his years. He gave them his best shot.

Winney McGee was another violent Jock! I met Winney in Parkhurst in 1976. One night he got a knife and chased all the screws off the wing. Winney loved a fight. He served his ten stretch, got out and was stabbed to death. That's how it ends — death! Madness is just waiting for us madmen! And when it comes, you can't stop it. Few of us, if any, rot away in a hospital bed riddled with cancer, having our arse washed by some nurse.

Barry Robinson hijacked a police car with an Old Bill in it from Rhyl, North Wales, to Blackpool, back in the early '70s. They lifed him off. Barry was ex-Broadmoor and a great artist. I met him in Hull Jail in the mid-'70s. He did a painting for me. I got it framed and was gonna hand it out on a visit to my mum. Sadly, some Scottish prick upset me. Would you believe he came on heavy to me in my cell, so I nutted him and he fell on to my painting! That only upset me more, so I smashed the granny out of him.

Les Hilton was a man of fear; it oozed out of his paws. Les was a good pal of mine and so was his brother, Arthur — two hard men. Les was a big guy with a head of stone — one nut off him would put you in hospital. I used to play Scrabble with Les years ago, and I can tell you he took his game seriously. We played for Mars Bars. I was up a good 20, then some idiot upset him and off he went. When Les lost it, everyone knew about it; buildings trembled and bodies got busted up.

When Les was in Borstal in the '60s, a mob tried to take him out. He's lived with the welts and scars ever since. Ten could not put him away. Sadly, he got a 7in blade in his back in a Leeds street. He died free, as many in jail predicted he would die. Les was a hard man. He once bit a man's throat in a fight. An awesome fighter and mad as a hatter.

Vee Jay was a woman I'd met in Holloway. She began to write to me. We built up something between us. For a good year, we wrote to each other. She sent me photos ... she looked lovely. Then she got out; so she was up to see me, but she never said the photos she sent me were 20 years old! She had put on stones! It was like a fucking baby hippo walking into the room. Now I don't want to be nasty, but it put me off my porridge. For a week after it sort of shook me up.

Now I blame my old pal, Lord Longford (RIP), as I sent him up to see her in Holloway. He never told me she was a hippo! He should have warned me. I never saw her again. We were supposed to be getting married, but I soon put a stop to that by saying that, once we were married and I was released, we wouldn't be having sexual relations ... what else could I say? Fuck me, she frightened the life out of me. She had shoulders on her like Frank Mitchell and hands like George Foreman. I could have got badly bruised with her in a clinch.

When big Stevie Lannigan took a works screw hostage in Wakefield Jail in the '70s, they brought in armed cops. Steve got sent to Broadmoor for it. Would you believe he's still locked up? I bet he wishes now they'd shot him.

Peter 'Jock' Murray was and is a bully. He was on C-Unit in Parkhurst with us in the '70s. He was serving a six for violence, but all he ever did was cry about it, which was pathetic. At the time we had Ron and Reg Kray on the unit with a recommended 30 years apiece. One day, Murray got lemon in the kitchen area and I stuck a tool into his neck and told him if he ever moaned again I'd stuff it right in him. He was a big fat piece of dry shit, but sadly he got out and killed three youngsters up in Manchester and got life. He also abused and disrespected the Krays, who later made it known what a slag he was. I'm sorry I never plugged him that day, as it may have saved three youngsters' lives. Dirty, fat, useless Scottish rat, I hope you die in a cell, you scumbag, and so does every decent con.

Emma Humphreys was a lovely girl; she served 10 years of a life sentence, got out and died of a broken heart. Such a sad life she had; some prick put her on the game when she was 16 years old; she stabbed him to death, but she should have got manslaughter. Emma, I still remember her so well; such a sad girl!

Big Webby was a lunatic and still is – a lifer, 20st of him, it's his ambition to become the longest-serving lifer in history! What can you say to that? It's one title I don't fancy challenging! What a crazy fucking dream to have! If that's not the classic sign of institutionalisation, then what is? Webby has lost his soul, mind and heart; he's even lost his vision; that's sad! Insanity drove him mad!

Mad Mitch was an errand boy. Ron Knox used to use him for picking up 'bacca'. I met him in Parkhurst way back in the 1970s. Some of the tobacco would dwindle down, but you've got to make allowances for Mad Mitch (well, he had to be mad to fuck with Ronnie) and let's face facts, there is no escape, not in a jail there ain't.

It was just a normal day when my door hatch opened; it was Mitch, with his silly grin. He was on cleaning duty. 'How much will you give me for this?' he whispered while holding up a black wallet.

'Who does that belong to, Mitch?'

'I've just nicked it off a screw,' he said.

'What?'

'Yeah, out of the tea room, it was in a jacket.'

'Fuck me, let's see,' I say.

'There's no money in it, but there's documents and photos and the like.'

'Give it here, Mitch.'

'How much for it?'

'I'll get you some bacca!'

He slung it in and shut my hatch. Fuck me, a passport photo of one of the slags and his address and some other bits and pieces.

Now at this time in Parkhurst there was a lot of brutality going on, so it was only right to get back at them — but I had to work fast. I went on the yard and buried it in a bag, as I sensed Mitch would shout his mouth off ... and how right I was. At 1.00pm that day, my door burst open. 'Where is it?' Eight of them, all in those boots!

'Where's what?'

'The wallet Mitch gave you.'

'Fuck off,' I said.

After a good search, they fucked off. The next day, I got it back. The following day, a pal passed it out on a visit. It was all set. The screw got some strange calls. Funny how that place got better overnight. 'More cake, Charlie?' 'More spuds, Chas?' Life got so much sweeter for us all, but nothing lasts. That screw mysteriously left, plus Mad Mitch was never seen after that! Little rat. But the cake was nice while it lasted.

Scullion, the little prick, got two life sentences for murder. It was in Long Lartin in early 1992. He was a hobbit, a strange one. His cell was done out like a shrine — candles, Bibles, etc. He spoke little to anybody and he was a scruffy fucker. All my pals were there — Noel Gibson, Alan, Chris Haig, Stan Thompson, John Anslow, Alec Sears, John Bowden, Dominic Gallagher — so many legends. Great guys. Respect. Now I love a lunatic. Something about a madman is like a magnetic force to me.

Scullion, I noticed, was a loner, the silent type. I peeped in his cell ... it told me the madness was there. I saw him in the recess. 'Hi ... I'm Charlie.'

'Yes, I know,' he said. I shook his hand.

'Scully, they call me.'

'Oh, right! Err ... do you like a drink, Scully?'

'Yeah, but I don't get much,' he replied.

'Sorted. You and me are on the piss later,' I said.

I got a bucket of hooch (prison liquor); it doesn't taste so good, but it works. I paid a tenner for it. I shot in his cell, but I had no clothes on ... all I had on was a white sheet like the Pope. I also had a big wooden cross on a lace. I love a laugh – it was a joke. The party began. Scully and me were about to enjoy some madness. It was about 6.00pm. Lockup there was 9.00pm, so we had three hours of supping time.

By 7.00pm, I was fucking gone. We got singing songs, religious ones, but I changed the words: 'He's got the whole life world in his hands,' I sang. 'He's got a sawn-off shooter in his hands,' or 'He's got a plate of fish 'n' chips.' I was laughing, screaming, I was rolling in madness. Scullion was dancing and I was rocking. It was madness at its very best. I even blessed him. How the fuck I got back to my cell, God only knows; I was out of this planet.

I fell asleep in my Pope's outfit, then – crash! My door flew open. Shields came at me: it was morning and all hell had broken out in my cell. They were trying to drag me out. I fought for my life. Fear, it drives you on. Madness is power. Would you believe they ran out, all ten of them with their shields and MUFTI gear on.

Next, all I heard was banging and shouting. 'Leave him alone, you cunts. Charlie's done fuck all.'

My head was whizzing and my mouth was cut. I felt like I was in a nightmare. Then a governor arrived. 'Charlie, you have to go into the block.'

'But why, governor?'

'A serious allegation is being made against you. I have no choice but to isolate you whilst we investigate it.'

'But I've done fuck all, governor.'

'Leave him alone, you slags.' More bangs.

'Look, let me speak to the lads,' I said as I walked out. The entire MUFTI squad was up the top. I went to Noel Gibson's cell. 'What's up, Noel? What the fuck have I done now?'

He said, 'Best you go down, and we will all steam into the office to sort it out.'

I shouted to the lads, 'But I've done fuck all.'

Simon Bowden, the block cleaner, came to my door. I got on well with him. He'd escaped from Durham Jail in the late 1980s. A lovely escape. He's also a good armed robber. The Newcastle boys can be proud of our Simon.

'Chas, what the fuck's up?'

'I've done fuck all, Simon. I had a drink last night and they come into me like a herd of cattle before breakfast. Go and find out, Simon.'

The governor said to me, 'You're alleged to have raped an inmate!'

'What!' I went fucking mad. 'Raped a geezer? Me? How? Why? I couldn't. I've never even had a women's arse, let alone a geezer. It's not me; so there it is.'

A police investigation — I could not believe it. The governor knew it was all shit. It turned out the inmate is a nutcase and he had made similar allegations three times before and all were the same lies.

The police came in! I took a blade with me on the visit, hiding it in my mouth. My lawyer was there and two Old Bill. I pulled the blade out. 'Move and I'll cut you all.' I shouted to the screws, 'Get me a plastic mug.' I then sliced open the back of my hand. Blood rushed out like a tap. I then let it drip into the mug. Those mugs hold one pint. When it was three-quarters full, I then tore my T-shirt off and wrapped it around my hand. I gave the Old Bill the blood. I said, 'Right, let's stop fucking about. If I've shagged this inmates arse then test it. Here's my blood to prove I haven't. Now fuck off and get me the examination I need, as I've not fucked nobody's arse, but I sure will with a table leg if this isn't sorted out ... and fast.'

It took three weeks to examine all the forensics. I got six copies of it, and I personally hung them on the notice board on each of the six wings in Long Lartin. The inmate stayed in the hospital wing, then moved on to Wakefield, where he belongs with his monster pals. That dirty piece of shit almost pushed me over the edge. Good guys helped me through that bad spell, as they all know it was insanity.

We have to seriously question this incident. If I was Joe Bloggs I may have been stabbed up over it. But everyone knew me and after more than 20 years in jail, a man doesn't just start pumping arseholes. It's not in me to do it. And what was the inmate doing on the landing? It was known that he had made such statements before that were also of no substance. Or was he put up to it? Was it a plot to life Bronson off? Was it a plot to make me a target? Whatever it was, it was evil.

Days later, a screw called Brittain fell over outside my door. I grabbed his neck and lifted him up. He ran off shouting, 'Bronson attacked me.' The truth is, I never, but I wish I had now. I was moved; such a shame it wasn't to Wakefield so I could fuck that inmate for real ... with a table leg ... without any Vaseline!

Delroy Showers is a top legend from Liverpool. It was in Walton Jail in 1974 where we had a sit-in. I got a pair of scissors to stab a screw with, but Delroy calmed it down. Maximum respect.

They made these fishhooks with feathers on and plastic kids' watches in this workshop. I got half-a-dozen of these hooks, very sharp. This big, fat, useless, beer-bellied screw was on. A rat. Always nicking cons over silly things. We called him the 'Walton Walrus'.

I said to a con, 'Get the Walrus off his chair for two minutes.'

'Here, boss, look at this,' the slave said.

I strolled over to his chair and pushed some hooks into the cushion. If I only had a camera as the Walrus sat back down on it! He went red, purple, you name it – you could see the pain in his eyes. Our eyes met. He knew. He knew I knew he knew. I just smiled. Fuck you, Walrus. Next time it's in your neck. We all despise bully screws; even other screws despise them. How can you respect a bully? You can't. They're scum.

John Childs was one evil bastard – the supergrass. He got a taste for murder and he started to enjoy cutting them up, putting them in a mincer and then burning them in his fireplace; they call him the 'Butcher of the East End'. But, strangely enough, he was a fucking good armed robber; he had some lovely bits of work. But like that slag Berti Smalls he had to go and open his fat mouth and put good people away. He may as well have put Big H in the mincer as put him away for life. How the fuck can a grass sleep in peace after putting people in jail.

Bob Maynard and Reg Dudley got life in the '70s in the Headless Corpse Trial. After they got life, the head turned up in a London toilet. Someone went in for a shit and a fucking head was in the pan, looking at him! A fucking nightmare or what? I met Bob in Wandsworth and then later in Parkhurst where he kept protesting his innocence. In July 2002 both Maynard and Dudley were cleared of the murder by the court of appeal. Good luck, lads.

If a man's into shaging arses, prison's got to be home from home. Me, I've never even shagged a bird's arse, let alone a geezer's. I'm afraid I'm old fashioned – arses are just arses to me. Sometimes I wish I could, as I'd not be as frustrated as I am. I'm just one of many who has to go without sex and pull my dick when I fancy releasing some tension.

Steve Lannigan was a serious customer, another six-footer, a Manchester lad; he got life when he was 17 years old. He's still in, 30 years later! He took a screw hostage up in Wakefield; they sent him to Broadmoor over that, but Steve caused so many problems there they slung him back into the prison system. He pulled the roof off at Parkhurst; he's just in a vicious circle! Last I heard he's got a bad ticker; at 47 he's looking 87 and he won't make it ... he knows it only too well; the body bag awaits! Just another statistic, sad but true.

Look at that Lily Savage geezer, heart-attack at 40-something! If you don't look after your body then you pay a price. That's why I'm constantly keeping fit. Wait 'til you read my book *Solitary Fitness* ... it'll blow you away!

Ferdie Lieveld is a big black guy. He got life in '88 over some stabbings, but in the 14 years he's been away, no man has survived so much violence as Ferdie! He's been stabbed up, scalded and brutalised. You name it and he's had it! Personally, I like the guy 'cos I love a survivor and he fights the system, so I admire that. But in Brixton, D-Unit, he had a problem with Charlie McGhee. Charlie was at the time on remand for armed robbery and shooting a 'pig'. He was a seriously respected face; everyone respected Charlie.

Ferdie stabbed him with some scissors; in that attack, Mickey Reilly, another armed robber, smashed Ferdie with a table leg. Charlie was rushed to hospital and survived, but Ferdie was now a marked man amongst the London faces. Headquarters knew this, so it was their duty to keep Charlie and Ferdie apart.

Two years later, they put them both in the same jail up in Frankland. It happened on the yard. Ferdie got jumped on and stabbed up, but survived. So the question has to be asked, why were they together? Simple – it was planned. They are both Cat

A' and both dangerous; the 'pigs' and the system hate both. Putting them together, one will die or get hurt. That's the only reason, but the headquarters will not admit it. How can they? But they haven't commented on how they made the mistake! Why? 'Cos they're gutless, spineless pigs! That's why, and it happens all the time!

Basically, they're responsible for a lot of the violence in jails and they cause it! They love it when we attack and kill each other. Last time I saw Ferdie was about two years back in Woodhill unit; he's still the same — smiling. The system can't beat that man and it never will! These 14 years he's served, I bet ten of those years have been spent in solitary. He sings, he laughs and he does his press-ups. Ferdie is a good man! Max respect!

John Cannon was three cells away from me in Whitemoor seg unit. I kept telling him to be a man and do the right thing and top himself; amongst the prison fraternity, they all believe he knows about the Suzy Lamplugh murder.

Old Bill Taylor was a nice old boy, ex-professional boxer; he got lifed off for killing his wife. She was playing about and he snapped and killed her. It was in Full Sutton about ten years back, I walked into the bathroom for a shower and Bill was in the bath. 'Hey! Charlie, I don't want to bother you, mate, but look at this.' I looked at him standing in the bath. 'Look, Chas.'

I couldn't believe it; his bollocks were like blown-up balloons! 'I can hardly walk, Chas — I'm in pain.'

'Fucking hell, Bill, how has it got like that, have you seen a doctor?'

'Few months, Chas, I think it's cancer!'

'Look,' I said, 'you gotta get some treatment, you can't live like that!'

He finally saw the doctor and it was cancer, but it had spread to other organs; he had left it too late. He was a proud old boy; he died within six months. Insanity never had time to drive him mad; it just killed him. I used to have some nice chats with Bill about all the old-type boxers; he idolised Marciano, poor old sod.

Paul Sykes was in Walton Jail with me back in '74. He got out and fought John L Gardner for the British Heavyweight title. Sadly, he lost. Gardner went on to manage a pub near Newcastle. During an attempted robbery in the '90s, he was stabbed in the gut and became a shadow of his former self, refusing to ever leave his home.

Paul's a big Yorkshire guy who was born to fight. When he hits you, you go down and stay down – few get back up. In Strangeways on a protest in the yard, he knocked out the biggest screw in the jail. Only to be sticked and restrained by 20 more.

Paul's got no fear; he is what he is ... man amongst men. The crazy thing is his old dad was a screw in Wakefield. I bet his old dad lost some sleep over him. I remember when Paul got the prison cat and made a Davey Crockett hat out of it ... he killed it and cut off its fur. That day, a lot of the cons hated him, but it's incidents like that out of which legends are made!

Some of the best cons I ever met were in Liverpool; Scousers to me are such funny people – good hearts and a good sense of humour. Sadly, over the last ten years drugs have destroyed the Liverpool people and scumbags are taking over Liverpool! Just as in Manchester, a lot of scumbags are taking serious fucking liberties! Even kids are getting shot dead in the streets over drug wars; it wasn't like that 10, 20 or 30 years ago. You had some proper villains up that way, men of honour and dignity with morals. The Scousers have always been decent to me, so it saddens me to hear about all the filth on the streets now.

Freddie Foreman, Eddie Richardson, Alan Byrne, Charlie McGhee, Ray Johnson, the Dunford brothers and my old pal Eddie Holland were all banged up in the '80s in Full Sutton;

some great guys there. I mean 'top men', real villains. Eddie Holland was a great fighter, a Leeds man. When I got out, I went to Leeds on some business and I met Eddie in the Trotters pub; he was on the door. That night, he knocked three out in the car park. That's Eddie Holland for you — top man! You don't mess with men of his quality. It was lucky it never got ugly, as that night I had three guns on me! Crazy! I actually thought at the time, Oh well, in for a penny, in for a pound! I was buzzing, just out of jail, so shooting someone's leg off would be fun — to me, at that time, it meant nothing. I'd probably have picked the leg up and bashed his head off with it!

Jack Cronin, my uncle, came to see me on a visit in Gartree in 1987. Kelly Anne was with him and she always used to smuggle me in a drink, vodka, a little treat for me. But on this visit I hadn't eaten for two days and I was on one of my 'clean outs'. I often stop eating for two or three days and I just drink fluids. I often like to clean out my system. You feel great; light, fast, healthy and even your shit shines. So on this visit the vodka hit me. I felt the room whizzing. How the fuck I got off that visit is beyond me. I don't even remember why I knocked out a screw, but I remember waking up in the box in a body belt. That cost me 100 days' remission and 56 days in solitary and a £10 fine, but that's how it is in jail — mad!

Only weeks earlier, the most infamous prison escape took place in the UK. Gartree Prison, up, up and away. Bear in mind it was where I was released from 69 days earlier. I was set free, a Cat 'A'. A Cat 'A' is a status of danger to the public; that's how fucking insane it all is — we are labelled dangerous one minute and then let out the next!

Sid Draper and John Kendall were the two to escape. I know both, but more so Sid. I met Sid in Hull back in 1974; he had just copped a life sentence and 28 years after a robbery that went wrong. On our first meet, we got on great. John I met in

Parkhurst some years back; he's just pure gold, an Eastender, we all love him. So they flew out. The chopper landed on the football pitch and the screws just freaked out; even the dogs looked puzzled.

Good cons held a lot of screws back, so John and Sid could get on the rope. If it were not for them cons, it could not have happened. Men like John Anslow, top guys. Anyway, I'm in the police station being quizzed over the James Tobin jewellery robbery in Luton when one copper just said, 'Nice little escape, Charlie, the other week.' I looked at him; he smiled and said, 'You wasn't involved, was you?' I looked again ... he smiled. I thought, fuck me, do they think it was me? Sadly, John and Sid got caught. John first and Sid a year later.

Andy Russell was the guy who hijacked the chopper, another Eastender who became a pal of mine. It was while in Leicester Jail, when he was on a hunger strike, I got up on the roof for him to get him some publicity, as they were taking fucking liberties with him and his case. He was a game fucker; he got ten years over that escape and another 16, consequently, for a slag. But he did his bird like a man. He's out now – well done. John Kendall's also out. Poor Sid, though, is still in; such is life, but that was a beautiful escape, the only one of its kind in the UK.

Imagine it! You're out on the exercise yard, walking around in max secure, screws watching, dogs and cameras; there's two walls, a fence, razor wire and then out of the sky comes a roar, all look up ... it's coming closer. Is it SAS, is it terrorists or could it be a VIP? All stop. It lands on the football pitch, dogs barking, screws running and cons cheering.

Then two cons run for it, get in and up, up and away. 'Tally ho ... toodle pip, old chap ... up yours, we shafted you pigs, have a nice Christmas.'

I've often thought about it. I believe if I were there that day, then I'd have run and hung on to the bottom of the chopper. I'd have had to. I couldn't let a golden opportunity pass me by; it was freedom on a plate ... flying out of hell. Leave the madness behind! I'd have dropped my pants and shit on the pigs as we went. I've always wanted to escape but I've as much chance of escaping as a pig can fly. It's impossible when you've a label like me; I'm just a piece of the machinery — that's what I am ... rusted in!

13

PRISON MADNESS

Prisons are the most shaming of all our public institutions. This country, the United Kingdom, imprisons more of its people than virtually any other country in Western Europe in conditions that are frequently an affront to civilised values, and at great cost to the taxpayer. Yet the vast majority of our prisoners don't present a serious threat to life or limb. Their crimes are such that they can be more humanely, economically and effectively dealt with in the community.

There would seem to be those who are highly enthusiastic when it comes to imprisonment, which isn't surprising. How else are these people to get their rocks off at night? They've got to have some nice thoughts in their head to wank over ... cunts!

Prison has a poor track record. I dare any one of those in power to show the relationship between a society's rate of incarceration and its rate of crime. Prison keeps some offenders off the streets, but it definitely doesn't deter the majority of offenders who go on to become recidivists; neither does it reform.

I ask you a question – for how long have they been locking people up in prisons? Thousands of years! So how do you evaluate the effectiveness of prison, which has been repeatedly condemned as a blunt instrument of torture, yet has been continuously used by those you class to be intelligent? Let me tell you this. One day, prison will be outlawed and laughed at as much as the slave ships of the past that became obsolete! Eventually, prison will only exist for the most dangerous of humans, mark my words!

Prisoners do not remain in prison for ever. Some will be living right next door to you; some will be your employers and employees and some will even be in positions of power. Only a tiny handful of the 70,000 behind bars will never be released. Those who are released should be encouraged to lead law-abiding lives and be fully integrated back into the community. If they, cons, are 'damaged' or disillusioned by their detention, then how easy will it be to integrate them back into society without any trouble?

Prison is the easy way out for the government of the day. Look at what's happened under Labour rule. The prison numbers rapidly increased; this reflects the fear of crime. 'Lock the fuckers up, that'll stop the crime' mentality is not always the most appropriate answer to how punishment should be dished out or served up. But when prison is the only option, then we must ensure that it is a just and effective punishment and that prisoners are encouraged and helped in their efforts not to return. Prison should not be used as camouflage for secret punishment beatings or mistreatment of its inmates like it currently is, and has been in the UK for the last few hundred or so years.

- Fact – Every prisoner costs about £25,000 a year to keep in custody. A night in a police cell costs more than a night in a London hotel. To keep me banged up costs between £100,000 and £150,000 per year.

- Fact — Only one in three prisoners are behind bars because of an offence involving violence, sex or drugs. Many of the remainder have committed only minor property offences.
- Fact – 20 per cent of all prisoners have not been convicted of any offence. Yet 40 per cent of these are not judged to need a prison sentence when they come to court.
- Fact — Half of all prisoners (and nearly two-thirds of young prisoners) are recidivists within two years of being released.
- Fact — Up to a third of prisoners have some identifiable psychiatric disorder. So why lock them up? Out of sight, out of mind.
- Fact — Remand prisoners, who have not been found guilty of any crime, suffer the worst conditions and regimes.
- Fact – Prison officers have a high rate of job dissatisfaction and a high rate of time off work due to sickness.
- Fact — Three-quarters of young offenders discharged from prison are reconvicted after two years.
- Fact — People who should be cared for by the mental health system wrongly end up in prison.
- Fact – Human rights activists are more interested in sensationalist international cases.
- Fact – Human rights abuses still continue against prisoners in the UK.
- Fact — Community penalties cost less than prison and can work better.
- Fact — On average, one prisoner commits suicide every few weeks.

- Fact – Not enough is done to stop prisoners returning to crime.
- Fact – Prison is ineffective and does not help reduce crime.
- Fact – Nearly all prisons are overcrowded.

I first hit jail in 1969, on remand. It was Risley. So I have experience of prison life; some would say I'm institutionalised. But I'm not. Now let me explain why and how prisons today are full of shit. It's simple – they're run by shit.

Years ago prison officers were responsible, smart people. They had morals. Ninety nine per cent were ex-Forces, so they had seen discipline. You could see your reflection in their boots and their shirts were crisp from being starched.

Screws today are a different breed; three-quarters of them are spineless prats, never done fuck all and never will do fuck all. They're not even has-beens; they're complete wasters, and their qualifications are fucking nil. But they still become screws in spite of this. If you don't believe me, ask some of the older screws.

Some screws chew gum, wear earrings, have ponytails and they don't respect themselves. Now don't get me wrong, I'm not painting them all with the same brush. But it's a fact; many are useless! We now have a large percentage of female screws. Now let's be honest, why do women want to work in a man's jail? We are men and only human. We go years without sex. Do we need the smell of fanny in our faces? Isn't it a tease?

Your door opens, the smell of sweetness, scent, a pretty face and lips enter; is it fucking normal? At times, I wake up with a big erection. I get out of bed to piss and a screw may look through my door flap ... or I'm having a shit ... is it normal? It's fucking insanity.

Governors – 90 per cent of them are not like the governors

of old, which is only natural with this accelerated promotion thing they've got in place these days. They're weak and they're afraid to make decisions without first securing the consent of Prison Service headquarters. They have no backbone. Many are straight out of college. They have no idea about how to treat humans; we're just a number and a photo in a book to them, we've no characters or personalities and no emotions or feelings. We're a one-dimensional picture. They have no idea about life. In fact, those pricks cause a lot of today's problems in jails, as there's no real authority.

Old governors had character, guts, were fearless and they were a smart bunch of bastards. We hated them but we admired their fairness. A governor has got to have a heart. He or she can be the meanest fucker on the earth, but a good governor will make a decision and stick to it — go down with the ship. Nowadays, they're rats on a sunken ship.

They say something on a Monday, and change it on a Tuesday. Prison used to be a regime with a routine. Everybody knew where they stood. The Prison Chief was the man who ran the jail. He was always a smart man, immaculately dressed and with the silver crown polished on his peaked hat. He would creep around the jail and catch the screws that were not liked.

Nowadays there are no Chiefs, they've been done away with. The Senior Officers and Principal Officers were once men of leadership. If you went to them with a problem, then you would get an answer and no passing the buck. Everything was routine, all timed. Nowadays, there are no bells. A prison without a bell is like having a car with no brakes.

The days of respect are over. Fat, useless, scruffy, gutless screws are the norm. In the old days you got bashed up and it was over. You either went back at them or you got on with it. Now they torture you. Not just with a kicking, but also mentally. They use psychology on us.

Prison was porridge for six days a week and cornflakes on a Sunday. Now we get porridge twice a week, if we're lucky. It's all Sugar Puffs now and soggy Rice Crispies.

Years ago we had piss pots, and we could press a bell to slop out and have a shit in a toilet. Now we have toilets in our cells. We live in a fucking toilet. It's not for our benefit! It's for the screws, 'cos now they don't have to unlock us so much. Screws of today are a disgrace and a joke. How can it all be justified? Just look at the slobs leaving the jail after their shifts — dirty shirts, unpolished shoes, crinkled trousers, long hair, earrings, gum chewing, fags in their mouth and tattooed hands with lots of rings. These are prison officers?

They're meant to teach us how to live, and these people have one of the highest rates of divorce, alcoholism, bullying and debt. It's a joke.

Prison of today — it's divide and conquer. Why put us into groups? Basic, Standard and Enhanced. It causes friction; cons fight cons. That's the idea of it, 'cos as long as we are fighting each other then the screws love it.

The Basic regime (which I'm on) gets fuck all; bad visits and no privileges, whilst the Enhanced regime gets it all. It's like at school ... prefects!

On the Basic prison regime, screws despise me and governors hate me. Doctors fear me, while cons dream of doing what I do. 'Cos at the end of the day, 90 per cent of cons are 'yes' men, strutting around the jails in their nice tracksuits, and they go on their visits acting the big one. But the screws are laughing at you all. If you were all on the Basic regime, we could beat the whole system and all would be treated decently.

The Strangeways riot was for everyone. These men lost years to better prisons. They suffered terrible brutality. They spent years in solitary. And all for what? 'Cos prisons today, years later, are worse. Me? I'm probably best off in a cage away from the scruffy fat screws and dykes trying to be men. I'm better off away from the drug mug cons and spineless governors. I'm best away from the whole shovel of shit.

Some will say, 'Who the fuck does he think he is?' Well, I'll tell you who I am; I'm the guy who tore off eight prison roofs. I'm the guy who's had eleven hostages. I'm the guy who's spent 24 years in solitary. I'm the guy who's fought for you lot. I'm the guy who's attempted to fight the bully screws. That's who I fucking am. I'm nearly 50 years old and I don't fuck with drugs. I don't poke arseholes and I don't sniff glue. I don't mug old women and I don't bully people and I don't strut around jails flexing my biceps.

Headquarters want me in a box, 'cos they're like that — they've no backbone; no guts and are too afraid to give an impartial decision. Let me tell you guys and girls, few cons ever get to see me, but all seem to know me. Lots like to slag me, condemn me. But why don't you turn your anger on the shits who abuse your rights?

A young man of 22 came into prison. Six months for a poxy driving offence; he's a worker. Never been in jail before, so it's all hell to him. The noise, the arrogance of the screws, the hate, the violence and the homosexuality are too much for him, he can't believe it. He's doubled up in a cell with a drug addict. Soon he's swallowing pills! Smoking dope! Snorting coke! The drug mug gets a needle, they inject. That young man of 22 is now hooked up big time! His life is now over.

He goes out evil; he steals and mugs to get money to buy his daily drugs requirement. He comes back into jail. He gets Hepatitis B or AIDS. He sucks a cock for a snort; he takes a cock for two snorts. He sells his soul. The system created this monster; is that not insanity? If not, what is it? And it's happening every day in the jails of the UK. Prison actually breeds these lost souls.

Category 'A' security status is another madness; we are a

separate breed of convict – assessed as high-risk, a danger to the public. We are moved in high-security conditions. Even here in jail, escorts move us about. They have a book with our photograph in. All movements are timed and signed in. Some of us get to be categorised; others never do. I am one of those guys who stays on category 'AA'. I've been released while on it and it's madness. How can it be right? There is no rehabilitation for us Category 'A' or 'AA', so how can we change or alter our ways?

HMP Belmarsh in the early and middle 1990s housed a lot of IRA men. One you might remember was that big 20st one caught in London; armed pigs got him at a bus stop. The police told him to put the parcel down and get on his knees and crawl away. There he was, all 20st of him, crawling all the way to a 20-year sentence, but that same guy lost 6st in about three months. The time he spent in Belmarsh he used it to get fit. I was right impressed with him; I told him, 'You've got a lot of determination.'

Then they nicked those Warrington bombers. They were all coming in. One had a rumble with the screws so all the screws did was bend him up and take him to the box. OK, he might have got a slap, but would you believe he was crying ... fucking crying! I told the cunt, 'Behave, grow up, get used to it because it's a long, hard road ahead.'

It was when Del Croxon died in Belmarsh, the IRA upset me. Del just died in his cell; a great guy, a big strong fucker who could bench press 500lb easy. The day of Del's funeral service, that same night they were playing Irish rebel songs. It fucking upset me! A big screw was on nights. Now this screw was a diamond, so I wrote a note out and gave it to him. I said, 'Give this to the Irish lads.'

He said, 'I will, but I'm not supposed to.'

The music stopped; I was very relieved over it, and I didn't need a war.

There was a big, fat, ugly screw in Belmarsh said I terrified him and he was in fear of being taken hostage. It was pathetic to hear all this and read it in the press; the screws and cons were all disgusted. This prick was 6ft 4in, 18st and about 40 years old! That's how it is in prison – mad!

It was 24 June 1993. I arrived in the special unit with six screws in the van with me; I had the body belt on – I go nowhere without it these days. In reception was a big mob waiting for me. I recognised the Principal Officer from way back up in Armley. He was a handful in the 1970s! We had words years back; I always found him fair, although he jumped me when I arrived at Armley years ago. But I don't harbour a grudge; I was a young nutcase in those days, so I probably was half to blame.

This PO told me the second I walked into Belmarsh that I was going in the block. The unit I went on is part of the special Cat 'A' wings. There were 48 Cat 'A' inmates, mostly IRA terrorists, drug barons, killers, bank robbers, all danger men in the eyes of the law. They could watch TV, play football, tennis, association and pool – only I couldn't.

My pal, Peter Pesito, was allowed to see me in the block. Pete's a great mate. Big Ronnie Johnson was also there; a gentleman. I always give it time before I kick off. The unit governor was a little fat rat whom nobody liked. I fell out with him, as he tried it on; he lied. This was in the first week; we had words.

He had no idea how to treat long-termers so I fucked him off. I can't respect a sack of shit. So there I was in Belmarsh unit – alone. The first week went by feeling each other out; the second week was the easiest bit of porridge I've ever done, but I had one bad day when the sack of shit upset me, so I started to smash my cell door down but, fortunately, nothing came of it. They all knew who'd upset me! The block screws, I can only respect them, they treated me fairly.

I got a bit of gym, plenty of exercise and extra food. One particular screw, Mick Reagan, was one of the best screws I've come across; he was only in his late 20s, but a solid guy who does not stab in the back. He tells it to your face and if all screws conducted themselves like him then prison would be a better world.

He and several others went out of their way to make my stay comfortable. Mick slung the 12lb medicine ball at me and another one, Mark, helped me out in the gym. They even got me a tennis net to play tennis in the cage. Basically, I was happy. They gave me a lot of trust; bear in mind, I am Cat 'AA'. I've normally got six screws all over me, watching.

Right outside my cell was an electronic camera. This unit, even today, is the most up-to-date secure unit in Britain. Some doors even screws cannot open, as they're electronic. Cameras zoom in to all the doors; it's much like something out of a science fiction film. Security is the number-one priority – cons and screws alike, we're all being monitored! My only problem was not being allowed to go on the wings with the other Cat 'A's, but there was one inmate up there whom I had been told to stay clear of if I came up; a Rastafarian, a filthy rapist who was actually serving life and had come down from Wakefield Jail for accumulated visits. He was a fucking disgrace to our human race.

Yeah, I was getting back to sanity. I felt good there. I ate well, trained hard and slept peacefully; it was only weeks away until one of my famous trials. Then days later, on my twenty-eighth day there, Ben, a senior officer, came into the block with other screws. I knew by their expressions it was time to go. 'OK, Charlie, you're away!' I was gutted, fed up, depressed. Why move me again? It was the Home Office playing games and it was unjust. I stripped off and they put me in the body belt and that's how I left Belmarsh – naked and trussed up like a Christmas turkey.

A lot of the screws said it was a wrong decision and they were genuinely concerned. Two in particular shouted to me as I got in the van, 'Behave, Charlie, good luck.' Obviously, it's not their doing; they can only do as they are told. As the van drove out of Belmarsh, I felt betrayed, even more so to begin a 200-mile trek. It's no fun being tied up and travelling to destinations that you don't need! But nothing ever lasts, does it?

HMP Bristol had a new gate lodge when I arrived on 22 July 1993. It was four years earlier that I last hit this jail. Now I was arriving all trussed up and naked from Long Lartin and, exactly the same as the last time I arrived at this prison, I went into the strong box!

This box has three doors to get in to it; it's the old-type box, 'empty' except for a mattress, stone-cold floor, bad lighting and air vents blocked up with 100 years of shit. Armies of cockroaches, mice, damp and crap food, but what's new, it's all I know — I'm the ultimate survivor.

A Board of Visitors member, Mr Wicks, came in to see me. I explained the position to him — 'I am not leaving this box 'til the van comes; I will not wear clothes; I will not slop out or wash or shave; I will not see anybody, including my solicitor.' There I was, six weeks away from my trial, I'm 220 miles away, my mind is full of bad thoughts; I'm actually feeling dangerous!

My sights were set. I remained boxed up in the concrete coffin. A doctor called Brown, an old boy, kept coming to see me — it's no secret I despise the fuckers, so I shouted at him every day, 'I want some chocolate; fuck off if you ain't got me none.' Obviously, no prison doctor gives cons chocolates, it's unheard of, and then, lo and behold, he comes in with a big bar of Cadbury's Fruit & Nut for me. I nearly fucking fell over. It goes to show not all of them are vets! The governor, doctors and Board of Visitors came to see me twice every day.

On the fourth or fifth day, I started to hallucinate and felt a dry mouth. I'm convinced I had been spiked. The hallucination consisted of cracks moving in the wall. A mark moving on the wall, stains, maybe it was stress or my eyes were fucked, as I had not been washing at all and I was stinking.

On the sixth day, I got a cramp in my gut, a bad pain. I was sick and had the shits real bad. The box was now stinking, as I was marking the days off on the wall with my shit! I shit and shit; my pot was being taken out and slopped out for me, as I would not come out. It's really something to watch, six screws coming into the box to bring my food and slop my pot out.

Messages were coming to me from my solicitor, but I could not phone as they refused to bring in an extension line. I had nothing – no books, no radio and no bed. This was the old days all over again – real porridge. My thoughts were all 'bad'; every time they came in either to slop my pot out or bring food in, I thought of taking a hostage, but these screws in Bristol were not to blame. The odds of grabbing a governor in a box are almost nil. But these type of thoughts I have to fight, otherwise it's a never-ending pain.

My mail, surprisingly, was being redirected from Belmarsh. I got letters from my brother Mark who was out in Italy. I racked my brains. 'Why have they done this to me?' My only thought was Linda Calvey's appeal being heard at the time. (Calvey had been dubbed 'the Black Widow', but I renamed her 'the Black Rose'.) But why should that get me moved 200 miles away?

The fact is, whatever reason they gave me was unacceptable; it was a liberty, and I was dug in. I was not leaving this box! Fuck Bristol, fuck the system and fuck my trial. Until the van comes, I'm in my coffin!

I started to sleep by day and walk up and down at night with a few press-ups every once in a while. But with no water, soap or towel I couldn't let myself go, as a wash is essential after a work-out. I sang a lot, loud, Christmas carols and Tom Jones numbers. I find singing releases tension, but my shits never helped. At one point, I had a pot full of shit and I still needed another one. It must have been food poisoning as I was sick as well; I started shitting on the floor. That box stank like a cattle shed. Strange how you get used to it. Survival.

Yes, it's crazy how a man's pride can take him to the limits! It did my neck no favours sleeping on the floor; I must be getting old. On 30 July they came in with smiles. 'You're away, Charlie.' That was a breath of fresh air well needed, I can tell you. I refused clothes! They strapped me up in the body belt and off we went. As we got to the van, which was parked outside the block, there were dogs, screws and even a governor, all watching. I stopped and gulped in some of that beautiful air; it was like food!

People just do not realise how lucky they really are. Believe me, when I say this, I truly love the world. To see flowers animals, trees and even the sky is heaven. Anyway, I felt good. Obviously, I must have looked a mess; nine days of not washing, no shaving and no clothes. Two screws jumped in the front, four in the back and the madman – off we shot.

HMP Brixton was home to me in 1988, I was on D-Unit, maximum secure. I was held there in a cage a cell with two doors; a barred iron door that you could put your arms through, and the outer door was a solid steel door. In the daytime, they left my outer door open so I could see the day-to-day life on the unit. Cons used to come to see me, have a chat or play chess – the unit held Cat 'A' remand prisoners.

On the unit at the time was Valerio Viccei, the mastermind of the £60m Knightsbridge Safety Deposit Box Robbery. Valerio was eventually shot dead in a supposed bank raid in Italy, which is hard to believe. Some say he was riddled with eight bullets fired from an automatic as a reprisal attack. All will come out though, be sure of that. I felt at home with the likes of Charlie McGhee, Ronnie Easterbrook, Mickey Reilly and Tommy Hole.

There were terrorists, IRA, a Mafia drugs baron and even a fucking spy ... and yours truly. I was held in the cage owing to my unpredictability; those cunts are considered dangerous to civilian society, whereas I am considered dangerous to prison society.

Liam McOttor was on remand for IRA activities; his co-defendant was Paddy 'Fatso' McLaughlin — two fair guys! I don't like what they do outside, never have and never will, but they acted like men inside, with respect. Obviously, if they had bombed my manor up, or blew my people's legs off, it would have been war! In fact, they were only nicked because of a gun find. Every day Liam would come to my cage to have a chat, which I looked forward to, as I did with all the lads' chats.

Two days passed and he didn't come, so I thought, Funny! Dennis Wheeler was a drug-smuggler (20 tons of cannabis); he used to play chess with me through my bars, as did Valerio. I said to them, 'That IRA cunt is blanking me!' Like I'm some sort of prick.

Another day went by, and another. I stopped sleeping. I got ill. I developed a violent mood; all night long I'd pace my cell like a mad tiger. He's fucking blanking me ... he comes over here, kills my people, blows legs off and now he thinks he's better than me! I gave him friendship, he gives me disrespect!

The screw let me out at 7.00pm to get my supper, which was a bun and cup of 'Rosy Lee'; it was in a big steel bucket, red hot. I picked the bucket up to pour myself a pint mug when out of the corner of my eye McOttor was coming out of an office. Cunt! I rushed him and slung the tea bucket all over him. Then I let him have the bucket. The screws jumped me and slung me back in the cage.

Later, Valerio and some of the lads came to see me. 'What's up?'

I told them.

Then I'm told, 'Chas, the reason he wouldn't come to see you was because he was on trial all week ... he wasn't here!'

I shouted, 'Paddy, come to see me!' I said to Paddy, 'Look, tell Liam I want to see him.'

'He won't come,' said Paddy.

'He has to come,' I said.

'Why?' Paddy asked.

''Cos I want him to chin me or cut me through the bars.'

McOtter sent a message: 'He doesn't want to.'

I sent a message: 'He must.'

He said, 'Forget it,' so I chinned myself! Now that's madness at its best! Brought on by prison paranoia!

Isolation does affect you. So prison does and can often cause problems. And remember, I've lived alone in solitary for 24 years out of 30 years inside, so imagine how my mind gets! My diagnosis by one doctor is sensitivity, paranoia and psycho. Whatever I am, I'm me, a complete man. If I had had a gun that day, McOtter would have had a hole in his face, plus all the guards and that fucking spy!

McOtter never did speak to me again. McOtter in later years was one of six to escape off the SSU from Whitemoor Prison. I've no problem with him, but he should have chinned me when I gave him the chance, now it's still madness with me! I wish him well, but I cannot ever turn my back on him. After all, he's a terrorist and he kills people!

At HMP Full Sutton in the mid '80s, I saw a man break up into a million pieces. Have you ever heard or seen a grown man cry? Cry like a baby, lose the plot? I have, many times. Some guys I've known, others I didn't. But I've seen it; it's not nice.

One guy, he was about 40-ish, a tough-looking guy, tattoos and scars. It was crazy how it happened. He was out in the yard when he just lost it. Fuck knows how, but he caught everybody's eye. He ran up to a wall and butted it. Then he lay on the floor, screaming, crying, howling. Fuck me, I thought I was back at Broadmoor. Cons were open-mouthed, amazed and stunned in shock.

I walked over to the guy. As I looked down at him I could see the tears flowing out. It was like a boy in a man's body! Screws came over. It was embarrassing. 'What's up with him, Charlie?' they asked. Fucking idiots could see he was crying.

I bent down and said to him, 'Fuck me, mate, pull yourself together, every cunt's looking. Why not cry when you're alone?'

'Chas,' he babbled through his tears, 'Chas ... I can't take no more, I can't fucking handle it no more.'

The madness had eaten into him. Not nice to see! Sort of upsets people. They put him over in the hospital wing, and pumped him with some tranquillisers. What else could they do? He was serving 25 years. I wonder if he ever made the end. Poor sod.

HMP Hull had its fair share of loonies. It was back in 1975 when some loony came into my cell. I knew he wasn't the full shilling by the way he put himself across, plus he was just one of those guys you don't feel safe with. You just want to punch his fucking lights out. Well, this guy was for real; he was a conman, up to no good and with too few brains in his head to see his scams through.

His latest scam was for money; he wanted some cash, and his brainwave was to come into my cell, and discuss a way to get some readies. If he got cut or stabbed up, he could get compensation. I said, 'Yeah, sure ... but are you sure?' So we discussed it – the deal was he would bung me half.

So I got a couple of razors and sliced his body, but I caught his eyelid and it was a nasty one. Blood all over the place! It even squirted on me. I thought, Fuck it, I'll give him some more, as the more stitches he'd need, the more 'compo' we'd get. So I cut him from his right shoulder down to his mid back. Opened up like a glove. Then I got carried away and smashed the clown in the head with my table leg. Crazy, but I do like the sound of a skull cracking – there's no noise quite the same. I also did his legs. I never did get paid, I don't even know if he did. In fact, I've never seen him since! I doubt he ever got a penny, as he probably forgot why he did it – fucking lunatic.

Another time in Hull in the '70s, they slipped in a granny basher. Some con came into the association room with a newspaper article. We all went white with rage. We had to bide our time. Gently and easily! A game of patience – build up his confidence. Gently slide up to him ... then crush the victim. All sounds a bit evil, but it's great fun.

We drew the straws ... I got the baby; he was my take. I went whistling into the shower. 'Hey, you're the new guy, ain't ya?'

'Yeah,' he said with a cocky grin.

'One of the chaps said you're good stuff,' I said. I built him right up. I stripped off and got in the shower. Whistling like a good 'un. My razor was checked. The fucker was whistling away with me. I bet he was whistling when he beat the fuck out of the granny.

Stripe! I sliced his back down to his arse. Blood – fuck me, it was like *Psycho III*. I was soon out of there, still whistling. Once the shock kicks in, no noise. Hit 'em when they're not expecting it. But after years of cutting 'em up, you do get fed up with it, but you also get experience – you become a 'pro'. I was like an abattoir worker. Fuck knows how I never killed any of them.

My paranoia was extreme, and in another incident I could only see one way out. 'Sorry, mate, accident ...' Was it, or was he just a cunt trying it on? Did he mean to tread on my foot? Did he? Has somebody told him to do it? Did he smile? What's his fucking name? Again, for days I brooded on it 'til I could take it no more.

Those days, around the mid-'70s we used to have the weekly film on the end of D-Wing in the gym, and I'd make sure I sat behind this cunt! It was a Mafia movie; the lads loved a good gangster film. In my head, I re-examined the foot-treading incident. Did this cunt step on my foot on purpose? Too late now ... Crash! I stuck it in his neck and continued to watch the movie; he got up, staggered and fell. Some people will bleed all over the place ... got no consideration for others watching the film. That's how it is ... insanity! Did he? Didn't he? Who gives a fuck? He did it!

HMP Liverpool had its fair share of nonces, so one day I eyed up my target and I got this guy in the queue. Bosh! Right in his ribs as I passed by. I left it in him, fucking nonce. Six inches of steel went in that prick. I'm not a great stabber, but at times you've no choice. It needs to be done! We can't have filth mixing with us, can we? If there were more like me, there wouldn't be so many nonces about today. Now there are more nonces than robbers.

I remember up on the Liverpool roof, screws were shouting up to me, 'We'll break your fucking legs when you come down,' and they fucking meant it! These screws were not joking. They can get nasty, as some of them are ex-SAS. Believe it, they can kill you and think nothing of it. I've always said to young cons, 'Don't do what I do. Best you just do your time and get out fast. Don't get caught up in this madness, as it will eat you up! Let's say they've got to let us out some day, so who cares?'

Well that's bollocks, 'cos they don't ever have to let you out. If the system hates you so much, then you'll never get out; you will die inside, so don't kid yourself; it's a cruel, hard, cold fact and truth hurts, so don't allow it to destroy you.

HMP Manchester (Strangeways) had a very memorable riot in 1990; it had to happen and it was great that it did. If it hadn't, we would all still be in the Dark Ages – slopping out, overcrowding, and so on. Strangeways was a godsend: it blew the lid right off the system, but those guys who fought became victims. They still suffer for it.

Yeah, I'm sad I missed Strangeways — I've always been unlucky like that! I've never been in jails where it's blown up like that. Madness unleashed; a violent explosion of hate, heads cracked, bodies smashed and spilled blood! Keep on stabbing 'til the angels call. The system caused it. They degraded and abused men but they could not face the truth. They lied; they made it look like the system was the victim. I'll tell you now, those cons were driven to rebel; they had taken years of brutality.

Did you see the screws run? They ran out. I thought they were hard. They're only hard when they run into a man's cell in mobs of ten — basically, they're cowards. Yes, Strangeways was the riot of all riots, only, sadly, no dead nonces. Oh well, maybe next time.

At HMP Parkhurst in the 1970s, I had a dream in the back cell. At this time, my life's existence was just a shithole. I had nothing but a bare cell; two doors, one in front of the other, no window and my bed was a lumpy straw mattress with one canvas blanket. Flies, bugs and spiders; I was in hell! The screws were devils; they spat on my food, pissed in my tea, beat me and abused me. I cut one. I told them, 'I'll cut the both of you if I get half the chance.' So they brutalised me. Turned me mad.

My dream was this: my doors opened up. There was nobody there. Just a beautiful light and a voice, this voice was so gentle, warm and friendly ... 'Come, walk out.' I walked out naked, but the light had this warm effect on me; it was like a tunnel. I followed the light and as I came to the end there was an open door. 'Go in,' the voice said. So I did ... I wish I'd never ... it was hell! Bodies broken up, decapitated heads and eyes in jars! There was this stench of rotting flesh. I was standing in blood and then all hell broke out, screams, shouts, crying, moans and groans.

I was in madness. I froze – I could not move. But the crazy thing was, I was laughing, too. I was laughing so much it hurt. Then blows rained down on me ... sticks, boots, fists and more abuse. 'Kill him ... kill the fucker!' Why? But as they beat me, I still laughed. I began to crawl for the door ... I had to get back to the light ... follow it ... get back into the safety of my hole. My cell was my safety, my home – a shell, my armour.

'YOU'LL NEVER MAKE IT BACK,' they screamed. But I kept crawling: I had to get back. I thought of my family; I could not die in hell. I had to get back for them. My heart felt like it would blow up and rip through my chest. My eyes were blacked out. I was slipping away and nobody or nothing helped me. I was alone.

I'd wake up, sweating, shaking. A dream maybe, but it was a nightmare of madness.

I'd lie awake not wanting to sleep. The back cell light was on 24 hours a day. The blood was on the walls. This cell, with two doors, was hell. It put this dream in my head. At times, I'd test the door to see if it was locked, to see if it was real. It was a dream. No normal, sane man can live in such hellish conditions and stay sane.

Terry Waite, the Archbishop of Canterbury's envoy, had company when he was kidnapped and held for so long, but I had only my shadow for company. That shadow is all I've had. At times, I never even had that. When I look back to those sad times, is it no wonder I went mad? Is it no wonder I went to Broadmoor?

Did I tell you about the time I had a cockroach crawl inside my ear? Fuck knows if it ever came out. Maybe it laid eggs in my head. Could that be the madness? It sure went in, as I felt it. The itch inside my eardrum. I felt it crawl behind my mastoid. I stuck a piece of stick inside, but it vanished for days ... weeks. I was terrified. But you get used to anything. You overcome it. So that's why I sleep with my ears blocked up. You live and learn, even in a hole. It doesn't matter how big the hole is. You can always overcome it. Beat it. Make it a hole to be proud of.

I used to do the 'Lizard Press-Up'; I invented it. You assume the press-up position and in one go you jump, holding your feet inches off the floor. Then dip. You move six inches, slowly. I used to do it the length of the unit and back. Ron used to shout, 'WATCH OUT, LADS, HERE'S THE LIZARD!' This exercise pumps up the entire body; lungs included. At other times, I'd find a nice quiet spot, and hang upside down on the rails, or from a pipe or gate. Why? Well, why not? It's me and it's different. It's my life.

When the cell door slams up at the end of the day, that's when the real battle begins. Those other guys at that time all had life. For me, at that time, I had an end, a date, something to work at. A goal, hope, faith, call it what you will. All they had were prison lies ... dreams. They could tell them anything, but with me they could tell me dog shit. Or so I thought! Yeah, sweet memories.

Another mad moment was when I walked past the medical officer who was carrying a big bag over from the pharmacy. I bumped into him and carried on. He never even saw me nick a plastic bottle of blue liquid. Chilly and me drank the lot. How the fuck we liked it is beyond me. Why I drank it is beyond me. But that's how insanity is — you do things that you rarely plan or believe you'd do.

I remember one day, out on the yard, I got two loose bricks, from a drain. I got one in each hand and went on my jog, around and around and around. Fuck me, do you realise how heavy they get after half-an-hour of jogging around a yard? My arms were hanging off! But every time I passed the screws in their sentry box, their eyes darted away from me, as if not to notice. Why? I suppose in case I smashed their stupid skulls in. You guessed it!

I later got a call up by Dr Cooper. Same old shit – 'Why?' Same old answer – 'Why not?'

It's just me. I can't change. I'm just impulsive, but when I start, I can't fucking stop. That's the problem. The lads will remember the small wall in Parkhurst near the tennis courts, by the SSU. That wall was maybe 4ft high, but on one side it had an 8ft drop. The width of the wall was two bricks. The length of that wall was maybe 30 yards. I used to run up and down it 50 times. Screws used to sit in their boxes praying I'd fall, but did I ever fall? To be honest, I did once or twice, but nobody is perfect. But how many saw me fall? All saw me do it.

One day Kev Brown was out on the yard; this was in the '80s. I stood on the wall with Kev on my shoulders, so he could shout over to Andy Russell who was on the SSU. Now Kev's no small guy and, remember, this wall is only two bricks wide. I'm just a natural balancer. I could have been a big star in the circus.

It was in Parkhurst when I bumped into 'Psycho', a block screw. Yeah, a screw called Psycho! Amazing, eh? Now this Psycho prat was just a bully. It was 6½ years since the riot and this guy still thought he was the bollocks. I was slopping out this day, and Chilly Chamberlain was in the next cell to me. He had left me some toothpaste and soap in the recess, in a hiding place we used when we slopped out one at a time. I went straight to it; it was empty. As I turned round, Psycho was smiling at me, it was all over his face. I smiled back and ran at him. What a row that was. It was worth it, but when it ends up 10–1 against, it's never good odds.

Psycho was so hard he went on sick leave for three months; that's how that sort are, they don't like a bit of their own. The best block screw in Parkhurst in the '80s was old Tim Cotton; he was a gentleman, one of the true old school – hard but fair. But there are far too many psycho prats; they see a weak person and play on it, but they ain't got the bollocks to do anything outside.

It was a beautiful summer's day on the Isle of Wight. I was on the exercise yard on C-Unit, Dr Cooper's wing for dangerous and insane inmates – con killers, psychos, schizoids and trouble-shooters. It was called the 'Psycho Wing'. A lot of psychotropic drugs were used to control certain inmates; one in particular was big George Wilkinson. George was a Giant Geordie, a violent man, feared by many. But deep down he was smashing, he just had mental problems and the system could not handle him. George had had many years of torment and suffered terrible brutality.

I recall the hostage siege in Parkhurst '76 when big George Wilkinson and Taffy Beecham took a screw hostage; that screw has since retired – his nerves went. They both got ten years for that, but George was on a mission. There were no brakes on the machine when it came to George ... he just smashed his way through! A mission of madness, I think he knew he was dying inside.

I met George in the Dungeon in Wandsworth in '76; some days we would go out on the yard together. Back in those days we weren't allowed to talk on the exercise yard of the block, but George and me did; who was gonna stop us? We talked about outside life, normal stuff like guns and robbing banks, but George was on his mission and nobody could or would stop him.

He died in Walton Jail in the box; he had been on a hunger strike for two weeks. But I believe he's one of prison's mystery deaths. They were so afraid of him that he had to die. That man was and will always be a legend to me. A fearless man, but not a bully, as he fought the system. George was born to fight. What a soldier he would have made; he would have got a chestful of medals and ribbons. In prison, all he got was stamped on, and he left in a zip-up bag.

One day on the yard I saw Dr Cooper coming over with four of his super troopers – all in white coats with their evil, eagle eyes and size-10 boots. 'Nurses from hell,' I used to call them. Prats in the POA, brain-dead rats, scum of the planet ... bully-boys. You get the picture.

Dr Cooper was a strange man, but a gentle man. I liked him for several reasons – he gave me Marmite, milk and peanut butter, and he once gave me vitamins. He also helped the Parkhurst rioters at their trial, speaking up for them, how they'd been beaten. The screws hated Dr Cooper for that. Basically, he was an honest man trapped in a very evil system. He was the Prison Medical Officer, the top man, as well as a psychologist. He was still a nasty fucker when he wanted to be, but as prison doctors go ... tops.

'Dr Cooper,' I shouted.

He stopped in the centre of the yard, surrounded by his troopers. I walked over to him; the atmosphere was tense. 'Yes,' he said, and the madness hit me. I froze! I could not speak. My throat went dry. I just stared at him, I never saw the four goons standing beside us. 'Yes?' he asked. What do I do? I wanted to see him about my milk, I wanted more. 'Yes?' he said, 'I've not got all day.'

I logged on to his nose. He had a lot of nose hair sticking out. I stared at it! 'Look, what do you want?' I just did it. I shot my hand out, fast, like a snake. All froze and, in a split-second, I grabbed the hairs out of his nostril with my finger and thumb and ripped them out! It happened so fast, too fast, nobody could believe it; I looked at it; they all looked at me. Cooper was white; the screws were ready to jump me. I blew the hairs away. 'That could have been your brains!' I said, and walked away, madness over!

Seven years later, I returned to Parkhurst. Dr Cooper was still there. It was then he asked me, 'Why did you do that to me that day?'

I told him the truth; I did it to take away my own problem; I was embarrassed; I couldn't speak, I wanted to, but I just couldn't get a word out. He actually smiled. So did I. That's insanity. Nobody can explain it, just enjoy it.

I originally landed in Parkhurst in '76, when only 23 years old. It was B-Wing. Berti Costa, John Hilton, Billy Gentry, the Ape Man and Joey Martin were some of the faces there. Tap, tap on my door, association time. This guy walked in — oldish, Scottish, long hair, crazy-looking. 'Hi, I'm Malcolm,' he stuck his hand out. As I shook it, it felt limp, no strength. It was a seriously weak handshake! I was on red alert.

'Oh, you do have lovely eyes,' he said. Fuck me, is he for real? He went on, 'Oh, your skin is so soft.' Fuck me, he fancies me! Well, I had two options — be nice or nasty. In that cell at that time I could only see one way. Smack! My head went in like a bullet — teeth, bone and blood.

Malcolm was a lifer. Served 20 years, then he was sentenced to hang, but was reprieved and commuted to life. He was also the raunchy fairy of B-wing. After that introduction, he gave me respect. That's insanity, that's the madness that surrounds you in prison every day of your fucking life. God, give me strength.

I had a brilliant idea to get grub out of the kitchen. I started it off in Parkhurst and in no time the whole system was doing it. My pal at the time was Henry Wallace, a Leeds guy serving 12 years for a robbery. He worked in the kitchen. At the time I was on the unit so I got a message to him: 'Drop me a big lump of meat in the tea urn.' So he did. One day a leg of lamb and then a massive lump of beef; it was fucking brilliant and it worked every time. Now it's all muggy tea kits; nothing lasts in prison and they call it progress, technology, a 'better' time. It's all shit now, pathetic; bring back the cat, I say, let us be men, not mice.

HMP Risley in 1974 was where I caught my first cell thief. They're scum and filth. I never actually caught him, but I was there with three Scousers who did. He nicked a watch and a radio. The Scousers had him in a grip and covered his mouth. I said, 'He has to learn!'

The Scousers were just going to bash him up a bit; I grabbed his arm and stuck his hand in the door ... a finger dropped to the floor! That's life in jail, violent and mad.

In the same prison, three of us went into a nonce's cell. I hit him, he went down. I sat on his chest and stuffed an old rag in his mouth while the chaps did what they had to do. Not nice, but was it nice what he'd done to the old lady of 69 years of age? Put it like this; he never did it again. Such is life in jail.

It was in Risley in 1970 when I first came across women prisoners. I was on remand having nicked a lorry and was involved in a crash. While there I had a job collecting boxes from the women's workshop. Risley was split in two: men's and women's sides. So once a week I'd go over to that side with three other lads and a trolley, all accompanied by a screw. Fuck me, what a laugh, we used to leave there with red faces. Wolf whistles, grabbing our bollocks, showing us their tits. Some even spread their legs and we were told by the screws to take no notice. Fuck me, we were young lads with hormones racing around! My dick was pumping! Take no notice!

One used to slip me a note; I'd read it later in my cell, and it was pure filth. One used to bend over a work table, arse in air, flashing it; it was winking at me! A big juicy fanny. I was 18. Even the screws would cherry up. Those girls were having a laugh, but did it affect us. How the fuck we controlled ourselves is beyond me!

They loved it; it was the girls' highlight of the week to see us and get a squeeze! And some of them were tasty birds. Fuck knows what they had been up to; not for nicking milk bottles, I'm sure! One of the girls we knew was nicked for six armed robberies, as her boyfriend was on remand with us, a real-life Bonnie and Clyde! I think they got ten years each.

The Ma Bakers and Bonnie Parkers of the world really do exist. They do say a 'real' female gangster is the equivalent of ten male gangsters; when it comes to women being cruel, they make us men look like pussycats! More vicious, too, and more determined! The pigs must thank their lucky stars so few women turn to crime, as they would have some serious trouble if they did!

HMP Wandsworth in 1976 I'll never forget. I was in the old dungeon block, doing 56 days' solitary confinement for shitting the governor up. I was just lying on a blanket on the floor as I had no bed, when I heard two guys arguing outside my window. I got up to have a look and found two screws toe to toe, arguing. 'Don't you fucking tell me my job,' one said.

'Bollocks to you!'

'Don't you swear at me!' Blah, blah.

I thought, Daft bastards. Then ... crash! One knocked the other clean out; it was so funny. I shouted, 'Oy, you should be locked up for that.' He just shot off. It was for a good five minutes the other lay spark out, then he got up all shaky! 'Oy,' I shouted, 'you can't stitch me up for that one.' It really was a sight to see.

Wandsworth in the '70s was, without a doubt, the toughest jail in the country. It was a hard jail but a fair jail and everybody knew where they stood. A con was a con; a screw was a screw; step over the line and you got it big time. I spent a long time in the block — at one stage for 11 months and all of it was punishment! I had fuck all, not even a newspaper, no radio, no bed ... it was hard bird, but it was good for testing a man's character! Looking back I loved it, even the kickings, 'cos I always got a few of my own in. The violence in those days was raw! The screws never had riot gear; they just slammed into you and lashed out with truncheons and big size-10 boots. Fucking good old-fashioned rules — do it or get it! I must admit ... I got most of it!

Looking back over my three decades of imprisonment I would say I was at my most dangerous in the '80s, simply because I had lost the plot. I was driven insane beyond cure! They tried drugs, they tried brutality and they tried isolation. In the end, I was just actually moved every few weeks from jail to jail. One solitary cage to the next. I used to wake up and have to think which jail I was in. It got so bad that my family actually lost track of me.

In six months I'd have nine or ten moves. It was their policy to confuse a man, cause him problems, and that's exactly what it did to me. They created the problem. Back then, their only way of dealing with it was to jump me, wrap me up and sling me in a van ready for the next problem. My life and my world was madness. But it made me dangerous and totally unpredictable, but I now want to confess I was in fear of myself. Yes, I was frightened of me and I was no longer a sane man.

Imagine this if you can! You're in a soundproof box, with two steel doors to get in, no windows and no furniture. You're naked, but alive, and aching and bruised from the beating you've just had to endure. You know they're coming back into you. They may have big sticks, shields and whatever ... they're coming back.

You've just attacked one of theirs up on the prison wing and they dragged you down into the seg block and threw you naked into the box. You wait for the second attack. This was me in Wandsworth back in the early '70s.

Nowadays it's mostly restraint, but they can still strangle you. But in the '60s and '70s it was pure violence with violence and a bit of shit thrown in. You may lose, but lose with dignity!

There was this con who had one of those faces you just had to punch in. Fuck knows who or what he was in for. But as soon as I set eyes on him, I knew I'd end up hurting him. Up on D-Wing, in Wandsworth, I was watched like a hawk, but at slop-out time we used to all slop out together and this rat-faced con seemed always to be in my face.

He made my skin crawl. He seemed to look down on me: 'I'm better than you' sort of thing. I seemed to see him in my dreams. That face ... I used to wake up angry, mad, sweating. As the door would unlock to slop out, I'd see him again. I'd have killed him 20 times in my sleep. There he was again!

I walked into the recess with a pot of shit and piss and there he was, looking as if to say, 'Look, everybody, he's shit in his potty.' I emptied my pot and rinsed it. I looked over and there he was, still fucking looking my way.

I just lost it, I mean totally lost it! I ran at him and grabbed his reptile neck and began to squeeze it. I believe I was laughing. I then smacked his head and face into the wall about 20 times. I then picked him up and slung him at the sluice, where the pots of shit get emptied. Cons were walking in with pots to empty. 'Over him,' I said. 'Stick it over him.'

Within ten minutes he was covered in shit. Prison is a mad place. Cons were emptying pots of shit over him – me, I did not know who the fuck he was. But I'm not a bad judge; it turned out he was a filthy rapist. 'Better than me, eh?' Fucking rat.

I had another good scrap but this time with a screw in Wandsworth block in '76. He actually put up a good show in my cell, but once I was on top the rest steamed in. Believe me, you can't have a straightener with a screw, 'cos if you beat him, the rest are in; if he beats you, the rest love it. It's a catch 22.

I've had enough of it; memory lane for me. But rest assured, they did not beat me, ever! They never could! How do you beat a man who won't lose?

Insanity has been my best friend; it's helped me through. It kept me sane. Now, almost 30 years later, I've got Saira, my beautiful wife, and Sami, my beautiful daughter. Insanity has left me; I no longer need it. What's left to do? What's to prove? Who cares? I'm tired of it! It's time for a new chapter, a new life and a new challenge. So many gone, dead, dying, forgotten, even the dreams are different.

I'm now no longer a part of the shit; it's time to fly! A few big TV interviews, if Parkinson is still alive when I get out! Maybe a movie about my life, a few book signings – six months on the road and then you will have had your fill of Bronson, let someone else take over and I'll willingly give them my mantle to carry for the next 30 years of hell!

Wandsworth, 30 July 1993. I was here for my legal visit, before moving off to Woodhill, where I'd be tried for robbery, which I'd committed during my 69 days of freedom. The first night in cell 13 I heard somebody shout my name – it was not Jacko. He was in the cell opposite me! We had a chat through our doors, but two days later he was moved to Whitemoor. In the next cell to me was Paul Ross's brother, Gary Ross. We passed a couple of days chatting through the pipe; he left to go to Downview Jail in Surrey. He was in the block for three days for slagging a screw off. Jacko, like me, is forever in the dungeons – we have no choice. Unlike most cons, we are just sent from block to block.

My next couple of days passed peacefully. On 5 August, Maggie (my solicitor at that time) and my barrister were due to visit. My barrister, Issy Forshall, was a diamond. The visit was booked in for an afternoon, but in the morning I was told it was cancelled, owing to a mix-up, as legal visits are supposed to be in the morning at Wandsworth. I saw the governor. I said, 'If I don't get my visit, then fuck everything. I will be going to my trial, bollocks showing and in a belt, and I'll tell the judge what you filthy scum have done to me to justify this.' I had my visit!

It now seems there was additional evidence. The police said I was waiting to hit a security van delivering to the bank. What are the police ... mind-readers? They're living in Disney World! My legal visit was held in the block. It was the first time I'd met Issy; she certainly made me feel better. I gave Maggie my cross, which I promised her; it was made out of matches by my pal Kirk Barker.

I was exactly four weeks away from trial and it couldn't come soon enough. Maggie had been informed why I'd been moved a lot; it was because six screws are needed to unlock me, and the prisons haven't got the manpower to keep me any longer than a month. Don't they come up with some blinders? There is only one reason to keep moving me — it's to fuck me up, to confuse my state of mind and to cause me unnecessary problems.

They soon find 40 or more screws when my van arrives at all these jails.

Cell 13 seems to have a magnetic force; it's become my second home, and absolutely nothing changes! Even the flea-riddled pigeons outside are the same, the little sparrows the same, the flying shit parcels, the soldiers of cockroaches are the same, the stench of shitty pots — everything is the same. Am I the same? Maybe I am! I'm older. I've a few more scars on my body; my eyes are tired; I've arthritis in my neck and wrist but I'm still the unpredictable man I've always been.

I just hoped I would win that trial. If not, God help this Prison Service, as I couldn't see me taking too much more of that bollocks. I was certainly the only remand prisoner ever to be on a block circuit, being moved from one high-security jail to another.

My next move would be my sixth in six months; it would never be repeated, as it's illegal to keep moving a remand prisoner. I still awaited being charged with the siege at Woodhill when I wrapped up the librarian, Andy Love, and took him hostage. I guessed right that they would eventually be charging me with the siege! So I expected another police visit soon. Maggie said they might wait to see how my trial went. If I was to walk, then I'd have been charged for the siege, so I wouldn't be walking anyway. As it turned out, I was to receive a handsome prison sentence.

On 13 August 1964 at Strangeways and Walton Prisons, we had our last official hangings in Britain. Peter Anthony Allen, 21, was hanged in Walton Jail, Liverpool; and Gwynne Owen Evans, 24, was hanged in Strangeways Jail, Manchester. They were both convicted of the murder of John Alan West, while robbing him in his house on 7 April 1964.

But whatever you thought about the abolition of capital punishment, you have to ask yourself, how many innocent men and women were topped? Look at the posthumous pardons given to the likes of Timothy Evans in 1966, Derek Bentley and Mahood Mattan, both posthumously pardoned in 1998. It doesn't bring them back to life, does it? If you just go on the last 38 years alone since hangings stopped, look at all the miscarriages of justice, scores of innocent people have spent years rotting in prison on life sentences and then being freed on appeals.

Take the Birmingham Six and the Guildford Four, that's ten who would have hanged, so imagine the full horror of it all. Just how many did hang who were innocent? Doesn't it send a shiver up your spine?

So Britain is finished with capital punishment, right? Wrong! In May 1999, British law lords dismissed an appeal against the death sentence by a Trinidadian drug baron and eight gang members. The law lords of the Privy Council, based in London, acting as a final court of appeal for several Caribbean countries, decided against the motion of a stay of execution. They also rescinded a stay of execution granted to the nine men in the previous week.

On 4 June 1999, Dole Chadee, Joey Ramiah and Ramkalawan Singh were hanged. The other six men were hanged on 5 and 7 June 1999. They were the first executions in Trinidad and Tobago in five years.

I've been in jails where my cell has been very close to the old gallows and the condemned cell was next door to the trap door. The actual gallows itself was three cells high.

In Wandsworth, the actual bottom cell of the gallows set-up was on E/1, which is the punishment block, and my old cell was just yards away from that cell. And every time you passed it, you felt the hairs on the back of your neck prick up.

It's not just Wandsworth. I've been to all the old hanging jails and lived feet away from the old condemned cells — Leeds, Walton, Winston Green, Durham, Bristol, Strangeways and Winchester. But Wandsworth was the spooky one! This one sort of crept into me.

They hanged Derek Bentley in Wandsworth; he should never have swung. He had the mind of a 10-year-old boy; they murdered a boy! Gutless pigs. But I've heard the ghosts many times. I've heard the screams in the night; I've laid awake and heard crying, banging doors. I've even felt it; I've seen shadows move in my cell; I've smelled death!

Wandsworth is a nightmare full of mental torture! But the strange thing is, you get used to it, you become a part of it. Same as all the other dungeons, they all have ghosts and strange noises in the night. Noises that can only be ghosts. Screws have seen the ghosts many times; some screws have refused to work nights over it. One screw's hair went white overnight! Cons have gone mad and taken their own lives over it, and men have had breakdowns. Me? A ghost is a ghost; I quite like them. If I was a ghost, I'd do a lot more than just make a few noises! I'd be back to cause heart-attacks.

I was on D-Wing in '77 for a very short spell. I'd just had a couple of years in solitary. I was slopping out one morning when a big guy bumped into me. I don't know if it was on purpose or not, but I went back to my cell and brooded. Did the screws tell him to do it? Was it to get me upset? Did he want a fight or was it a genuine accident? All fucking day I brooded on it. Out on the exercise yard, I clocked him; how he walked, how he moved and how he spoke. Cunt, he was enemy; shall I stab him, cut him or just break his face up? Wait, what if it was an accident? In the morning, I put my square PP9 battery in a sock, slopped out and waited for him — crunch! I hit him six times and left him on the recess floor with all the piss and filth. A bit strong, but that's madness at its worst! That's prison! Did he do it on purpose? Who knows? But he sure never did it again.

I suppose in those days, when I was starting out, you could have called me a 'predator'. I'd spend ten months of the year in solitary, then pop up on a wing to smell out some monster! I also became a bounty hunter and, occasionally, if I got lucky, I'd trap a dog screw. I remember one screw we called the 'Rat'. I caught him with a bucket of shit. He was on the second landing, with me on the third. WHOOSH! All over him. I was gone. All I could hear was swearing. I got a serious hiding for that, but it was worth it ... a bit of shit works miracles.

HMP Whitemoor is out in the middle of nowhere. It might as well be on the moon for all I care, but when John Allen got assaulted by the MUFTI squad — punched, kicked, etc. — I saw his injuries, so I'm a major witness. The screw who threatened to poison my porridge, we believe, was one of the MUFTI who beat John.

John's a placid man; he's never attacked a screw in all his years. The last time I was there, I was assaulted twice, once so badly that I later had to have surgery on my wrist. My lawyer at the time never got the police involved and didn't even get photographs of the injury to my wrist. It was at my insistence that I had photographs taken of the injury, and to date that little matter is outstanding.

HMP Woodhill special unit — what a hellhole and a complete disgrace to the prison service, a fucking joke. It was built and designed for one purpose, to dehumanise men and turn them into vegetables! But it never worked ... it had the opposite effect. It became a hate factory. It was designed by a prison governor, but when he saw what it had turned into, he washed his hands of it. I mean, what fucking prison has concrete sheep in its grounds? Mad or what?

Woodhill CSC unit opened up in 1998. I was the third con to

arrive there. Anyone who's anybody in the system arrived there; it was just a way of saying 'behave'. They used it as a sort of punishment and we were locked up in cells for 23 hours a day, which was nothing new to me. Our beds were a concrete plinth raised some 6in off the floor, with a thin mattress. We had no windows to open, our toilets had no lid or no seat and our furniture was made of compressed cardboard.

With no fresh air, it became inhuman; it caused claustrophobia, mental breakdowns and depression. Men were acting like they had never done before — hate was in the air! Some attempted suicide, others lost the plot and turned violent; some went on dirty protests. We all had to live in a hellhole, run by fascist, evil pigs. They were all part of the psychological destruction.

This place was soon put in the media spotlight and soon to be condemned by Sir David Ramsbotham, HM Inspector of Prisons. They all condemned it — doctors, social workers, Board of Visitors, organisations, ex-screws and ex-governors. But it's still a hellhole, even now in 2002! They will say, 'Well, it's changed and it's better,' but I say, ask the cons there and they will tell you it's just the same.

One day, I had just had enough. It was a hot day; my cell was like an oven and I could barely breathe. I felt trapped ... I was panicking; I knew it was a serious bout of madness coming on. There was no stopping it. When my door was unlocked to feed me — seven screws brought my food to the door — I ran out; I had to!

I went insane ... I wrecked the godforsaken place. That day, I left Woodhill in a body belt, all wrapped up like a Christmas turkey. They took me to Whitemoor for a couple of months, but they then moved me back to Woodhill. Again it went off on the yard. They got in 20 riot screws to take me in and again I was wrapped up.

Some incidents in Woodhill CSC unit are hard to believe, but let me tell you about Sean 'Sharkie' O'Connor. He's serving 12 years for armed robbery, aged 30. Now Sharkie is a big, strong East Londoner from a good family, with a good set of morals. He says something and it's as good as done but, as violent as he is, he's a very polite man who gives respect. One day he said through his door, 'Excuse me, gov, sort us out a milk sachet.' The screw never sorted it. So the screw basically denied him a cup of tea.

The next day on exercise, Sharkie sees the screw who'd ignored his request for a sachet of milk. Sharkie spat in his face twice.

I said, 'Good shot.'

Sharkie says, 'I've had enough of this shit hole.' Sharkie starts bandaging up his hands and says, 'Come and get me, let's have a rumble!'

I said, 'Yeah, me too!'

All this is over a $\frac{1}{2}$p sachet of milk. Governors came out; screws are all tense; riot mob on stand-by. I say to the governor, 'Look, you lot want it, so let's cut the talk and get it on. Come in and bash us, but I'll bash some of you!'

Now Sharkie is probably the number one in the system at attacking the shields. In Woodhill he's had a good dozen rows with them so they're not playing with an idiot.

Me? Well, I prefer a wrap up, torture the cunt, but at times a man needs to attack, empty his haze! So it's on! I'm ready! The governor promises Sharkie he will get a move if he comes in. Me? I don't care, what's it matter any more? It will take 20 screws in riot gear, two vans and a police escort, all for a $\frac{1}{2}$p sachet! The screw who never gave him a sachet, what happens to him? I'll tell you — fuck all!

This is the insanity of it all. That $\frac{1}{2}$p will cost them 30 grand. But the joke is, why wasn't the screw reprimanded?

Talk about miscarriages of justice! Our penal system is one of the worst offenders in Europe! One sad case was 'Kizcuff. He was branded a sex killer, but he was just the village idiot, a mummy's boy! It was so easy to use him as the scapegoat, it took 20 years to prove his innocence. In those years in jail, he was beaten up so many times that to him it was all part of prison — spitting on him, abuse, kicks in the nuts — after so long he became immune to it. Once out, he died within six months of being free.

I remember a lifer at Woodhill called Ian Wallbey. He was a suicide risk, always cutting himself up, or if he was depressed he'd cut others up. One day he was in solitary, they gave him a razor. Now the rules are simple — the screws have to watch him shave, but they fuck off and leave him for half-an-hour! So he cuts himself up big time and almost lost his life. Sack the fucking lot of them, I say. Ian gets 80 stitches and they get a nice fat wage packet.

HMP Wormwood Scrubs has been in the news regarding brutality dished out to prisoners. They were out of control in the Scrubs; they had too much power, but at the end of the day it's the governor to blame. They know what's going on. They can stop it. So why did they allow it to go on? Why?

The insanity never stops — mysterious deaths, very mysterious. So who's the maddest of the mad? Shall I tell you who? The maddest fucker in the system is ... the system. It's also a fucking disgrace.

It's all right for cons like Aitken and Archer who come in and get the cushy jails and nice treatment, or the Guinness mob, or the paedophiles who all get parole. It's a fucking cesspit of shame, corrupt and insane.

Around '85 I realised I was losing my senses. The things I used to do were not normal. When I dived on the governor and started to strangle him, I had lost my way. Every time my door unlocked I faced ten screws — it was a war. It was forever tense; nobody knew what would go down, not even me.

So in the end I became a dog — a mad dog! I was bashed and degraded all round the system! So now you know why I attacked so many screws over many years. I had no choice. The same went for the governors; if I got the chance, I'd attack them, sometimes with a pot of shit all over their nice new suit and their false face. Governors, to me, were no better than sewer rats. All they deserved was a pot of shit; the doctors got it as well. I hated everybody and I was at war!

So the journeys became a battle of wits, but let me say right now, I lost every battle I had and suffered severe consequences for it. I've even been strangled to unconsciousness. Only an act of God saved me.

I myself have suffered at the hands of the screws in the Scrubs. The criminal investigation into some of the Wormwood Scrubs brutality led to the prosecution of 27 screws and to the conviction of six, three of whom have been sentenced. Brutality against us prisoners at Wormwood Scrubs has been going on for years and did not consist of a few isolated incidents. The police investigation looked at claims of brutality made by 40 inmates and former inmates of Wormwood Scrubs, covering the period from October 1996 to March 1998, including beatings, burning with cigarettes, verbal abuse and an incident in which a black inmate was forced to eat a poster.

Of the 43 staff members named in the files, 15 screws were suspended on full pay, and 28 left the service or are continuing to work. The then Home Secretary, Jack Straw, said he found the claims 'very disturbing'. Bollocks! I believe Jack Straw has seen CCTV footage of brutality dished out against me with his own eyes, and he's done nothing about it!

In September 2001, the Prison Service Director Martin Narey accused Sir David Ramsbotham, HM Inspector of Prisons, of 'talking nonsense'. This was in relation to Sir David's comment that, 'There must be absolutely clear understanding that this sort of treatment of prisoners will not be tolerated and it must be supported by a system that warns a person that if they go on behaving like this they will be out.' It's people like Sir David that need praise for revealing this sort of thing.

Martin Narey said, 'There was no evidence at all for Sir David's accusations. He knows that I have made it absolutely plain that anyone who lays a hand on a prisoner will leave this service. I have not just relied on convictions in court. Quite recently we sacked senior staff at Northallerton and Portland because they've laid hands on prisoners. All my staff know that if they lay a hand on a prisoner, then they will be out of a job.' OK then, why not sack the screws from HMP Birmingham that have been caught on CCTV? Put up or shut up!

The biggest ever set of criminal trials of prison officers ended in September 2001 when three screws were jailed for a 'sadistic' attack on a man at Wormwood Scrubs. What a load of bollocks – three out of fucking thousands!!

The last two Chief Inspectors of Prisons, Sir David Ramsbotham and Sir Stephen Tumin, called for public inquiries into the extent of violence at the jail and why it had continued for so long despite repeated warnings. Another 36 claims of brutality, with at least 41 civil claims against the prison service for alleged assaults, are pending.

In March 1998, in the jail's segregation unit, screws got Steven Banks in a headlock, and said how easy it was to break his neck and threatened to kill him. Nothing new in that; I've had that for years. Steven was then punched and kicked and smashed into a wall with such force that his head caved in.

The Senior Officer in charge of the seg unit, John Nicol, got four years' imprisonment. Another two screws, Robert Lawrie and Darren Fryer, also got four years and three-and-a-half years respectively. Three other screws were convicted of bashing up a lifer, Timothy Donovan, who was held down, just like I was, and beaten. Three other screws were jailed for 18 months, 15 months, and 12 months respectively.

Sir David said that former Home Secretaries Michael Howard and Jack Straw, to whom he had reported his concerns about brutality at the jail, should be summoned before a public inquiry to explain why they failed to act. 'The responsibility to ensure that custody is exercised according to the law and in a civilised manner ultimately rests with ministers.' Too fucking right it does! Sir David went on to say that he feared an internal Prison Service inquiry could lead to a cover-up and that senior managers failed to do anything when they knew what was happening.

A solicitor acting for group litigation against the Prison Service said, 'Some prison officers felt they had the permission of society to go beyond the normal punishment of imprisonment and beat certain people up. There was also persistent racism.'

The General Medical Council has also received 20 complaints about medical staff at Wormwood Scrubs jail and alleged failings on their part in treating prisoners and blowing the whistle. These doctors and other staff helped protect the violent officers, and you can't tell me that a large number of people knew nothing about it – prison officers, doctors, the Board of Visitors, chaplains, probation service! Every professional in that prison must have known or suspected something and said nothing for years, and that makes them just as guilty of brutality.

So now you can see why I've carried out these sieges and demonstrations over the years – brutality!

I am the only serial hostage-taker the United Kingdom has ever had, and probably the only one in the world. So I am qualified on the subject matter, as I see myself as a Professor of Sieges. I know more than the negotiators know. Basically, a negotiator is a mug, a clown, a messenger or a Joey. They only relate back to Prison Service headquarters.

Headquarters houses the top brass who decide what demands can or can't be met and what cover-ups can and can't be revealed to the media. Let's face facts, a siege is only a bargaining tool. We want, we demand ... and we either get or we don't. A siege is a very complex thing, as you're dealing with humans, and humans are unpredictable. Where one will shit his pants, another will try to escape. You have to weigh up each individual siege. But let me say now, each one is as mad as the next one. It's all insanity.

In June 2009 I was up before the Parole Board for a hearing about my release. Surprise, surprise, it was decided that Charles Bronson would not be let out. They don't ever want to let me out – my next parole hearing will be in March 2011 and it will be the same bollocks all over again – and again in 2013, 2014, 2015, blah, blah blah.

The Board recommended that I talk to a psychologist but I WILL NOT be working with prison shrinks – not today, not tomorrow, ever. I couldn't, even if I wanted to, not after my asylum years of hell. I'll work with my probation officer and independent doctors and that's all.

No man can rip off nine roofs, take 11 hostages, fight a 36-year battle and ever be freed – it's political now.

On 8th October, out of my window, I watched a plane with a banner saying 'Free Bronson – Enough is Enough' circling the skies above the jail – that shows I'm never buried and forgotten! My case will never be swept under the mat and one day I'll find myself back at the appeal court, or in the European Court of Human Rights.

The day I walk free from a court of law, there will be the biggest party that the UK has ever had. And then I'll write my 'freedom book' on a beach with a few ice-cold beers.

It's never over til the sun goes down, so watch this space ...
The insanity of life goes on – a journey of extreme madness.
Adios amigos

THE CAMPAIGN TO FREE CHARLES BRONSON

Dee Morris is a close friend of mine and she runs an active campaign and support group that has been set up to fight for my immediate de-categorisation which is part of the progress towards my freedom.

Talking is not enough. Talk is cheap and actions speak louder than words – action is what is needed. People need to raise awareness by writing to their local MPs and the Ministry of Justice about my case and demand answers.

My family, friends and supporters have organised protests to gain attention for the cause. Protests have been held outside 10 Downing Street, in Trafalgar Square as well as outside the Houses of Parliament. There is another protest arranged to take place outside my prison.

Protests will continue to be held on various dates and at various locations around the country. Everyone is welcome to attend and give your support!

Further information on how to support my campaign for freedom can be obtained by contacting freecharlieb@yahoo.co.uk

We hope to have your full support – enough is enough!

TIME SERVED

1968	Risley Remand Centre, two months (criminal damage)	
1969	Risley unknown period, banned from driving for life (hit and run)	
1970/71	Risley unknown period, suspended sentence (smash and grab)	
1974	Risley Remand	normal wing
1974	Walton	normal wing
1975	Hull	block (dungeons)
1976	Armley	block (dungeons)
1976	Wakefield	block (dungeons)
1976	Wandsworth	block (dungeons)
1976	Parkhurst	special unit
1977	Wandsworth	block (dungeons)
1977	Walton	block (dungeons)
1977	Wandsworth	block (dungeons)

1978	Parkhurst	certified insane
1978	Rampton	block (dungeons)
1979	Broadmoor	block (dungeons)
1984	Park Lane	normal wing
1985	Risley	remand wing
1985	Walton	certified sane
1985	Armley	block (dungeons)
1985	Walton	block (dungeons)
1985	Albany	block (dungeons)
1985	Wormwood Scrubs	block (dungeons)
1985	Wandsworth	block (dungeons)
1986	Parkhurst	special unit
1986	Winchester	block (dungeons)
1986	Wormwood Scrubs	block (dungeons)
1986	Parkhurst	block (dungeons)
1986	Wandsworth	block (dungeons)
1986	Parkhurst	normal wing
1986	Wandsworth	block (dungeons)
1986	Albany	block (dungeons)
1986	Winchester	block (dungeons)
1986	Wandsworth	block (dungeons)
1987	Gartree	block (dungeons)
1987	Leicester	block (dungeons)
1987	Gartree	block (dungeons)

Released October 30th from Category 'A'
from the block at Gartree

7 January 1988	Arrested, Luton

		Police Station
1988	Leicester	remand block (dungeon)
1988	Brixton	remand cage (special unit)
1988	received 7 years' imprisonment	
1988	Wandsworth	normal wing
1988	Full Sutton	normal wing
1988	Durham	cage (special unit)
1988	Full Sutton	normal wing
1988	Armley	block (dungeons)
1989	Full Sutton	normal wing
1989	Long Lartin	normal wing
1989	Bristol	block (dungeons)
1989	Winson Green	block (dungeons)
1989	Winchester	block (dungeons)
1989	Wandsworth	block (dungeons)
1989	Albany	block (dungeons)
1989	Parkhurst	special unit
1989	Albany	block (dungeons)
1989	Gartree	normal wing
1990	Durham	block (dungeons)
1990	Parkhurst	block (dungeons)
1990	Frankland	normal wing
1990	Albany	block (dungeons)
1990	Parkhurst	special unit
1990	Wandsworth	block (dungeons)
1990	Full Sutton	normal wing

1991	Parkhurst	normal wing
1991	Wandsworth	block (dungeons)
1991	Albany	block (dungeons)
1991	Leicester	block (dungeons) there for just one day!
1991	Hull	block (dungeons)
1992	Lincoln	special unit

Released in November 1992

Remanded for a short time in January 1993 and released a few weeks later.

February 1993 remanded for other offences.

1993	Woodhill	remand
1993	Winson Green	
1993	Belmarsh	
1993	Bristol	
1993	Wandsworth	
1993	Belmarsh	
1993	Bullingdon	
1993	Belmarsh	
1993	Bullingdon	
1993	Belmarsh	
1993	Wakefield	cage
1993	Frankland	
1993	Hull	special unit
1994	Leicester	
1994	Wakefield	cage
1994	Bullingdon	block (dungeons)

1994	Leicester	block (dungeons)
1994	Wakefield	cage
1994	Strangeways	block (dungeons)
1994	Walton	block (dungeons)
1994	Highdown	block (dungeons)
1994	Belmarsh	special unit
1994	Lincoln	block (dungeons)
1994	Wormwood Scrubs	block (dungeons)
1994	Wandsworth	block (dungeons)
1994	Winson Green	block (dungeons)
1994	Lincoln	block (dungeons)
1994	Bullingdon	block (dungeons)
1994	Wandsworth	block (dungeons)
1994	Bullingdon	block (dungeons)
1994	Full Sutton	block (dungeons)
1995	Frankland	block (dungeons)
1995	Armley	block (dungeons)
1995	Frankland	block (dungeons)
1995	Highdown	block (dungeons)
1995	Winson Green	block (dungeons)
1995	Lincoln	block (dungeons)
1995	Frankland	block (dungeons)
1995	Winson Green	block (dungeons)
1995	Belmarsh	block (dungeons)
1996	Full Sutton	block (dungeons)
1996	Walton	block (dungeons)
1996	Bullingdon	block (dungeons)
1996	Belmarsh	block (dungeons)
1996	Wakefield	cage
1996	Bullingdon	block (dungeons)

1997	Durham	block (dungeons)
1997	Full Sutton	block (dungeons)
1997	Belmarsh	block (dungeons)
1997	Wakefield	cage
1997	Belmarsh	block (dungeons)
1997	Wakefield	cage
1997	Belmarsh	block (dungeons)
1997	Wakefield	cage
1998	Woodhill	CSC (Close Supervision Centre)
1998	Hull	special unit
1999	Whitemoor	block (special CSC cell)
1999	Woodhill	A-Wing solitary no privileges.
1999	Whitemoor	40-day hunger-strike
2000	Woodhill	Seg Unit, stormed by 60 MUFTI
2000	Whitemoor	Seg Unit
2000	Woodhill	Seg Unit
2001	Wakefield	Monster Mansion
2001	Whitemoor	Seg Unit
2001	Frankland	block
2001/02	Durham	cage
	Woodhill	
	Whitemoor	
2004	Wakefield	
2006–09	Wakefield	
2009	Long Lartin	

Stephen Richards, the no-holds-barred investigative journalist and spokesman for the underworld is a regular contributor of gangland news to over 20 websites. Author of many successful true crime books, he has had his works serialised in the national press.

Branded a maverick of the publishing industry, he has made acquaintances with many of the more notorious underworld figures in the UK and around the world. Richards' Management Company, Crimebiz, represents many of these infamous figures.

Sought out by many top production and film companies from around the world for his expertise, he has been able to help and advise many popular investigative TV shows. Credits include: *Panorama*, *Trevor McDonald's Tonight* programme, *Real Lives*, BBC TV (and BBC TV digital Horizon channel), BBC Radio and independent radio, Channel 4 TV and Independent TV.

Richards has also contributed to numerous newspaper and magazine features. TV companies have praised his expertise and he has appeared in numerous crime-related, national and international TV documentaries.

Currently he is working on more investigative true crime books and is also involved in producing and directing crime documentaries, as well as formulating big screen gangster movie scripts.